PART-TIME EMPLOYMENT: A BRIDGE OR A TRAP?

For my parents, especially my mother

Part-Time Employment: A Bridge or a Trap?

MAY TAM

Avebury

Aldershot • Brookfield USA • Hong Kong • Singapore • Sydney

© M. Tam 1997

Published by
Avebury
Ashgate Publishing Limited
Gower House
Croft Road
Aldershot
Hants GU11 3HR
England

Ashgate Publishing Company
Old Post Road
Brookfield
Vermont 05036
USA

British Library Cataloguing in Publication Data
Tam, May
    Part-time employment : a bridge or a trap?
    1.Part-time employment - Great Britain
    I.Title
    331.2'572'0941

Library of Congress Catalog Card Number: 96-79119

ISBN 1 85972 532 5

Printed in Great Britain by the Ipswich Book Company, Suffolk

Contents

Figures and tables

vi

Preface

Lately, part-time employment has attracted a lot of public attention. There have been conflicting normative evaluations in terms of the benefits or disadvantages it brings to both employers and employees. Some critics regard it as a form of wage work which gives both employers and workers a high degree of flexibility. Others argue that it brings about employment inequalities and job insecurity to employees and would ultimately confine workers to a ghettoised arena of employment. It would worsen the employment conditions of women as compared to those of men.

In Britain, these two opposing views were used to buttress different arguments for and against the legislative changes which were introduced in 1994. The changes gave part-time employees the same extent of protection against unfair dismissal and redundancy as that of full-time employees. Supporters of the changes, unionists and the Labour Party alike, said that this then would enhance the employment security of part-time employees. They would also promote equality and justice between full-time and part-time workers. Those who opposed to the amendments, typically employer groups, claimed that the new legislations would lead to higher fixed labour costs. These extra costs would serve as disincentives for employers to create more part-time jobs and, therefore, would lead to further deteriorate the general unemployment scenario.

Both sides of the debate assume that the effects of the legislative changes would be translated directly and unproblematically into positive or negative effects on the employment conditions of and the demand for part-time workers. To supporters of the amendments, an unfettered labour market would bring inequalities to particular groups of workers and add to social inequalities. Those who oppose the changes uphold the principle of free market and argue that a de-regulated labour market would ultimately benefit everyone.

These two opposing evaluations of part-time employment are premised on two very different approaches to the way labour market operates. Those who herald part-time work as a flexible form of employment see the labour market as operating in an unfettered manner. Employers can get the type of workers they need and employees are able to secure jobs which give them the kind of job returns they merit. Opponents argue that there are market barriers which give rise to persistent unequal employment conditions.

However, critics who are engaged in the debate generally overlook the complex reality that underlies employers' demand for part-time workers, the employment conditions of part-time employees and factors that shape participation in part-time work. A betterment in the legal protection may not close off the gap between part-timers and full-timers. There are a number of job returns which are as crucial as job security. Likewise, there are other advantages of employing part-timers which may offset the potential higher fixed labour costs that result from the legislative changes. These advantages would then lead to a demand for part-timers despite the higher fixed labour costs incurred by the legal changes.

In other words, neither of these two different evaluations of part-time work has been examined thoroughly with comprehensive and relevant empirical data. Existing studies on part-time work focus either on the demand side or on the supply side only. There has also been little systematic comparison of part-time jobs to full-time jobs in terms of various types of job returns. Studies that deal with participation in part-time work tend to be cross-sectional, instead of assessing the cumulative effect of previous working experience. Normative judgements of part-time work which are substantiated by a full understanding of the various issues involved are, therefore, still wanting.

By using a comprehensive dataset, this book seeks to examine the array of factors which underlie the demand for and the supply of part-time workers as well as the employment conditions of part-time employees by using Britain as a case study. The choice of Britain is particularly relevant and timely as the 1995 government statistics show that two-third of the newly created jobs were part-time jobs. In fact, in various members countries of the European Union, it has been noted that the expansion of part-time jobs has contributed significantly to new employment opportunities. The aim of this study is to provide a thorough empirical account of the various issues related to part-time employment. It also attempts to draw out some of the policy implications of the findings.

Acknowledgements

I would like to thank my doctoral supervisor, Dr Duncan Gallie, who gave me access to the various datasets for the research of this book, and whose suggestions have often helped me get out of what seemed to be a cul-de-sac. Dr Gallie's supervision made the whole process of research an enjoyable one. I still have a lot to learn from his meticulous comments on the various drafts of my written work.

My college supervisor at Oxford, Mr John Goldthorpe, often offered particular insights into areas which I neglected and how ideas could be further developed. His comments on the various earlier drafts of my work were both specific and general from which I have learnt a lot.

During the course of preparing this book, I have benefited from various people's suggestions and assistance. The advice of Dr David Firth, Nuffield College, on the statistical part was tremendously helpful. So were the comments by Dr O'Reilly and Joan Payne. Some of the staff members and graduate students of the Department of Sociology at the Chinese University of Hong Kong have also given valuable comments on some parts of the analysis. Dr T.L. Lui offered very sharp criticism and the late Bryan Wilkinson's help on the literature on labour laws related to part-time workers was much appreciated. Although we were miles apart, Ah Wai, Ah Ping, Ah Wah, Karen and Milly were always supportive. I would also like to thank Chris Green who kept assuring me that I could make it and cheered me up with his humours throughout the process of researching and writing.

Due acknowledgment is hereby given to John Swire & Sons Company Ltd for offering me a scholarship for my study at the University of Oxford.

1 Introduction

This book is about part-time work. Using Britain as a case, both the supply side and the demand side of part-time employment will be examined. The main issues which we shall address are : (1) the determinants of employers' demand for part-time workers; (2) the extent to which part-time workers differs from full-time workers in terms of their respective employment conditions; (3) the long term effect of part-time work experience on the labour market fortunes of women; (4) the different explanations for participation in part-time work. By analyzing these four aspects, this study seeks to examine the ways in which two labour market theories help us understand part-time work and the labour market experiences it brings to women.

This Chapter will first give a brief overview of the trends of part-time employment in various advanced industrial societies as well as in Britain. We shall then discuss the two major theoretical approaches to the study of labour market and the implications which can be drawn from them with respect to the four issues addressed in this book. This will be followed by a review of the existing studies on part-time work and a discussion of the way in which the present research seeks to overcome some of the deficiencies of these studies. The Chapter will then conclude with a brief description of the focus of each of the Chapters to follow.

The use of part-time work in Europe and in Britain

In this section, we shall examine briefly the use of part-time work in a number of industrialized economies to note some of the commonalities between Britain and her European counterparts. Official labour force statistics show that part-time work has been expanding in most OECD countries, as illustrated in Table 1.1.

1

Table 1.1
Size and composition of part-time employment in OECD countries, 1979-92
part-time employment as a proportion of employment (percentages)

Country	Total Employment			Male Employment			Female Employment		
	1979	1986[a]	1992[b]	1979	1986	1992	1979	1986	1992
Australia	15.5	+4	+5.6	5.1	+1.6	+3.9	34.5	+3.4	+5.4
Austria	7.6	-	+1.5[c]	1.5	-	+0.1[c]	18	-	+2.5[c]
Belgium	6	+2.6	+3.8	1	+1.9	+0.2	16.5	+4.6	+7
Canada	12.5	+3.2	+1.2	5.7	+2.1	+1.5	23.3	+2.6	+0
Denmark	22.7	+1.2	-1.3	5.2	+3.2	+1.7	46.3	-2.4	+7.2
Finland	6.7	+1.4	-0.2	3.2	+1.7	+0.6	10.6	+0.9	-0.9
France	8.2	+3.5	+1	2.5	+1	+0.1	17	+6.1	+1.4
Germany	11.2	+1.1	+1.9	1.5	+0.6	+0.1	27.6	+0.8	+2.3
Greece	-	-	4.8[d]	-	-	2.8[d]	-	-	8.4[d]
Ireland	5.1	+1.4	na	2.1	+0.3	na	13.1	+2.4	na
Italy	5.3	+0	+0.6	3	+0	-0.1	10.6	-0.5	+1.4
Japan	9.9	+1.8	+8.8	5.2	+0.3	+4.9	18.4	+4.1	+12.0
Luxembourg	5.8	+1.5	-0.4	1.0	+1.6	-1.3	17.1	-0.8	+0.2
Netherlands	11.1	+13	+8.8	2.8	+5.9	+4.7	31.7	+22.5	+8.7

Table 1.1 (continued)

Country	Total Employment			Male Employment			Female Employment		
	1979	1986[a]	1992[b]	1979	1986	1992	1979	1986	1992
New Zealand	14.7	+2.9	+4	5.7	+0.9	+3.7	28	+3.2	+4.7
Norway	27.3	+0.6	-1.2	10.6	-0.3	-0.5	51.6	+0.3	+4.2
Sweden	23.6	-0.1	+0.8	5.4	+0.6	+2.4	46	-3.2	-1.5
UK	16.4	+4.8	+2.3	1.9	+2.3	+2.1	39	+5.9	+0.1
United States	16.4	+1	+0.1	9	+1.2	+0.6	26.7	-0.3	-1

Note :
[a]'+'/'-' indicates an increase/decrease over 1979
[b]'+'/'-' indicates an increase/decrease over 1986
[c]refers to the increase over 1979
[d]data refer to the absolute proportion in 1992
na means not available

Source : OECD (1987 & 1994), Employment Outlook.

3

The percentage share of part-timers in the total working population has risen between 1979 and 1986 in a number of OECD countries except in Sweden, and then started to decrease slightly by 1992.[1] Nevertheless, the general trend is a net gain over 1979 except in the case of Denmark and Norway. Table 1.1 also shows that the increase comes mainly from the growth in female part-time employment. The rise in male part-time employment is generally lower than that of women, except in Finland, Sweden and the United States.

Table 1.1 also indicates that the pattern of part-time work varies considerably between countries in Europe. Part-time work as a proportion of total employment is higher in Denmark, the Netherlands, Norway, Sweden, Britain and relatively lower in Ireland, Finland and Italy. Between 1979 and 1992, the Netherlands has the greatest rise in part-time work as a proportion of its total employment, followed by Britain. In 1992, in terms of the share of part-time workers in the female employment, the Netherlands also comes first among all European countries (63%), followed by Norway (47%) and Britain (45%).

Besides its growth, another notable feature of part-time employment is the dominance by women. As shown in Table 1.2, women invariably make up two-thirds or more of the total part-time workforce. In a number of countries like Austria, Belgium, Sweden and Britain, women make up over 80% of the part-time workforce. The age distribution of part-time workers is also skewed. Neubourg (1985) recorded that in a number of western economies, the average age of part-time employees was 35, and they were concentrated in the age group 35-44.

Another distinct feature of part-time work is its disproportionate distribution across different industries. Part-time employment is concentrated in service industries like distributive trades; finance and insurance; social, community and personal services and public administration, as shown in Table 1.3.

While these national patterns highlight the similarities shared by different countries, there are differences between the British situation and those of other European nations. Britain has a relatively higher proportion of working women who are in their child-bearing age working on a part-time basis, as compared to a number of European countries. As illustrated in Table 1.1, among a number of European countries, Britain comes after the Netherlands and Norway with the third highest proportion of working women who are part-timers. Dale and Glover (1990) also noted that Britain had a higher proportion of female part-timers who were between 30 and 44 years old, as compared to Italy, Belgium, France, Luxembourg and Ireland. Other studies have noted that there are differences with respect to certain industrial sectors. Schoer (1987) compared the industrial distribution of part-time employment in

4

Britain and in the former West Germany. He found that the full-time/part-time ratio in the distributive retail sector was higher in Britain. O'Reilly (1994) found in her case studies that the French retail banking sector had a limited use of part-time work, as compared to the British one. Gregory (1991) noted in her comparison between the French and the British grocery retailing that the contracted working hours for part-timers were longer in the former than in the latter.

Table 1.2
Women's percentage share of part-time employment, 1979-1992

Country	1979	1986	1992
Australia	78.7	78.7	75.0
Austria	87.8	-	89.1
Belgium	88.9	86.1	89.7
Canada	72.1	71.2	70.0
Denmark	86.9	80.9	75.8
Finland	74.7	68.7	64.3
France	82.2	83.0	83.7
Germany	91.6	89.8	91.0
Greece	na	na	61.3
Ireland	71.2	74.3	na
Italy	61.4	61.6	68.5
Japan	70.1	70.0	69.3
Luxembourg	87.5	76.6	88.5
The Netherlands	76.4	76.1	75.0
New Zealand	77.7	79.0	73.3
Norway	83.0	79.2	80.1
Sweden	87.5	86.6	82.3
Britain	92.8	88.5	85.2
USA	68.0	66.5	66.4

Key : na = not available.
Source: OECD (1987 & 1994), Employment Outlook.

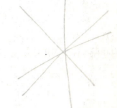

Table 1.3
Part-time employment as a proportion of total employment by industry, 1985&1986

Country	Industry						
	(1)	(2)	(3)	(4)	(5)	(6)	(7)
In 1986							
Australia	18.9	20.8	7.9	25.4	18.1	24.2[b]	
Canada	15.6	15.3	3.6	23.5	11.6	24.4	7.0
Japan	11.8	-	9.6	16.2	10.7	14.3	7.1
Norway	23.1	26.0	12.3[a]	29.7	17.3	32.4[b]	
Sweden	24.5	19.7	12.6[a]	28.9	21.2	36.5[b]	
United States	16.3	-	4.5	29.7	10.7	22.4	6.2
In 1985							
Belgium	8.6	7.2	4.3	11.2	10	17.4	7.4
France	10.8	15.6	5.8	12.1	10.8	19.4	13.4
Ireland	6.5	7.9	2.9	9.7	4.7	12.52	2.5
Italy	5.3	14.3	4.3	5.1	3.3	7.7	1.7
Luxembourg	7.3	13.4	5.0	8.6	5.7	12.5	7.0
The Netherlands	24.0	17.6	10.3[c]	24.9	19.85	45.5	33.7
Britain	19.1	14.9	12.2	35.5	15.3	38.8	10.3

Keys :
(1) = all industries
(2) = agriculture, forestry, fishing and hunting
(3) = manufacturing
(4) = distributive trades
(5) = finance, insurance and real estate
(6) = social, community and personal services
(7) = public administration
[a]included in this percentage is the mining industry.
[b]this percentage combines both (6) and (7).
[c]this includes the industries energy and water; mineral extraction and chemicals, metal engineering and other manufacturing

Source : OECD (1987), *Employment Outlook.*

6

The expansion of the part-time workforce in Britain is notable when it is considered in the context of rising unemployment. Rubery and Tarling (1988:101) indexed the employment and unemployment rate of men and women between 1971 and 1986. They found that within this period, there were decreases in the proportions of men and women who were in full-time employment and rises in the female and male unemployment rates. Alongside with these changes is the increase in part-time workers as a proportion of all employees, and a rise in part-time employees as a percentage of all female employees. As illustrated in Table 1.4, the share of the part-time workforce in total employment has been increasing between 1976 and 1993. Casey (1991) noted that much of the total employment growth which Britain experienced between 1981 and 1987 was contributed by the increase in part-time employment. Employment projections have estimated that there would be over a million extra part-time jobs in Britain by the year 2,000. A major part of this increase would be due to the expansion of part-time employment in health and education services, in the retail distributive sector, and in hotel and catering industries (Wilson, 1991).

Approaches to the study of part-time work

One of the approaches to study part-time work is through analyses of aggregate time series data. Specifically, time series data on unemployment rates, aggregate figures of the demographic composition, and of employment by industrial sectors would unravel the ways these aggregate trends are associated with the growth of part-time employment. For example, Tilly (1991) used American data to examine the way in which the unemployment trend was related to the growth trend of part-time employment between 1973 and 1989. He found that the unemployment rate was positively associated with the rate of part-time employment. Ehrenberg and his associates (1988) used American data to study the relation between the relative wage rates in different industrial sectors and the growth rate of part-time employment in these sectors. They also estimated the time trend of the percentage of non-agricultural workers employed as part-time workers between 1955 and 1984 in relation to cyclical economic factors. Sundstrom (1987) investigated the growth trend of the Swedish part-time workforce by analysing changes in the employment rate of different industries. Rubery and Tarling (1988) examined the growth rate of the British female part-time workforce in different industries between 1971 and 1984. They found that within this period, the growth of part-time employment was closely associated with the overall expansion of service industries.

7

Table 1.4
Trends in the growth of part-time workforce in Britain, 1976-1993
part-timers as a proportion of employees (percentages)

Year	All employees	Male employees	Female employees
1976	19.4	5.3	40.1
1977	19.4	5.2	40.0
1978	19.7	5.3	40.2
1979	20.2	5.5	40.7
1980	20.5	5.6	41.2
1981	21.0	5.8	41.6
1982	21.5	6.1	41.9
1983	22.0	6.5	42.3
1984	22.0	6.8	42.5
1985	22.8	6.9	42.6
1986	23.5	7.3	43.2
1987	23.8	7.6	43.0
1988	23.8	7.8	42.5
1989	24.3	7.7	43.0
1990	25.3	8.5	44.1
1991	26.3	9.2	44.7
1992	26.9	9.6	45.2
1993	27.6	10.0	45.6

Source : HMSO (1994), *Employment Gazette, Historical Supplement,* October.

Disney and Szyszczak (1984) derived an econometric model to examine whether the extension of protective employment legislation and social security contributions in Britain had reduced the demand for part-timers. They used aggregate time series data of the relative wage and working hours between full-timers and part-timers. They argued that the extension of employment protection legislation to part-time employees induced employers to vary the working hours of part-timers, rather than to reduce the absolute number of part-timers they employed.

These studies provide some general pictures at the aggregate level about the ways in which the growth of part-time work is related to the rise in the unemployment rate, the expansion of the service sector, and the increase in the female labour force participation rate. However, they cannot reveal the way in which part-time work is used by employers and experienced by individual employees. Observable behavioural patterns at the aggregate level are often outcomes of diverse actions undertaken by different individuals. An analysis of aggregate data would overlook these heterogeneities and would not enable us to understand the ways through which the different demand-side and supply-side factors shape the British part-time workforce. Employers may well differ from each other in terms of their demands for part-time workers. There would also be variations between individuals with respect to their participation in the labour market and their preferences for and experiences of a particular form of wage employment.

Instead of a study at the aggregate level, this study examines data collected at the level of individual workers and employers which will enable us to unravel these variations. In this book, the way unemployment is related to the individual's part-time work experience will be analyzed, rather than the relation between the aggregate trend of unemployment rate and the growth rate of part-time employment. Likewise, the relation between the life cycle of workers and part-time work participation will be examined, rather than the relation between the fertility rate of the whole female population and part-time work participation rate as in the study by Joshi and her associates (1985).

Our interest in part-time work at the individual level rather than the aggregate level is related to the theoretical relevance of part-time work experience in explaining disparate employment returns, especially those of women who, as we have noted, make up a major part of the part-time workforce. The amount and the kind of employment returns which a worker gets through specific forms of paid work are affected by a number of factors. In accounting for the different employment returns between individuals, labour market theorists generally distinguish between 'pre-market', 'in-market' and 'out-market' experiences. 'Pre-market' experience refers to the resources which an individual has prior to his or her entry into the labour market. These resources can come from one's social origin, the type of schooling experience and the level of formal qualification attained by an individual. 'In-market' experience refers to the different processes which an individual goes through while in the labour market, generally when he or she is in paid work. 'Out-market' experience generally means non-wage activities which an individual engages in when he or she withdraws from the labour market, for example, returning back to full-time education, or taking up domestic work.

In the next section, we shall discuss two major approaches to labour market studies and the different implications which can be drawn from them with reference to the issues addressed in the subsequent chapters. These two approaches differ from each other in the way they treat part-time work as a kind of 'in-market' experience and the working experience it brings to the individual.

Labour market theories and part-time work

Labour market theories are generally concerned with processes of job allocation, their implications for financial and non-financial job rewards, and the reasons for the unequal job returns between individuals. There are two main approaches to labour market studies - the neo-classical approach and the institutional approach.[2]

Neo-classical approach I : human capital theory

The neo-classical approach to the functioning of the labour market is epitomized by human capital theory which focuses primarily on explaining differential earnings. Underpinning the neo-classical approach are the assumptions of a rational economic man model and a perfectly free and competitive labour market. Both employers and employees are posited as rational and calculative actors, with perfect information about the market and about each other. The former compete against each other for the most productive worker and the latter contend for the best-rewarding job. The guiding principle of behaviours of both the employer and the worker is the maximization of benefits and the minimization of costs. Employers are concerned solely with the potential productivity of workers. They recruit and reward individuals according to their productivities which, in turn, are determined by the worker's innate ability or their investments in human capital by way of training and education. Workers are capable of moving freely between employers in search for jobs with the highest possible wage rates which match with their personal resources. The impersonal law of the labour market equalizes any inequalities in wages which are not due to disparate labour productivities.

The approach regards the labour market to be in an equilibrium state when workers with the most productive resources are matched with jobs which have the highest level of reward. Persistent pay differences between workers with similar kinds and amounts of human capital are explained by human capital theory in several ways. They may be short-term phenomena owing to imperfections in the information which employers and/or workers have about each other. The wage gap will disappear in the long run when eventually workers have more information about the ability of different employers to reward them, or when employers know more thoroughly about the productivities of different workers. Another explanation for persistent pay differences is some kinds of irrationalities either on the part of the employer, such as sex or racial discrimination; or on the part of the worker, such as a set of preferences and tastes not dictated by economic rationality. Deliberate actions or strategies adopted by either the employer or worker or both are treated as distortions and exogenous to the allocative mechanism of the market, rather than being regarded as endogenous to the way in which the labour market operates.

A central premise of the neo-classical approach underpins human capital theory, that is, labour is infinitely divisible into homogeneous units. One of the divisible forms which neo-classical theorists assume labour power would take is hour units. The supply of and the demand for labour are seen as continua of working hours, rather than as discrete ranges of working hours. Full-time and part-time work are not distinguished from each other as distinct forms of wage work. Instead, they are regarded as merely numbers of working hours the demand and supply of which can be incrementally increased or decreased unit by unit.

The primary concern of human capital theory is with the ways through which workers are allocated to jobs with higher or lower levels of rewards. The theory does not seek to explain the diverse methods which employers use to differentiate jobs. Nor does it deal with the issue that employers may well differ from each other in terms of their demand for particular types of workers. Employers are regarded as primarily concerned with maximizing profits and minimizing the labour costs in production. The labour market is assumed to be a perfectly competitive one in which no single employer has advantages over the other to pay job-seekers a wage rate which is above the going market rate. Employers are posited as price-takers - they face a market wage rate which they are not capable of altering unilaterally. In their recruitment of workers and the allocation of jobs, employers are guided by the market wage rate and the productivity of the worker. Their demand for labour is regarded as in equilibrium when the additional cost of employing one extra labour unit is equivalent to the marginal revenue of the product which the additional labour unit produces. The demand for part-time workers is treated as a demand for hours of labour and is determined primarily by the marginal productivity of the worker.

Some recent developments of the neo-classical approach have attempted to introduce variations to the perfectly competitive labour market model and to ascribe a role to firms or organizational structures in determining labour market outcomes. One of these developments is the recognition of the specificity of human capital investments. This implies that individual workers differ from each other not only in terms of the *amount*, but also in terms of the *kind* of human capital which they possess. Another development is the introduction of information and transaction costs, as well as other fixed labour costs, into the formulation of labour contracts or the recruitment of new employees. These costs could discourage employers from constant recruitment of outsiders to replace existing employees. These two developments, however, pose a dilemma for the approach itself. Specificities of human capital investments imply that there would not be one single market wage rate. Instead, there would be several wage rates each of which corresponds to a specific type of human capital. With respect to the second development, the various non-wage costs associated with frequent recruitment imply that existing employees have an advantage over outsiders in holding onto job positions within the firm. The competition between workers for job positions is not as perfect as human capital theory postulates. The approach would then have to give up its claim that the behaviours of employers and employees can be explained by one single behavioural model. Despite the recognition of specificity of human capital and non-wage labour costs in labour recruitment, these two developments share the basic feature of the neo-classical approach - employers are seen as passive adjustors to costs and constraints, rather than as actively designing jobs and deploying workers to these jobs which have unequal rewards.

Human capital theory explains disparities in the job rewards of full-time and part-time work in terms of the individual characteristics of job-holders. It postulates that workers will invest in productive resources as long as the expected returns of the investment exceed the expected direct and indirect costs. The job rewards which a worker receives is a function of his or her earlier investment. The more investment a worker makes, the greater his or her productivity is, and the higher the level of job rewards he or she can reap. The reason why some workers have jobs which offer lower levels of job rewards is because of their voluntary choices to invest less in human capital. Thus, following the reasoning of human capital theory, any differences between the job rewards of part-time and full-time work would be explained by the lower human capital investments which part-time workers have, as compared to full-timers.

Investments in human capital take place in both 'pre-market' and 'in-market' experiences. Individuals vary from each other in terms of their human capital endowment due to different social origins and the level of formal education they attain before they enter the labour market. However, the various kinds of 'in-market' experiences are treated simply

12

as an absolute number of years of paid work. Few human capital studies consider the possibility that different types of working experience may well carry greater or lesser opportunities for workers to enhance their productivities and hence can result in unequal employment rewards and job prospects. Moreover, the acquisition and accumulation of human capital is regarded as determined primarily by the choice of the worker. The way in which employers allocate jobs and thereby affect the chance and the ability of workers to acquire different levels and kinds of human capital is a blackbox in human capital theory, and is treated as a non-problematic issue. It sees the labour market as merely translating resources accrued through both 'pre-market' and 'in-market' experiences into different levels of earnings through a perfectly competitive allocation mechanism.

As an 'in-market' experience, part-time work is, generally, not distinguished from other kinds of 'in-market' experiences which would give a higher or lower rate of returns to an individual, as compared to other types of work experience. The cumulative effects of different kinds of work experience, in our case, part-time work experience, on the labour market returns of an individual are often not distinguished from each other and not considered as separate factors in the earnings analyses of human capital theory.

With regard to participation in part-time work, human capital theory does not consider it as a separate and distinct form of wage work participation. Labour is supplied in the form of unit hours, instead of as discrete ranges of working hours. The primary factor which determines the individual's choice of the number of hours of work is the market wage rate. Other things being equal, a higher market wage rate would motivate a worker to supply more hours of work. Tastes and preferences which may well be shaped by normative forces are generally considered as exogenous to the choice schema of the individual.[3] Human capital theory does not consider constraints which arise from the labour market structure as its primary theoretical problem. It offers us an explanation about the way through which labour supply decisions are arrived at. However, the theoretical logic of human capital theory would not enable it to explain why it is women, not old people or youths, who dominate the part-time workforce.[4] We need to turn to new home economics which, by relating labour supply to the domestic household, provides an account of why part-time work is dominated by women.

Neo-classical approach II : new home economics

One of the many concerns of new home economics is to relate labour market participation to the situation of the household and, in particular, to the division of labour between husbands and wives. The emergence of new home economics is a major development of the neo-classical approach to the study of family. It is concerned with a wide range of topics which are related to the family and the functioning of the household, for example, dating and marriage behaviours, fertility behaviours, household consumption patterns, investments in human capital and the sexual division of labour between wage work and domestic work. We shall focus on its ideas about the last item as this is more relevant to the general issue of labour market participation and the specific issue of part-time work participation.

Just as human capital theory posits individual employers and workers as utility-maximizers, new home economics also assumes that households seek the highest level of well-being. In the maximization process, households are subject to time constraints and the financial resources available to them. Every household has to design a routine pattern of time allocation between wage work and domestic work. The decision involves two related questions : how much time will be allocated and whose time that will be. New home economics explains the allocation of time to wage work and to domestic work in terms of the comparative advantages of different household members. Since specialization brings increasing returns to scale, one household member will specialize in wage work and the other will bear the primary responsibility of housework. This does not dictate whether husbands or wives will eventually specialize in wage work. To explain why wives are generally home-makers and husbands are wage-earners in modern nuclear households, new home economics theorist Becker (1981) resorts to the biological differences between the two sexes which make women more suitable for infant care and hence they specialize in housework. Men are primarily responsible for wage-earning and specialize in wage work.

According to new home economics, the participation of women in various forms of wage work involves a process of calculative choices. In choosing the amount of time to be allocated to wage work, a woman balances the time which housework demands of her against the income brought into the household by other family members, typically by her husband in the case of a married woman. While housework and childcare take priority over wage work, a woman may still be driven by the financial needs of her family to take up wage employment. The form of wage work which a woman takes up would still be subject to the time requirements of her domestic duties. The implication of new home economics on the choice of working hours is apparent. The number of working hours supplied by married women are negatively associated with heavy domestic duties and positively related to the financial needs of their households which cannot be met by their husbands.

New home economics offers us a set of propositions which relate major household factors to the extent of wage work participation of women. With regard to the form which labour supply takes, new home economics, similar to human capital theory, makes no distinction between full-time and part-time forms of participation. The two forms differ from each other merely in terms of their numbers of working hours. New home economics also takes preferences and normative values as given and these are treated as a blackbox the formulation of which it does not attempt to deal with. Gender norms which prescribe the male and female roles in the household and in the labour market are not considered in the theoretical framework of new home economics. Nor does it take into account the possibility that the utility functions of individual household members may well differ from each other and cannot be aggregated into one single function. The way the total utility is distributed inside the household is also not a theoretical concern of new home economics.[5]

Neither human capital theory nor new home economics have much to say about the distribution and the variation of employment opportunities and job choices which employers' labour use policies engender for different workers. In contrast, the other major approach to labour market studies, namely, the institutional approach, emphasizes the role of employers in the differentiation of jobs, the distinctness of different types of working experiences and the consequences these have on the labour market experiences of individuals.

Institutional approach I : segmentation theory

The neo-classical approach came under increasing criticism as a general approach to labour market behaviours when studies in the 60s showed that American urban blacks repeatedly took up inferior jobs and earned a lower wage rate. Researchers introduced the dual labour market hypothesis to account for persistent labour market inequalities between different social groups. This perspective was later developed and articulated into various versions of segmentation theory which offer a more complex analysis of the labour market structures and processes in advanced industrial economies. Generally speaking, segmentation theory argues that there are social and institutional factors which inhibit the labour market from functioning in a perfectly competitive manner. Labour markets are divided up into segments. There are institutional barriers between the segments which limit the operation of market forces. Moreover, these barriers are not of short-term existence. They arise from and are maintained by the deliberate actions of employers and/or employees. These barriers restrict the free movement of workers between different employers and thus give rise to persistent disparate job rewards

15

between workers.

There are different versions of segmentation theory. They vary from each other in terms of their explanations of why the labour market is divided up into segments. We shall discuss the major ones which have greater relevance for part-time work. Doeringer and Piore (1971) attributed the cause of segmentation to the changing skills needs which were associated with advanced technology. The use of modern technology requires a stable and committed workforce so that the returns to staff training and human resources investment which employers make is maximized. An unstable workforce with a high turnover rate would incur high cost in training new recruits. To retain workers with firm-specific skills and to foster a strong sense of allegiance in these employees, employers offer them job careers which are intimately tied with the organization. A labour market segment develops in which the recruitment, the allocation of jobs and their levels of financial and non-financial rewards are determined by administrative rules rather than by market forces.

The subsequent work of Piore (1980) also emphasized political instability and economic uncertainty as primary causes of labour market segmentation. Product market fluctuations engender a production environment which is characterized by flux and uncertainties. Labour market segmentation is a response undertaken by employers to reduce or resolve these uncertainties. Employers offer some portions of the workforce better employment conditions and job security. These workers are not treated as disposable factors of production. Their careers and employment prospects are linked closely to their employing organizations. They would subsequently have a lower turnover rate. With a reliable workforce, employers would then be more capable of planning production and thereby reduce uncertainties.

A second version of segmentation theory was propounded by Edwards (1979) and Gordon et al.(1982). They sought to explain labour market segmentation in terms of the historical development of capitalism and the dynamics of capital-labour relations. When the capitalist system made the transition from the competitive mode to the monopoly mode, the workforce became increasingly homogeneous as workers were deskilled. The employer-employee relations became more tense and conflictual. Labour conflicts at the workplace escalated into political conflicts and labour movements. As a result, various legislations were enacted and statutory arrangements were set up to protect and advance the interests of workers at the workplace. These, in turn, had repercussions on management-labour relations. Labour market segmentation grew out of the desire of employers to exercise and maintain more effective control over work performance in the face of a unionized workforce. Control over the labour process enables employers to make greater profits. Edwards argued :

> The explanation I advance is straight forward : hierarchy exists and persists because it is profitable. Employers are able to increase their profits when they have greater control over the labour process (Edwards 1979, p.viii).

He argued that in differentiating employment conditions for various sections of the workforce, employers eroded the basis for common worker identity and opposition, thereby preventing the emergence of collective action which challenged management prerogatives. In response to the finer distinctions between job positions and the bureaucratic regulations at the workplace, unions increasingly accepted the organization of work and the basic principle of capitalism. The efforts of unionists were directed towards making job criteria more explicit and openly articulated, instead of towards winning over the power to control the labour process from the management. By offering a section of their employees preferential employment conditions, employers 'divided and conquered' the workforce and avoided labour conflicts and disruptions to production. The following remark aptly sums up the stance of this version of segmentation theory :

> Labour market segmentation arose and is perpetuated because it is functional - that is, it facilitates the operation of capitalist institutions....... it helps reproduce capital hegemony (Reich, Gordon and Edwards, 1973, p.61).

Edwards argued that there were different modes of control over the labour process. A more detailed discussion of the ways through which the labour process is controlled and their relations to labour market segmentation will be given in Chapter five when the work situation of part-time jobs is examined.

Piore (1980) also ascribed a role to union and militant labour movements in generating labour market segmentation. He traced the historical development of union movements in Italy, America and France and explicated the ways through which labour movements and organized political pressures resulted in protective legislations and institutional arrangements. These served to curtail the ability of employers to lay off and fire workers at will and thus incurred on them higher labour costs. As a result, employers relocated their production and reorganized their workforce to evade union pressures and legislative requirements. They used pockets of the labour force like migrant workers, women and

17

peasants to evade the statutory obligations imposed on them. Non-standard ways of organizing productions were devised, like the putting-out system in Italy, relocating plants to non-unionized areas, subcontracting etc to reduce the rigidities which legislations and union practices imposed on their use of labour.

Labour movements and the responses of employers resulted in a sharp division between the unionized and non-unionized workforce. The unionized workforce enjoys better employment conditions which are governed by formalized rules and collective agreements between unions and the management. Workers have better employment protection and a higher level of job security. Pockets of the labour force which fall outside the scope of union influence or statutory employment protection form another segment. Workers in this segment are more vulnerable to the 'hire and fire' prerogative of the employer. They are deployed by employers to achieve flexibility in the use of labour which employers cannot accomplish with the unionized workforce.

A common feature which variants of segmentation theory share is their argument that the labour market is made up of discrete and qualitatively different segments, rather than having a homogeneous structure. Basic economic processes like wage determination, job allocation, education and training, are fundamentally different between various market segments and cannot be captured by one single model of human behaviours, as assumed by human capital theory. Piore argued that the significance of segmentation lay in the fact that:

> various segments of society organize around different rules, processes, and institutions that produce different systems of incentives and disincentives to which individuals respond. These 'lumps' or social segments are coherent wholes that derive their unity both from the consistency of their internal rules and organization and from the stability of their relationships with other parts of society (Piore, 1980, p.2).

Segmentation theorists generally distinguish between primary and secondary labour markets. Earlier work in segmentation theory focused on the primary labour market. Piore (1980) further divided it into an upper and a lower tier. Workers in the lower tier enjoy a stable work environment. Work skills are acquired on the job and in the process of production. However, compared to workers in the upper tier, these workers do not have steady progress up job ladders. The upper tier of the primary sector consists of professional and managerial jobs. In addition to substantial job security, employees in these job positions have extensive opportunities for career advancement. Unlike workers in the lower tier, these workers have prolonged periods of formal education prior to their entry into the work organization.

Edwards (1979) also sub-divided the primary labour market into a subordinate one and an independent one. In the subordinate primary labour market, the labour process is subject to a technical mode of control whereas the bureaucratic mode of control characterises the independent primary labour market.

Subsequent segmentation theorists further refined the notion of an internal labour market which was put forward by Doeringer and Piore. Althauser and Kalleberg (1981) drew up a different typology of labour markets which conceptually distinguished internal labour markets that exist within firms from those which span across several employing organizations. They suggested a three-part structural definition for the term internal labour market. Jobs form an internal labour market if (a) they form a hierarchical ladder; (b) with entry limited to the bottom; and (c) upward movements are accompanied by a progressive development of skills and knowledge. Job structures are in the form of well-defined pathways. Steady and predictable movements of workers along these pathways is a defining feature of internal labour market. Althauser and Kalleberg delineated two types of internal labour market, namely, firm internal labour market and occupational internal labour market. The former is established and confined to a single employer.[6] The latter exists for incumbents of an occupation or two or more associated occupations. Job ladders in an occupational internal labour market can span across several employers. Entries to this type of internal labour markets are limited by administrative procedures, or by standards set up by professional and union organizations, for example, through licensing, certification and registration.

Secondary labour markets received only brief discussion in the early literature of segmentation theory, as compared to the theoretical and empirical work on internal labour markets. The secondary labour market is portrayed almost as a negative mirror image of the primary labour market. While employment in the primary segment offers generalized advantages, workers in the secondary segment have unfavourable employment conditions. In the primary labour market, the terms of employment are governed by a set of formalized, administrative rules, instead of by market forces. Jobs in the primary segment offer higher wage rates, employment stability, job security, chances of advancement and training. Workers are subject to due process of administration which is guided by institutional rules and regulations. The secondary labour market, on the contrary, offers less favourable returns. There are few limitations on entry or notable entry requirements to these jobs. Hence, wages and employment are more susceptible to market forces. Secondary jobs offer lower wages, fewer fringe benefits, and little chance of advancement. There is a paucity of training opportunities and a higher level of employment insecurity in the secondary segment. Jobs are unskilled, either requiring no skills at all or utilizing only very basic and general skills. Significant investment in training by either the employer or the employee is absent. Workers are subject to arbitrary and capricious supervision at the workplace. In other words, jobs in the secondary labour market lack the elements, or sources, of structure and employment stability that define the primary segment.

Segmentation of the labour market has significant implications for the job movement and the employment (in)stability of workers. In a segmented labour market, the movement of workers between the primary and the secondary segment is minimal. Where there is mobility, the movement is more likely to be intra-segment rather than inter-segment. Jobs in the primary segment are filled by promotion within the segment rather than by recruitment from outside. Workers who belong to the primary labour market have steady progress and orderly movements along their job ladders. They are stable workers who are committed to their employing organizations and have a lower turnover rate.

In contrast to workers in the primary labour market, workers in the secondary segment do not enjoy orderly movements into other jobs. They tend to have a higher turnover rate and move more frequently in between different firms, as compared to workers in the primary market. However, unlike movements in the primary labour market, these job moves are not accompanied by an upgrade of work skills and knowledge. They are also unlikely to be moves which bring the worker into the primary labour market. In other words, occupants of secondary jobs are trapped in the secondary labour market. They constantly switch between low-paid, dead-end jobs and unemployment. Doeringer and Piore (1971) suggested that employment instability and frequent unemployment were hallmarks of secondary employment.

Thus, regarding the role of employers, the structure of the labour market, the job mobility of workers and their employment experiences, there are major contrasts between human capital theory and segmentation theory. Instead of positing workers as perfectly mobile between different kinds of jobs and employers as in human capital theory, segmentation theory emphasizes the restrictions imposed on job movements by institutional factors like firm, trade unions and occupational associations. While human capital theory treats employers and workers as passive intermediaries through which perfect competition shapes the functioning of the labour market, segmentation theory stresses the active role which employers play in organizing and structuring the labour market. Unlike human capital theory, the different 'in-market' experiences are not aggregated together as absolute number of years of work. Instead, distinct kinds of 'in-market' experiences which arise from labour market segmentation are distinguished from each other. The employment experience of a worker depends on which labour market segment he or she has been involved in. Employment in the primary labour market enables workers to enjoy cumulative advantages leading to more favourable job rewards; secondary employment involves a vicious cycle of low-wage work and unemployment. Employers' labour use policies is the main explanation for differences in earnings and in other conditions of employment. Furthermore, the different employment conditions trap workers in their respective segments and restrict inter-segment movements. Workers are channelled to different segments and the boundaries between these segments are maintained by the minimal inter-segment mobility of workers.

Another major difference between human capital theory and segmentation theory is their views of unemployment. While segmentation theory sees unemployment as a persistent feature of secondary employment, human capital theory regards it as a short-term phenomenon. The unemployment experience of an individual is explained by the neo-classical approach in terms of imperfect information, or some forms of intervention in the perfectly competitive labour market, for example, minimum wage laws. When these interventions are uplifted, and/or when job-seekers have better information about the labour market, unemployment would disappear. The duration of an unemployment spell and the kind of job which an unemployed person will get eventually depend on his or her individual characteristics. In other words, the fate of unemployed people is not related in any systematic way to certain forms of employment. On the contrary, secondary labour market theory sees unemployment as a systematic feature of unstable employment conditions which can be explained by the ways which employers use different workers to suit their production needs. Workers of the secondary segment do not have an asset-like status. They are employed and dismissed according to business fluctuations and contingent manpower requirements which arise from production. These workers are more liable to experience job insecurity and unemployment.

The earlier works of segmentation theory concentrated on the internal labour market, or the particular form which labour market segmentation takes. While it argued for a distinction between different labour market segments, the secondary labour market was dealt with in very generalized terms. The theory allows for the possibility that working hours are segmented into discrete and unequal forms of wage employment, instead of taking the form of a continuum of unit hours as portrayed by the neo-classical approach. It also allows for the possibility that the

21

various labour use policies of employers may well shape the working hours of different jobs and the rewards associated with them. This implies that workers are not able to supply freely the number of working hours they prefer. However, the theory has made no specific claims about part-time work or about the way in which the primary/secondary distinction can be applied to the full-time/part-time distinction. It is not until the emergence of a set of arguments or predictions called the flexible firm thesis that we have a clear application of the notion of secondary labour market to part-time work.

Institutional approach II : the flexible firm thesis

In many ways, the flexible firm thesis can be regarded as a contemporary variant of segmentation theory. Segmentation theory arose as an attempt to theorize the emergence of distinct segments in the labour market when the structure of advanced industrial societies became more complex : firms grew in size, technology used in production became more advanced, product markets were increasingly dominated by monopolistic companies, workers organized themselves into various forms of organizations to protect their own interests vis-à-vis that of the management. Beginning from the 70s, advanced industrial economies have experienced vicissitudes and uncertainties in their economic growth. Researchers have noticed that employers are responding to economic fluctuations in different ways. Theories of flexibility are developed as attempts which seek to understand and explain these responses to these changing economic circumstances. While the term 'flexibility' can be pitched at different levels and with different meanings[7], the flexible firm thesis has been put forward in the British literature to analyse the different changes undertaken by firms to restructure their workforce and the effects these changes have on the structure of the labour market.

The flexible firm thesis argues that firms in Britain are increasingly conforming to a 'flexible firm' model. Proponents of this model claim that recession and intensified competition have made permanent reduction of unit labour costs a managerial imperative for British firms. However, this cannot be met by a simple across-the-board job cuts for several reasons. The reduction of employment levels is expensive due to the redundancy payments that need to be given out to workers. Uncertainties about the revival of the economy and the product market means that firms have to maintain a certain level of manning to meet unpredictable business improvements. Yet, these uncertainties also mean that firms cannot commit themselves to a high level of human resources investment for all sections of the workforce. However, technological advancements make it necessary to maintain and enhance the skill levels of employees.

22

The solution is to invest training selectively in certain sections of the workforce while simultaneously devising other ways to reduce the overall labour cost. The pressure from unions to reduce basic working hours has also led employers to deploy their workforce in a number of unconventional ways to avoid the rigidities imposed by union regulations.[8]

The result is that management adopts diverse labour use policies which are designed to increase the numerical, financial and functional flexibility of the workforce. Units of labour are employed and deployed flexibly to meet fluctuations in the levels of demand for goods and services. Different employment contracts and jobs with different working-hour schedules are designed to achieve numerical flexibility. The job content and skill levels of certain sections of the workforce are made functionally diverse so that new task requirements which arise from changes in customers' tastes and in technology can be met readily. As for the wage structure, the shift is from uniform payment methods to greater wage differentials and individualizations between workers.

There has been much debate about whether a trend towards flexibility has taken place in Britain. Regarding the flexibility in production techniques, Lane (1988) compared the pursuit of flexible specialization in Britain and Germany. She contended that Britain failed to achieve the level of flexible specialization which was attained in Germany. As for labour uses, Hakim (1987) claimed that a flexible workforce was taking shape in Britain and part-time work took up about half of this flexible workforce. Moreover, she argued that the trend was not a short-term response to recession. Instead, it is a secular and irreversible change. Rubery (1988) argued that the growth of part-time employment which the flexible firm thesis claims to be a 'peripheral' workforce is due to the growth of service industries rather than to employers' deliberate policy to substitute full-time by part-time workers. Hunter and Macinnes (1991) were doubtful whether flexible labour use policies could be characterized as results of the strategic calculation and long-term planning by employers. Procter et al. (1994) argued that the term flexibility had its unique meaning and should not be confused with other concepts like flexible specialization or variants of the concept post-industrialism. Pollert (1991) questioned whether the term flexibility carried any new and substantive meanings and whether the changes which the flexible firm thesis described were radical breaks or secular changes which industrial societies have been experiencing.

A full assessment of the various claims of the flexible firm thesis is not our purpose and is beyond the scope of the present study. With regard to part-time work, the flexible firm thesis offers a clear argument about its relation to labour market segmentation. Working hours are major levers of employers' labour policy. The various flexible measures divide the workforce into a core group and two peripheral groups. Core and peripheral workers have unequal employment conditions. Core workers are given employment security, training opportunities, more favourable work conditions and job rewards to retain them so that the labour requirements in times of business revival can be met readily and that firms can cope with technological changes. However, the size of the core workforce has to be kept small as it incurs on the firm a high level of fixed labour costs which is comprised of the payments which employers have to make to cover training, statutory employment rights payments, and social wages like national insurance contribution.

The core workforce is supplemented by two groups of peripheral workers. Workers in the first peripheral group are also full-time employees, but they are offered a job, not a career. Employers are not concerned with enhancing the general work skills of these workers or with investing them with firm-specific work skills. The opportunity for these employees to establish a career within the organization is minimal. The second peripheral workforce comprises of workers who work under various non-standard employment contracts. One of the major proponents of the flexible firm thesis has offered us a clear claim about the location of part-time work in this second peripheral workforce and explicitly associated part-time work with secondary conditions of employment :

> Part-time working is probably the best example of this [the second peripheral workgroup] - the jobs having all the characteristics of those in the first peripheral group, with their deployment often structured to match changing business needs - twilight shifts, overlaid shifts or peak manning etc. Jobsharing, short-term contracts, public subsidy trainees and recruitment through temporary contracts all perform a similar function - maximising flexibility while minimising the organization's commitment to the worker's job security and career development (Atkinson, 1984, p. 29).

Jobs with working hours which are shorter than conventional full-time jobs fall outside the core workforce. Part-time jobs as well as other non-permanent employment like temporary jobs which last for a short period of time, public subsidy trainees and job-sharers are classified as peripheral workforces. The flexible firm thesis argues that peripheral workers are given unfavourable job rewards, a lower level of job security, and have less access to career opportunities. Part-time workers are peripheral workers whose employment conditions are akin to those in

24

the secondary labour market. It has also been claimed that one of the major segmentation boundaries in Britain runs along the full-time/part-time distinction. Rubery argued :

> The more significant divisions in the employment sphere in the U.K. may not be between categories of employment contract but between employment in unionised or non-unionised establishments or simply between full-time and part-time jobs (Rubery 1989, p. 71).

Several other writers have made similar arguments. In their study of part-time work in Canada, Duffy and Pupo (1992) described part-time work as a ghettoized form of employment which helped employers save money but turned women into a peripheral workforce. Similarly, in her review of female employment in several OECD countries, Bakker (1988) claimed that part-time work was emerging as a form of labour market segmentation and gave rise to persistent inequalities.

The claim that part-time work forms a secondary labour market is often linked with the labour market positions and fortunes of women. We have noted at the beginning of this Chapter that women dominate the part-time workforce in Britain as well as in a number of OECD countries. The neo-classical approach and the institutional approach emphasize different factors to explain women's participation in part-time work. In the next section, we shall discuss the explanations offered by the two approaches.

Women's employment and part-time work

The distribution of workers between better or worse jobs is explained by human capital theory in terms of voluntaristic choices to invest in human capital. Workers who expect the opportunity cost of any current investments in human capital to be compensated by a higher level of future returns are willing to undertake job training and more formal schooling. Subsequently, they will get more rewarding jobs. Workers who are unwilling to bear such opportunity costs will get poorer jobs. The participation in part-time work is, therefore, explained by human capital theory as results of women's lower level of investment in education.

New home economics also regards the participation in part-time work as a voluntaristic and economistic choice. Time spent to shoulder domestic responsibilities is balanced against the opportunity cost because of non-participation in the labour market. As we have mentioned earlier, new home economics approach stresses that the demand which housework makes on a woman's time and the wage-earning capacity of other members of her household are two crucial factors in determining the amount of time she would allocate to wage work. New home economics shares the basic tenet of human capital theory in explaining women's participation in part-time work. The choice of numbers of working hours is made through rational calculation of costs and benefits derivable from wage and non-wage work.

Besides their reasoning about part-time work participation, both human capital theory and new home economics have crucial implications on women's mobility between full-time and part-time work. Since the neo-classical approach assumes that the labour market is perfectly competitive, this implies that movements in between full-time, part-time or non-participation would be unrestricted. It is just a matter of increasing or reducing the supply of hours of work. An open labour market implies that as the childcare duties of women become less time-consuming and the financial needs of the household are more pressing, women can change their employment statuses and adjust their involvement in wage work accordingly. In particular, switching in between part-time or full-time work could be easily accomplished to suit changes in personal preferences or needs of the household.

Very different propositions can be derived from segmentation theory and its contemporary variant the flexible firm thesis. Both segmentation theory and the flexible firm thesis are about job differentiation and the inequalities it brings to workers. They elaborate on the way jobs are designed, structured and differentiated by employers. They both emphasize the crucial role which employers play in shaping labour market structures and workers' employment experiences and prospects, although the two part company in terms of the extent to which employers are strategic planners in their labour use, or whether they are just responding in an ad hoc manner to changes which come from the wider legislative and economic environment.

Unlike the neo-classical approach, the institutional approach does not see workers as capable of adjusting freely the hours they work to suit their own needs or preferences. The number and the scheduling of working hours of jobs are subject to employers' labour use policies which are devised to meet the manning requirements of the production or service provision schedule. Taking up a part-time job would be a result of employers' job allocation strategies, rather than the outcome of personal characteristics or features of the household to which the worker belongs.

Another proposition derivable from the application of segmentation theory to the full-time/part-time distinction is about the mobility in between the two forms of wage employment. The secondary employment conditions of part-time work would give rise to cumulative employment disadvantages and a vicious cycle of confining workers to secondary jobs. These disadvantages would make it difficult for women to move from part-time to full-time employment. In other words, part-time work may be an alternative to, rather than a bridge between, non-participation and full-time employment in a woman's working life.

The third proposition which can be derived from secondary labour market theory is that part-time work and unemployment are closely associated with each other. Part-time workers would not be regarded as assets to the organization. Instead, they are treated as 'residual' factors of production. Workers on part-time jobs are employed to enhance the labour use flexibility of the firm. They are recruited and dismissed according to the needs of the employer. When a firm has to cut down its manpower, part-timers would be more likely to be laid off while core full-time employees are retained. In other words, part-timers would be more likely than core full-time employees to experience job insecurity and unemployment.

However, despite its emphasis on institutional barriers which divide the labour market and which inhibit the movements of workers, segmentation theory also suggests reasons which are not related to the employers or the job nature to explain why jobs in the secondary sector are dominated and repeatedly taken up by certain socio-demographic groups, for example, women, migrants and members of ethnic minorities. Piore (1972, 1980) suggested three sets of factors to explain the channelling of different kinds of individuals to different labour market segments : (1) formal qualification; (2) the political and economic power of different groups of workers; (3) class subcultures which shape the attitudinal dispositions of workers. Since the major proposition which we can draw from segmentation theory is the argument that part-time employment is a form of secondary employment, we shall focus on those factors which segmentation theory gives as determinants of the secondary labour market. Doeringer and Piore suggested that the employer, the nature of the job and attitudes of the worker all played a part in causing employment instability which characterizes the secondary labour market :

> This [unstable work relation in the secondary labour market] may occur because employers in the secondary sector cannot economically establish internal labour market conditions which are conducive to reducing turnover or because technical aspects of the jobs are such that reduction of turnover has little value to the employer. Second, the attitudes and demographic traits of the secondary labour force may be such that workers

place little value upon job security in particular enterprises (Doeringer and Piore 1971, p. 170).

Some employers, for example, monopolies, enjoy a better position in the product market and, therefore, are less constrained by market forces in setting wages and other types of job returns, as compared to firms which have little product market power. Larger organization may find it necessary to regulate employment relations according to administrative rules whereas the scale of operation of small firms makes it more difficult for them to establish primary employment conditions for workers.

In terms of job nature, Doeringer and Piore explicated that certain categories of jobs are inherently unstable. For instance, jobs in non-union construction work, or in manufacturing industries which produce goods for Christmas are of short-term existence and are not organized in the form of continuous employment. These jobs last only temporarily and workers who fill these jobs are thus more liable to experience job loss when the task of these jobs is accomplished.

The explanations in terms of employers and job nature follow from the theoretical logic of segmentation theory which stresses the labour use policies of employers and the limitations imposed on workers' job movements by the labour market structure. The third set of determinants which Doeringer and Piore suggested to explain participation in secondary employment and its employment instability are, however, related to certain attitudinal traits and dispositions of the worker. These are shaped by factors not related to drawbacks of secondary jobs, or limitations imposed by employers, or experiences at the workplace. Specifically, Doeringer and Piore gave working mothers, students and moonlighters as examples of groups of workers who are likely to place little value on permanent employment and chances of advancement. A common feature of the first two groups is that their major concern is not with participation in paid work. The gender role of working mothers in the household has priority over their role as workers in the labour market. They are secondary wage-earners of their households whose income is used only to meet minor financial needs. Their childcare responsibility restricts continuous participation in the labour market. Thus, they are likely to have a weak attachment to their employing organization and a low level of commitment to paid work. Young students' major concern is with school work and not with gainful employment. They take up paid work only for a short period of time to meet some short-term financial needs. Employers are less likely to offer these kinds of workers training and promotion opportunities. This, in turn, contributes to employment instability and the subsequent entrapment in a cycle of low-wage, low-skilled and dead-end work. Piore regarded the formation of the job or labour market attachment of secondary workers as exogenous to the economic system :

> .....the particular characteristics of secondary workers are largely 'accidents' which the economic system makes use of but which it does not create (Piore 1980, p. 26).

This view about the secondary labour force as existing independently of the economic production system is heavily criticized by other theorists as ignoring the ways other social institutions are integrated with the labour market in stratifying the supply of different types of labour. Humphries and Rubery (1984) emphasized the importance of social reproduction in understanding the supply-side of the labour market. They argued that the dependence of women on the earnings which men brought into the family enabled them to withdraw from the labour market. At the same time, this dependence provided the basis for employers to exploit women by giving them poor wages. Craig and her associates (1985) argued that the organization of the family and community shaped the supply of different socio-demographic groups to different segments. They suggested that the ways these social institutions interacted with the demand-side should be considered in labour market studies.

Criticisms also come from the different feminist theories about female wage work and the sexual division of labour (Beechey, 1987; Barrett and McIntosh, 1980). Generally speaking, these theories argue that women's roles in wage work and domestic work are used to maintain the viability of the capitalist system and the patriarchal power of men over women. The domestic labour of women serves to reproduce labour and enables capitalists to extract further surplus value from the labour power of male workers. Employers would offer female workers poorer employment conditions and legitimize their differential treatments of men and women by the rationale that women are not main wage-earners for their families. The labour market disadvantages of women exacerbate their economic dependence on men and the unequal power relations between the two sexes. For our purpose, these arguments amount to the implication that women's socially defined roles in the household and the ways which employers perceive these roles are crucial in understanding women's participation in part-time work and the employment conditions which they receive.

Segmentation theory thus offers us two different explanations regarding women's participation in part-time work. The first one can be called a 'job-centred' explanation. This explanation stresses the opportunities or constraints which arise from the labour use policies of

29

employers. It also focuses on the effect of cumulative disadvantages of secondary jobs on labour market positions. To the extent that the part-time work is a form of secondary employment, we would expect that it carries cumulative disadvantages and an entrapment effect in this form of wage work. The second explanation can be called a 'gender-centred' explanation which attributes the cause to the gender role and the related attitudinal dispositions which female workers themselves hold. Their attachment to their jobs and to the labour market is weaker than workers in the primary segment. The importance they attach to their family overrides success in their jobs. Their participation in part-time work is a result of their lower level of commitment to employment and their acceptance of their socially defined role in the household. One of the aims of this thesis is to assess these two explanations in accounting for participation in part-time work.

Existing British studies of part-time work

The various implications and propositions derived from the two major labour market approaches and discussed in the previous section have not been examined comprehensively in the existing studies of part-time work. In the following discussion, the literature on part-time work will be examined. We shall note the findings, the strengths and the weaknesses of these studies with respect to the four issues which this study addresses. The way through which this study attempts to overcome some of these inadequacies will also be discussed.

The demand for part-time workers

Existing empirical studies about the demand of British employers for part-time workers can be divided into two types : case studies and surveys. In the first type of studies, usually several organizations are chosen. The reasons for employing part-timers and the ways they are deployed to meet various changes and needs of the employing organization are then examined in details. Walsh (1990) analysed the use of part-time workers as well as other types of non-standard employment (for example, contract and casual workers) in nine cases chosen from retail, hotel and catering industries. He noticed that part-time workers were employed to meet peaks and troughs in the demands of customers. Gregory (1991) examined the pattern of working hours of French and British part-timers in large-scale grocery retailing. She noted that working hours in France were subject to a greater degree of statutory regulations than in Britain. O'Doherty (1993) used BankCo as a case to examine the way the organization's restructuring of its clerical workforce led to an increase in the use of part-timers. O'Reilly (1994:151-83) compared the use of part-time workers in the British retail banking sector to that in France by investigating four cases. She identified three main reasons why banks used part-timers : for managing fluctuations in workload; in response to the demands of employees for reductions in working time; and to resolve recruitment problems or reduce full-time equivalent staff.

These case studies are rich in details and often unravel the organizational dynamics associated with the use of part-timers. For example, O'Reilly (1994) combined interviews with bank managers and official documents of the banks to examine the changes in the use of part-timers and the way through which the current practices emerged. O'Doherty (1993) related the changes in the organization's employment policy to the increase in the intake of part-time clerical workers. However, given the small number of cases, these studies cannot tell us the extent to which their findings are applicable to firms across the full range of industrial sectors.

Some other studies examined more cases and covered a greater diversity of industrial sectors. Horrell and Rubery (1991) examined the working-time policies of 29 establishments in Britain. These establishments included manufacturing, public and private service establishments. They investigated in details various kinds of working-time arrangements and the extent to which part-time workers were involved in these flexible arrangements. They noted that there were sectoral differences in the degree of flexibility in working-time patterns. While the study contains details about the different types of working-time schedules in the routine manning schedule of the organization, there was no attempt to link them systematically to organizational features like size, unionization or industrial sectors.

Beechey and Perkins (1987) focused on seven cases in Coventry. These cases covered manufacturing and public sector establishments which provided health, education and social services. They recorded in detail the ways an upgrade in technology and changes in the organization of production led to reductions or increases in the intake of part-timers. They argued that flexible labour use is more important than substitution as an explanation for the growth of part-time work. Moreover, employers had gender-specific ways of organizing their labour force. In cases in which the labour force was dominated by female workers, employers used part-time employment as a major way to attain flexibility. Where the labour force was predominantly male employees, employers adopted other strategies like overtime or short-time working.

Robinson and Wallace (1984) noted in their case studies that part-

31

timers were employed for several financial advantages. Employers did not have to pay national insurance for part-timers whose earnings fall below the threshold for contribution. Part-timers were excluded from a range of fringe benefits which were enjoyed by full-timers. Part-timers saved employers the need to pay overtime premium to full-timers. Hunter and Macinnes (1991) chose 47 cases from the 1987 Employers Labour Use Strategies Survey (ELUS) to investigate the rationales for the employment of part-timers as well as other types of labour which the flexible firm thesis classifies as non-standard types of labour. Their sample covered a wider range of industrial sectors. They found that the two commonest reasons which employers gave for the use of part-timers were to match manning levels to demand patterns and that certain tasks require only a limited period of time to complete. The case studies approach which these studies adopt reveal the diversity of reasons why employers employ part-timers. However, the ways the importance of these reasons varies between different organizations are not systematically investigated.

The second type of study covers a wider range of industrial sectors and organizations with different features by drawing on data from surveys. Bosworth and Dawkins (1982) used the information of 764 establishments interviewed for the 1975 Women and Work Survey for their analysis. They drew up a comprehensive list of reasons which employers gave for employing part-timers and for increasing the proportion of part-timers. These reasons included both supply-side and demand-side factors. Supply-side factors include : to retain experienced workers who cannot work full-time, to overcome difficulty in recruiting full-timers, and to obtain skilled workers. Demand-side factors are : to provide manning levels which match with busy periods, to undertake jobs which do not need full-time cover, and to make extra shifts of production. Bosworth and Dawkins enumerated the frequencies of the different reasons which establishments gave for their employment of part-timers. However, they failed to examine systematically the ways the proportion of part-timers employed vary with the organizational features of these establishments. This deficiency has been redressed by other studies which are also based on surveys of establishments.

Blanchflower and Corry (1986) used the data of the 1980 Workplace Industrial Relations Survey (WIRS) to relate the use of part-timers to an array of factors. These factors included the nature of production, the industrial relations system and the use of other types of labour. They defined an establishment as 'part-time using' if (1) at least 25 part-timers were employed, or (2) in establishments of less than 50 employees, part-timers constituted at least 50% of the workforce. This way of delineating the dependent variable is arbitrary. Moreover, collapsing the dependent variable into a dichotomous one is likely to result in a substantial loss of information. It overlooks the finer distinction between the different levels of part-time employment measured as a continuous variable.

Mcgregor and Sproull (1991) investigated the variations between establishments in the proportion of part-timers employed as well as other types of labour which the flexible firm thesis classifies as peripheral workers. They attempted to relate the variations to both temporal influences like changes in the product market and structural factors like sectoral and industrial differences. The data they used were drawn from the 1987 Employers Labour Use Strategies Survey (ELUS). The sample of the ELUS was in turn derived from that of the 1984 WIRS. However, the sampling method of both the 1980 and the 1984 WIRS excluded establishments which had fewer than 25 employees. As the discussion in Chapters three and four will point out, this coverage leaves out small establishments which are crucial employers of part-timers. Thus, there is still the need for an adequate analysis which assesses the relative importance of both structural determinants and temporal changes in explaining different employers' demand for part-timers.

The difference between part-time and full-time work

We have noted that applying the secondary labour market theory to part-time work implies that workers who work part-time have poorer employment situations, as compared to those who work on the full-time basis. A systematic application of the secondary labour market theory to part-time work needs to make explicit comparison between full-time and part-time employment. Moreover, in the comparison, other relevant job and workplace features as well as individual characteristics of the job-holder have to be taken into account in order to ascertain the effect of part-time status *per se*. Previous studies have paid insufficient attention to these two points. Hurstfield (1987) analysed the pay of part-timers. The occupations which she included in her analysis were mainly semi-/unskilled manual occupations. We cannot tell the extent to which her findings can be applied to other occupations. As we shall see in Chapter four, part-time jobs span across a wider range of occupations than those which Hurstfield examined. Moreover, she only covered one aspect of a full range of employment conditions which segmentation theory uses to characterize secondary employment.

The studies of Beechey and Perkins (1987), Robinson and Wallace (1984) dealt with a fuller range of employment conditions of part-time workers. While these two studies are rich in details about the unequal employment conditions between full-timers and part-timers, there was no

33

attempt to assess the net effect of part-time working hours by taking into account the personal characteristics of the worker and other salient workplace features.

The 1980 Women and Employment Survey (Martin and Roberts, 1984) covered a wider range of employment conditions. These included wage levels, training and promotion opportunities, the availability of paid holidays, sick pay and occupational pensions for women who worked full-time and part-time. Since the sample covered only women, we do not have full-time working men for comparison.

Rubery and her associates (1994) compared in greater details the employment conditions, the job content and the skill levels of men and women working full-time and part-time. However, they did not attempt to control for other features of the job and of the workplace as well as individual characteristics to assess the distinctness of part-time as a stratum in the job market. The same criticism can be applied to the study of the part-time employment in Swindon by Court (1990).

We have noted in the earlier discussion that a proposition which can be derived from the secondary labour market theory is that part-time work is closely associated with unemployment. The few existing studies which address the employment security of part-time workers are case studies. Beechey and Perkins (1987) noted in their case studies that part-timers were the first group to be laid off when technological changes in production reduced the number of workers which employers needed. Robinson and Wallace (1984) found in some of their cases that part-timers had a higher chance of being made redundant and this is partly due to the 'last-in, first-out' redundancy criterion. We need survey-type of data to assess the extent to which these findings can be generalized to a larger population.

Payne and Payne (1994) used Labour Force Surveys to examine the association between unemployment and part-time work between 1979 and 1989. They examined the chance of unemployed people in getting a part-time rather than a full-time job. The data they used were collected at two fixed time points which were 12 months apart. This data do not allow us to assess the long-term cumulative effect of unemployment on part-time work participation. Work history data are needed to examine the way unemployment experience would affect the chance of getting part-time rather than full-time work.

Taking these studies together, the argument that part-time/full-time employment forms a segmentation boundary remains as a hypothesis which needs to be tested more comprehensively.

With respect to the long-term effect of part-time employment experience on the labour market attainment of women, previous studies have focused on two major aspects, namely, earnings and occupational mobility. The analyses of Dex et al. (1993), Joshi and Davies (1992), Ermisch and Wright (1993) show that part-time work experience has a negative effect on wage level. Similar results were noted by other researchers using Canadian, American data as well as in cross-national comparison (Cocoran, Duncan and Ponza, 1983; Long and Jones, 1979; Simpson, 1986; Gornick and Jacobs, 1996).

The effect of part-time work on women's occupational mobility is more contentious than that of earnings. Dex and Shaw (1986) analysed the data of the 1980 Women and Employment Survey and found that women who took up part-time work upon resuming paid work after their first childbirth were more likely to experience downward occupational mobility. However, her analysis is restricted to only one particular life-cycle stage of women. The analyses of Dale (1987), Brannen (1989), McRae (1991), and Joshi and Hinde (1994) have the same problem. The focus on occupational mobility of women before and after childbirth is too narrow to capture the effect of part-time work experience on the working life of women. Moreover, the issue is not always analyzed by using the appropriate method. In Chapter six, the ways through which these deficiencies can be overcome will be discussed.

Participation in part-time work

There are a number of studies about the labour force participation of British women. Most of them are applications of the neo-classical approach to the labour supply of women. They focus primarily on the ways the wage (potential or real) of a woman and that of her husband (in the case of married women) affect the participation rate. The dependent variable in these studies often takes the form of a dichotomous variable, for example, working versus not working as in the case of Stern (1981) who used the data from the Family Expenditure Survey; or active versus not-active in the analyses of Joshi (1984) which used the data of the 1980 Women and Employment Survey and that of Zabala (1983) which used the data of the 1974 General Household Survey. Alternatively, the dependent variable is treated as a continuum of working hours, as in the study of Layard and his associates (1980) who analysed annual working hours of married women by using the data from the 1984 General Household Survey. As we shall explain in greater details in Chapter eight, these ways of handling the dependent variable are unrealistic and often lead to the inappropriate method of analysis.

The second problem of these studies is with their underlying assumption about labour supply. Following the neo-classical approach, these studies consider the supply of working hours as shaped primarily by household factors and the market wage rate, and assume that the number of working hours can be varied freely and incrementally along a continuum. In more recent studies, it is recognized that working hours may not take the form of a continuum and that hours of work may well be constrained by demand factors. Ilmakunnas and Pudney (1988) attempted to deal with the impact of demand-side constraints on hours of work by using Finnish data. The inability of workers to supply working hours freely was also noted by Altonji and Paxson (1992) in their analysis of the data from the Panel Studies of Income Dynamics in America. Blank (1988) argued and demonstrated with American data that there were discontinuities in hours of work on a weekly basis. Arellano and Meghir (1987) used the data of the 1981 Family Expenditure Survey and argued that individuals could not choose freely the hours they worked. These studies call for an analysis which handles full-time and part-time participation as discrete forms of wage work participation, rather than as a continuum of working hours.

Few studies deal specifically with part-time work participation. Dale and Ward (1992) used the OPCS Longitudinal Study to examine the effects of ethnicity, life cycle and local labour market on female labour force participation. The strengths of their analysis lie in contextualizing women's labour market participation in the local labour market and in handling the dependent variable, in a more appropriate manner, as three discrete states : full-time, part-time and not working. However, the possible channelling effects of previous employment experience as suggested by segmentation theory and the explanation of human capital theory were not considered. Vogler (1994) focused particularly on part-time work participation. The dependent variable is unsatisfactorily handled as a dichotomy - to participate in part-time work or not.

The literature on part-time work participation up to date lacks a test of the explanatory strength of the theories of labour market which we reviewed in the earlier discussion. Chapter eight will explicate the way this study attempts to address the issue of part-time work participation.

Organization of the book

In this introductory Chapter, two major approaches to labour market studies were reviewed. The different emphases of human capital theory and segmentation theory (and its variant the flexible firm thesis), and their implications on part-time employment were noted.

In the next Chapter, the data and methods of analysis used for this study will be described. In Chapter three, we shall deal with the employers' demand for part-time workers. The main question which this Chapter addresses is which type of employer is likely to have a particularly heavy demand for part-time workers. This serves to map out the organizational context of part-time employment.

In Chapter four, the focus is on the job-level of part-time employment. The market situation of part-time job-holders will be compared to that of full-time job holders. The comparison involves two purposes. One of them is to assess the extent to which part-time work differs systematically from full-time work in the way which segmentation theory suggests for secondary employment. The other purpose is to examine whether it is pertinent to regard all part-time jobs indiscriminately as secondary jobs. Chapter five is a follow-on of Chapter four in which the work situation of part-timers is compared to that of full-timers. The long term effects of part-time work experience on the level of earnings and on the worklife occupational mobility of women are examined in Chapter six.

The analyses in Chapters seven and eight focus on the worker-level of part-time work. Chapter seven will address the self-selection argument about women's participation in part-time work. The work attitudes of part-time workers which have been held to be a crucial factor for their participation in part-time work will be examined. In Chapter eight, the different explanations of part-time work participation will be assessed. Specifically, we shall test hypotheses derived from human capital theory, the theory of gender division of labour and labour market segmentation theory in explaining the current employment status of women. Chapter nine will conclude this study and draw out some general theoretical implications it has on labour market theory.

Notes

1   It should be noted that cross-national comparison of part-time employment should be treated cautiously as member countries of the OECD use different definitions to enumerate part-time employment in their labour force surveys. Some rely on the self-definition given by the respondent, others take 30 hours or 35 hours as the cut-off point. Moreover, the method of enumeration varies over time. For details on the various definitions used by each member country in their labour force surveys, see note A of the Technical Annex of *Employment Outlook*, OECD, 1985. See Dale and Glover (1990)

about some other difficulties involved in the use of comparative data.

2   Granovetter (1981) pointed out that theories of the labour market often leave out the 'matching' question, that is, the question of the ways through which individuals with certain characteristics are matched up with various kinds of jobs. He argued that other than the demand and supply factors, a third set of factors which explain the differential employment returns are those which pertain to the matching process. Granovetter suggested that the social network which individuals are embedded in is closely associated with the type of jobs they get. See Granovetter (1974) for a study which examined the relation between job entry and social networks.

3   Amsden (1980) criticized human capital theory as treating workers, men and women alike, as atomistic, a-social and a-historical individuals, rather than stratified and differentiated in certain systematic patterns.

4   Some empirical works show that part-time is also taken up by other socio-demographic groups, for example, young people and retired persons. Dale (1992) discussed why few British part-timers were young people as compared to the situation in America. Hayward and his associates (1994) noted an increase in retired people who re-entered the labour market as part-timers in America.

5   For a critique of new home economics, see Folbre (1986). She commented that new home economics ignored inequalities between different household members. She also made the criticism that the assumption about altruism as the prevalent distributive norms within the household is made on an *a priori* ground.

6   Some recent studies attempt to trace orderly job pathways within organizations and for closely related occupations. See Gaertner (1980) and Althauser and Kalleberg (1990) for two examples of such studies.

7   For a review of the context and the different ways the notion flexibility is formulated, see Pollert (1991).

8   For a historical review of the way working-hour changes under different epochs of capitalist-labour relations, see Hinrichs and Siranni (1991).

2 Data and methods

The data of this study are drawn from the Social Change and Economic Life Initiative (SCELI). This Chapter will describe briefly SCELI and the nature of the data which are used for our analysis. The methods of analysis used in this study will then be explained. In the third section, we shall also discuss two features of the data : (1) the reliability of the retrospective data in SCELI some of which this study draws on; (2) the extent to which the data resembles that of a nationally representative sample.

The data

SCELI focused on six local labour markets - Aberdeen, Kirkcaldy, Swindon, Coventry, Northampton and Rochdale. The first three localities experienced a lower unemployment rate in the 80s than the latter three. In each locality, four surveys were carried out between 1986 and 1987. They were the Work Attitudes/Histories Survey, the Household and Community Survey, the Baseline Employers Survey and the 30 Establishment Survey. These surveys were designed to provide considerable comparability between the six localities. For each of these surveys, the interview schedules for each of the six localities share a set of common questions, as well as some area-specific questions.

The four surveys were linked. The pivotal survey is the Work Attitudes/Histories survey. This provided the sampling frame for the Household and Community Survey and the Baseline Employers Survey. The Employer Survey in turn provides the listings from which organizations were chosen for the 30 Establishment Survey.

The analysis of this thesis is based mainly on the data collected in the Work Attitudes/Histories survey and the Baseline Employers

Survey. As far as possible, it uses data for that part of the interview schedule which is common to six localities. Where appropriate, data from the Household/Community Survey and the 30 establishments were used to supplement the analysis from the two main surveys.

The Work Attitudes/Histories Survey

This survey is concerned primarily with people's past work history patterns, their current experience of employment or unemployment, attitudes to trade unionism, work motivation, broader socio-political values and the financial position of their household.

The main fieldwork was conducted between June 1986 and November 1986. The achieved sample is about 1,000 from each of the six localities, making a total of 6,111 respondents in the overall sample. The overall response rate was over 70 percent. The sampling areas were defined in terms of the Department of Employment's 1984 Travel to Work Areas, with the exception of Aberdeen. A random sample was drawn from the non-institutionalized population aged 20 - 60.

The interview consists of two major sections. The first one is a life/work history schedule in which information was collected about various aspects of the individual's current employment and work history over the entire period since they first left full-time education. In the life history section, information about marital, childbirth and residential history was collected on a year grid basis. In the work history part, information was collected as spells of employment, unemployment and economic inactivity in the form of dated sequential events. In the case of an employment spell, further information was collected about several essential features of the job, including the occupation, whether it is a full-time or part-time job, the number of employees at the workplace, the extent of gender segregation, trade union membership, pay comparison, public/private sector and whether the job involves supervisory responsibility. With this data, it is, therefore, possible to examine the involvement of the respondent in different economic (in)activities throughout his or her working life. In this sense, the data are particularly relevant for addressing the cumulative effect of part-time work. We can also examine the way in which different kinds of previous work or non-work experiences shape current employment prospects.

The second part of the interview schedule consists mainly of attitudinal questions, with a core of common questions combined with separate sub-schedules designed specifically for the employees, the self-employed and the unemployed/economically inactives. For those who were employees, questions were asked about their current employment conditions, situations at their workplace and their work experience in their employing organizations. The analysis for this thesis draws mainly on data collected from interviews with employees. The detailed data about the different market and work situations as well as information about the individual characteristics of the workers in SCELI enable us to examine theories of the labour market which were reviewed in Chapter one.

The Baseline Employers Survey

SCELI also collected data from employers. The Baseline Employers Survey involves a sample of establishments. The major part of the sample was drawn from the Work Attitudes/Histories Survey. Each of the 1,000 individuals interviewed in each locality was asked, if currently employed, to provide the name and address of the employer and the address of the workplace. The sample covers all types of employers, and includes both public and private sector establishments. The method of sampling differs from a straight random sample of the list of establishments from the Department of Employment. The latter method would have resulted in a very large number of small establishments being included. The method used in SCELI weights the probability of an establishment being included by its size : the greater the number of employees at an establishment, the greater its chance of having one or more of its employees included in the sample of individuals (and hence itself being selected).

However, there are generally too few medium and large establishments to generate a true probability-proportional-to-size sample. To increase the number of medium and large establishments, a booster sample of private sector employers with 50 or more employees was drawn up. In practice, 70% to 85% of the sample in different localities were provided through the listings from the Work Attitudes/Histories data, while only 15% to 30% were from the booster sample.

Nearly all the interviews for the baseline employers survey were conducted by telephone. The response rate was 71%. The interview schedule was standard across all six localities. No locality-specific questions were included.

The interview involves collecting data on several topics. A considerable part of the questionnaire is devoted to gathering information about the employment structure of the establishment, in terms of seven pre-defined job-groups, their sex composition, the number of full-time and part-time workers in each job group, and their recruitment and promotion rates. The seven pre-defined job groups are : lower-skilled operatives, higher-skilled operatives, technicians and lower

41

professionals, technologists and higher professionals, lower administrative and management jobs, middle and upper administrative and management. Other topics include the introduction of new technologies, the use of workers who were on non-standard employment contracts, relations with trade unions, and changes in the product market. Different questionnaires were used for large and small organizations. The latter were asked fewer questions. There are also minor variations in the schedules for public and private organizations, and for different industries. The four industry sub-schedules were (1) manufacturing, wholesale, transport, extractive, agriculture; (2) retail, hotel, catering, personal and other consumer services; (3) banks, financial and business services; (4) construction. The variations were designed to provide functionally equivalent questions with respect to product market positions for different types of organizations.

The data about the establishment's workforce composition enables us to derive information about the proportion of part-time employees in the total workforce of the establishments. In addition to these information, the interview also asked questions about changes in the level of part-time workers employed as compared to that of five years ago; whether the establishment has been substituting full-time employees with part-timers; the frequencies with which part-timers were transferred to full-time jobs; and whether the management negotiated with unions about the use of part-time employees.

In each locality, there were follow-up interviews with at least 30 establishments - the 30 establishment survey - designed in particular to explore the motivation behind specific types of employment policy. The composition of this follow-up sample was not a random one. The analysis in Chapter Three draws mainly on the data from the Baseline Employer Survey and where appropriate, is supplemented by the analysis of 30 establishment survey.

The Household and Community Survey

The Household and Community Survey (HCS) was carried out in 1987. It involved re-interviewing about one-third of the respondents in the main Work Attitudes/History Survey. This survey focused primarily on household strategies, the domestic division of labour, leisure activities, sociability, the use of welfare provision and attitudes about the welfare state.

The sampling lists for the survey were generated from computer listings of respondents to the Work Attitudes/History Survey who had agreed to be re-interviewed. For the six localities taken as a whole, an average of 87% of respondents indicated they were willing to be re-interviewed. Attrition due to people leaving the area between 1986 and 1987 was 7% to 9% for the six localities. Response rates (for those that had agreed to be re-interviewed and were still in the area) were 75% or higher in each locality.

The questionnaire for this survey consisted of three sections : an interview schedule including questions for both respondents and partners, a respondent's self-completion section, and a partner's self-completion section. The questions included an update of the life and work history of the original respondents and a full work history was collected for partners interviewed.

Methods of analysis

The research strategy chosen for this study is a quantitative, secondary analysis of survey data. As was pointed out in the previous Chapter, a number of existing studies about part-time work are case studies which are based on several organizations to examine the demand of employers, or on one or a few occupations to analyze job returns. These studies do not examine systematically the effect of different factors. For our purpose of assessing the explanations offered by the different theories of the labour market about part-time work, statistical modelling is an appropriate approach. Modelling enables us to distinguish between different systematic empirical associations in survey data. It permits many interrelationships to be considered simultaneously. This allows us to assess the effect of a particular variable independent of other relevant variables. It also enables us to test rival hypotheses which is a major purpose of this study.

In addition to bivariate analyses, several modelling techniques are used for multivariate analyses. They include linear regressions of ordinary least square type and tobit type, binary and multinomial logistic regressions. The modelling method which is used depends on the level of measurement of the dependent variable. Linear regression is commonly used in analyses of dependent variables which are measured on a continuous scale. Ordinary least square method is used for earnings analysis in Chapters four and six. Tobit modelling is a special technique in linear regression which deals with truncated data structure, that is, for a sample in which a considerable number of cases has no value or observations on the dependent variable, and the normal distribution curve is truncated at certain threshold. This is the case for our dependent variable in Chapter three in which the data structure is truncated at the value zero at the lower end of the normal distribution curve.

For categorical dependent variables, the use of linear probability is

43

inappropriate. For issues which involve this kind of dependent variable, we are interested in the ways in which the probability of being in one category of the dependent variable instead of the other(s) vary according to a range of independent variables. In other words, we are concerned with the proportion of respondents in one category as compared to the other(s). Linear regression estimated with ordinary least square method can give fitted values for the proportion which lie outside the admissible range of 0-1. Hence, it is not a suitable method of analysis when the dependent variable is a categorical one. The logit transformation of the proportion overcomes this problem. Two logistic regression methods are used to deal with categorical variables in this study, one is binary and the other is multinomial. The binary type is used in cases where the dependent variable takes a dichotomous form, that is, there are only two levels. This is the case for the issue of promotion prospects in Chapter four and the issue of employment commitment in Chapter seven. Multinomial logistic regression is used in Chapters Six and Eight to deal with categorical dependent variables which have three or more categories. In a multinomial logistic regression, we are interested in the relative odds of A rather than B (or C, D etc, or any pairwise comparison for any two categories of a dependent variable which has three or more categories) and the way it varies with a number of predictors. In Chapter six, this method is used to examine the way the relative odds of being in one current class category rather than another varies with the amount of part-time work experience. This method is also used in Chapter eight to analyse the current employment status.

The software used for the estimation of parameters in ordinary least square linear regression is SPSS-x, LIMDEP is used for tobit modelling, and GLIM is used for both binary and multinomial logistic regression.

The problems of retrospective data

The work history and life history data of SCELI were collected through retrospective recollection by the respondent. It has been suggested that there are several problems with the use of retrospective data. One of them is the problem of sample selection bias which is due to the different survival rates of different socio-demographic groups. For example, middle class people may have a higher life expectancy and would thus be over-represented in a retrospective study. Another possible source of sample selection bias is out-migration. The second problem is the accuracy of the data, that is, the extent to which the data collected is affected by memory failure of the respondent.[1] For this thesis, the memory failure problem is a cause of concern when the work history data of SCELI were

44

drawn on for the analyses in Chapters six and eight. This is less of a problem for the analyses in Chapters three, four, five and seven as the data used are mainly about the current situations of the respondent (or the organization he or she belonged to). Part of the work history data which are used for the analyses in Chapters six and eight are major time points in the working life of the respondent : their first job and current status. These events are critical ones and hence are less susceptible to memory failure. This mitigated, to a certain extent, the seriousness of the problem regarding memory failure.

Reliability and accuracy are two of the many possible problems with retrospective data. Dex (1991) gave a comprehensive literature review of the reliability of recall data. She discussed the various types of errors that could arise when respondents were asked to recall their past experience; the methods which social scientists used to test and improve the accuracy of this type of data. I shall not repeat her discussion fully here. She concluded that in SCELI as well as other similar retrospective data collection exercises in Britain (for example, the 1980 Women and Employment Survey and the 1976 National Training Survey), the recollection and dating of periods of employment were felt not to present serious problems of data quality. The work history data in SCELI was collected by first obtaining a broad framework of the fertility and marital histories of the respondent. These then were used to help the respondent recall his or her employment history. Respondents were asked to provide a broad framework of working periods with some of the details filled in subsequently. This way of asking respondents to recollect their employment history was found to improve the quality of data collected from recall. It has worked particularly well with female respondents.

Buck and his associates (1994) also discussed different types of longitudinal data and their respective strengths and weaknesses. They remarked that for data collected in a retrospective way, inaccurate recall produced mostly random errors in the detailed timing of events, instead of systematic errors. In general, it can be reassured that the quality of data is adequate for the type of analysis which we are concerned with. Nevertheless, as it will be pointed out in Chapter eight, in view of the collection of unemployment experience in the work history, that it is still necessary to further develop methods to collect more precise retrospective data.

Locality data and the national picture

The various surveys of SCELI collected data from six localities. The fact

45

that it is not a national sample raises the question about the extent to which the data represent Britain taken as a whole. This question is addressed by Marsh and Vogler (1994) in their discussion of the historical development of the six localities. They documented the changes which each of them underwent from their first industrialization up to 1971, and from then on until the recession in the mid-80s.

The six areas started to industrialise in different industries. Aberdeen was dominated by primary industries (farming and fishing) before the oil industry flourished in the local economy. The industrialization of Rochdale was closely associated with the textile industry. Swindon developed on the basis of railway engineering and later diversified into steel and electronic industries. Coventry was dominated by the car and related industries like metal-manufacturing and the making of machine tools. Footwear industry started off the industrialization process in Northampton while Kirkcaldy shifted from coal mining to the production of linens and canvas which were then followed by other light industries.

Marsh and Vogler also examined the subsequent economic development of the six areas in the 70s and early 80s as well as the impact of economic recession on their economic conditions. They noted that many of the differences associated with the early stage of industrialization declined over time. The six towns underwent similar changes. They all registered a net loss of jobs in manufacturing industries between 1971 and 1981. Alongside the shrinking of the manufacturing sector was the expansion of the service sector. To assess the extent to which the six areas, taken as a whole, resembled the national pattern, Marsh and Vogler compared five national economic indicators with the averages of the six localities. These indicators were : population change between 1971 and 1981, employment change between 1971 and 1978, employment change between 1978 and 1981, unemployment rate in May, 1985 and percentage of households with two cars. Their results show that the average picture of the six areas taken together does not differ substantially from the national picture (Marsh and Volger, 1994:60).

While Marsh and Vogler examined mainly economic indicators, we can also compare the distribution patterns of class and economic activity status of SCELI to those of the 1986 British Social Attitudes Survey (BSA86) to assess the extent to which the sample resembles the national pattern. The BSA86 was designed to give a representative sample of adults aged 18 or over living in private households in Britain.[2] A sub-sample of the BSA86 who were between 20 and 60 years old were selected from the overall sample for comparison.

Table 2.1 shows the percentages of all SCELI and BSA86 respondents and of men and women separately in different classes using the

Goldthorpe class schema. The distributions of the economic status for the whole sample and for men and women separately are given in Table 2.2. It can be seen that for both distribution patterns, the sample of SCELI resembles the national picture to a considerable extent.

Table 2.1
Class distribution of SCELI and of the 1986 British
Social Attitudes Survey (BSA86)

Class	% of all respondents		% of female		% of male	
	SCELI	BSA86	SCELI	BSA86	SCELI	BSA86
Upper and lower service class	25.5	25.6	20	19.1	30.9	32.8
Routine and non-manual	22.0	24.4	37.6	39.8	6.7	7.6
Small proprietors	5.7	7.2	3.2	3.4	8.2	11.1
Technicians & supervisors	4.9	5.5	2.9	2.8	6.9	8.5
Skilled manual workers	13.5	10.7	6.9	4.8	20.0	17.2
Semi-/unskilled manual workers	28.4	24.1	29.5	27.2	27.2	21.4
N	6,111	2,237	3,041	1,627	3,070	1,439

We can, therefore, echo the remark which Marsh and Vogler made in their conclusion :

> The six study towns, which entered the recession which ended the long postwar boom looking strikingly different, and bearing

47

the birth marks of their very different economic histories, came out of it looking much more similar in economic terms. Moreover, we have suggested that these areas, whose experiences have been placed under a microscope by the SCELI initiative, provide an economic profile when added together which looks not dissimilar to that of Britain as a whole. (Marsh and Vogler, 1994, p.61)

Table 2.2
Economic activity status distribution of SCELI and of
the 1986 British Social Attitudes Survey

Economic status	% of all respondents		% of male		% of female	
	SCELI	BSA86	SCELI	BSA86	SCELI	BSA86
Self-employed	6.6	7.4	9.7	12.8	3.6	2.5
Full-time employees	50.6	49.7	70.1	69.1	30.9	32.0
Part-time employees	12.5	11.8	0.7	0.9	24.5	21.6
Unemployed	10.7	8.5	14.4	10.0	7.1	7.1
Non-employed	3.8	5.8	4.7	6.8	2.9	4.9
Unpaid housework	15.4	16.9	0.1	0.4	30.7	31.9

Nevertheless, the diverse industrial structures which the six localities have may still render them, taken as a whole, differ from the national picture. Cautions should, therefore, be taken in generalizing the results beyond the six localities. However, the data which SCELI has about the employer, the characteristics of part-time jobs, the household conditions of part-time workers as well as their attitudes towards the gender role of men and women are remarkably rich. This feature is shared by very few studies which are on a scale similar to that of SCELI. The 1976 National Training Survey covered an array of issues related to part-time work. However, it lacks information on the demand-side of part-time work and on the work attitudes of part-timers. It was noted in Chapter one that the 1980 Women and Employment Survey has detailed information about many aspects of the issues which this study seeks to deal with. However, the Survey does not have data on the employment conditions of full-time working men for comparison. The richness of the data of SCELI makes it a particularly good data source through which the issues of this study can be studied, despite the fact that it is not based on a nationally representative sample. The findings in this study, therefore, await a nationally representative sample ascertain their extent of generalizability.

Notes

1   Of all 3,041 female respondents in the SCELI's main survey sample, 42 failed to give the starting year or the season for some of their employment events. In computing the work history data, these were excluded. I am grateful to my colleague at Nuffield College, Sheila Jacobs, for pointing this out to me.

2   See Jowell, et al. (1986) Appendix I for a description of the technical details of the survey.

3 Employers' demand for part-time workers

We noted in Chapter one that while the neo-classical approach ascribes a passive role to employers, segmentation theory and the flexible firm thesis stress the part which employers play in shaping the labour market structure and the employment experiences of workers. In the early stage of the formulation of segmentation theory, the focus was on the way employers differentiated distinct employment policies for different employees. In more recent debates, the role of employers is further emphasized. It has been argued that a single employer actively deploys and combines diverse types of labour use policies (Craig et al., 1982; Atkinson, 1984; Atkinson and Meager, 1985). Discussions and empirical studies revolving around the flexible firm thesis have gained much currency in the recent literature of labour market studies (Pollert, 1991; Davidson, 1990; Harrison and Kelley, 1993; Procter et al., 1994).

The flexible firm thesis is about the ways in which firms combine and distinguish various types of labour use policies in response to a number of changes in their business environment. A detailed examination of these policies, whether as individual ones or as policy mixes, which employers adopt is too broad an analysis to be undertaken here.[1,2] With respect to part-time work, we noted in Chapter one that the thesis characterizes it together with other workforces which are not full-time permanent staff as peripheral employment. The part-time workforce is a major lever which firms use to attain numerical flexibility. It is expanded and contracted to enable firms to cope with product market fluctuations, uncertainties in business revival and technological changes. It is argued that the employment conditions of part-time workers are determined primarily by the labour use policies of the employer. It is, therefore, pertinent to begin this study with the demand side of part-

51

time employment. The major issue which this Chapter addresses is how the level of demand for part-timers varies between different employers. More specifically, the questions which this Chapter deals with are : what type of employers are heavy users of part-timers? How important are the influences which are emphasized by the flexible firm thesis in explaining the expansion of the part-time workforce? This chapter will set the organizational context of part-time work and the backcloth for the job-level analyses in the next two chapters.

The rest of this chapter is divided into seven sections. In the next section, a brief description of the sample which is used for the analysis will be given. The third section will review the reasons, as identified by previous studies, given by employers for using part-timers. Sections four and five will examine the situations in the private sector with which the flexible firm thesis is primarily concerned. In the fourth section, two major reasons, namely, product market changes and technological improvements, which the thesis put forward to account for the pursuit of labour use flexibility will be examined. In addition, the effect of shift-working will also be analysed. In the fifth section, four structural features of the organization and their impacts on the level of demand for part-timers will be examined empirically through a series of bivariate analyses. This is followed by Section Six which, through a multivariate analysis, will assess the net effects of product market changes, technological advancement and the structural factors on the level of demand for part-timers. In the last section, the use rate of part-timers in the public sector will be examined.

The Baseline Employer Survey

The data for this Chapter is drawn from the Baseline Employer Survey of SCELI. The survey involved a sample of establishments. The way the sample of this survey was drawn up has already been described in Chapter two. Here, a brief account of the industrial sector and size distribution as well as the incident rate of union presence in the sample will be given. Industry, size and union are the major structural factors which will be examined later. The total sample size is 1,308 establishments, 75% of them were in the private sector and 25% were in the public sector.

Table 3.1 shows the distribution by industrial sectors for establishments in the private sector. There were a total of 327 public sector establishments : 70% of them provided education, health and social services, 30% provided services like police, fire brigade, cleansing and recreation.

52

Table 3.1
Industrial distribution of private sector establishments

Agriculture	0.7%
Extractive	3.4%
Chemical	4.3%
Engineering	18.1%
Other Manufacturing	16.6%
Construction	6.2%
Retail	34.9%
Transport	3.5%
Finance	12.2%
Total	100% (N=981)

In terms of the size of the establishments measured as the number of employees, this survey has a better coverage as compared to previous studies. In their studies of the use of part-timers at the establishment level, Blanchflower and Corry (1986) and McGregor and Sproull (1991) drew their data from different sub-samples of the 1980 Workplace and Industrial Relations Survey (WIRS). The sampling method of WIRS excludes establishments which have fewer than 25 employees. This method neglects small establishments which, as indicated by SCELI and other surveys, are important users of part-timers. In using the data of the 1980 WIRS to analyse part-time employment at the establishment level, Blanchflower and Corry themselves recognized this problem and remarked :

> As we argue in the following chapter, part-timers employed in the population of establishments from which the WIRS sample was drawn, are more likely to be represented by unions, have better terms and conditions of employment and be more highly paid than their counterparts in the excluded establishments. Hence the results reported here, if anything will understate such differences as do exist between full and part-time employment (Blanchflower and Corry, 1986, p. 5).

We shall see in Chapter four from the employee survey of SCELI that full-timers and part-timers are disproportionately distributed between workplaces of different sizes. Part-timers are more likely than full-timers to be employed in small workplaces which have fewer than 25 employees, and less likely to work in large workplaces with 500 or more employees. Other studies have also noted the concentration of part-timers in small firms. Using the data from the 1976 National Training Survey, Elias and Main (1982) noted that a substantial proportion of female part-timers worked in small establishments. Blanchflower (1992) used the data from the British Social Attitudes Survey (1983-1987) and calculated that 47% of part-timers and 28% of full-timers were employed in small workplaces.[3]

Although it does not involve a nationally representative sample of establishments, the Baseline Employer Survey of SCELI, is more comprehensive than WIRS in terms of its coverage of establishments of different sizes. Establishments with fewer than 20 employees were included. In the final sample, the size distribution of public and private sector establishments is shown in Table 3.2.

Table 3.2
Size distribution of establishments

Size	Private sector (%)	Public sector (%)
fewer than 20 workers	30	15
20 - 49 workers	18	29
50 - 99 workers	17	15
100 - 199 workers	15	16
200 - 499 workers	13	13
500 or more	7	12
Total	100 (N=981)	100 (N=327)

We can see from Table 3.2 that there were more small establishments in the private sector than in the public sector. The two sectors also differed considerably with respect to unionization. While unions were present in 96% of all public sector establishments, this is the case for 44% of all private sector establishments.

In addition to collecting information about the workforce composition, the survey included questions about the recent product market changes, the various measures which establishments had adopted in response to

54

these changes, the different kinds of new technologies which they had installed and the consequence these new technologies had on the skill levels and the needs to train or retrain current employees. Before we discuss the ways these changes are related to the level of part-timers employed, a summary of the reasons why employers use part-timers as identified by previous studies will be given first.

Reasons for the use of part-timers

Previous studies have identified a number of reasons which employers give for their use of part-time workers. These reasons can be classified into three main types. The first one is the various relative cost advantages of employing part-timers rather than full-timers. Sproull (1989) noted in his survey of 107 service establishments in Glasgow that national insurance contribution had a significant effect on employers' choice between full-time and part-time workers in their labour recruitment. Other cost advantages of employing part-timers which have been noted in other studies include the fewer fringe benefits which part-timers are entitled to and their exclusion from an occupational pension (Robinson and Wallace, 1984; Puckett and Frederico, 1987; Ginn and Arber, 1993; Frenken and Maser, 1992). Bosworth and Dawkins (1982) found that some employers recruited part-timers to do extra shifts and over-time work. Robinson and Wallace (1984) noted in their study that employing part-timers to do shift work and over-time work enabled employers to make optimal utilization of capital equipments while simultaneously saved them the need to pay shift or over-time premium if full-timers were used.

The second commonly cited reason for employing part-timers is to meet variable demand patterns. In their analysis of the 1987 Employers Labour Use Strategies Survey, Wood and Smith (1989) found that this was one of the three reasons which were given most frequently by the establishments in the survey. Bosworth and Dawkins (1982) also noted in their study that a common reason given by employers for using part-timers was to cover busy periods. Employing part-time workers to match peak periods of demands for products and services help employers avoid the under-utilization of full-time labour during slack periods of demand, thereby reducing the total wage and non-wage labour costs. Walsh (1990) noted that in restricting pay for hours actually worked, the total wage cost was minimized.

The third reason for employing part-timers, as noted by Bosworth and Dawkins (1982) and Wood and Smith (1989), is to carry out tasks of certain jobs which are done for a limited number of hours and which, therefore, do not require a full-time cover. Recruiting part-timers to fill these job positions would avoid the under-use of labour and the higher level of wage and non-wage payments which need to be meted out if full-timers are employed to fill these jobs.

These relative cost advantages make part-timers an appealing labour force to recruit. However, as the discussion in the next two sections will explicate, the primacy of labour cost minimization through the use of part-timers depends on changes in the business environment which a firm has experienced. Furthermore, whether firms can capitalize the cost advantages of part-timers would depend on their structural features. In other words, whether employers find part-time work an attractive labour use option and their levels of demand for part-timers may well vary according to their structural characteristics and the type of changes they have undergone. In the next section, two major changes will be examined, namely, product market changes and technological advancement, and their relations to the proportion of part-timers employed by the establishment.

The pursuit of flexibility and the use of part-timers

One of the major determining factors of a private firm's success in maximizing profit is its performance in the product market. With respect to product market changes, the flexible firm thesis claims that companies in Britain are faced with uncertainties of business revival amidst the general economic recession, intensified competition in their product markets and increasingly selective demands from customers. To respond swiftly to these contingencies and to maintain long-term competitive viability, the thesis claims that firms actively adopt and devise flexible labour use policies. The numerical flexibility and the cost advantages of part-timers would be particularly appealing to firms which are faced with these changes that necessitate them to seek for labour use flexibility and cost reduction measures. We shall first examine the various product market influences which establishments had encountered.

Product market pressures

In the baseline survey of employers, establishments which had 20 or more employees were asked a series of questions about recent changes in their business conditions. Of all these establishments, 32% had been affected by more intense foreign competition and 48% had experienced greater competition from within Britain.

Besides more intensive competition, British firms were also faced with changes in the purchasing patterns of their customers in the 80s. Of all the establishments with 20 or more employees, 29% said there was an increase in small orders and 40% experienced a shortening of delivery periods. A considerable number of firms had experienced more stringent financial conditions. While 39% of the establishments had had significant increases in the amount of credit they were expected to give, 42% said their customers had lengthened the time they took to pay their accounts.

Product market pressures had also come from changes in the demands of customers. A majority of the establishments said their customers had become more selective about different aspects of the products or services they provided : 82% said their customers had become more selective about prices, 80% said they were more demanding about quality; 60% reported that customers had become more concerned with product designs and 74% said they were more selective about the availability of the product or services.

Establishments were asked whether changes in competition had led to significant increases in (1) the range of products or services they supplied; (2) the effort they put into developing new services or products; (3) the attention they paid to scheduling the work of their staff. Establishments which had experienced intensified competition (foreign or British) were more likely than those that had not to report an increase for each of these three items. Table 3.3 shows that for each of these three areas, the percentages of establishments which reported an increase were higher among those which had been affected by an increase in competition than among those which had not been affected by intensified competition.

We can see from Table 3.3 that of the three areas, scheduling the work of staff is the area with which the greatest proportion of establishments said they were concerned. In terms of labour use, we noted in Chapter one that the flexible firm thesis argues that management are actively transforming their workforce into one which is functionally, financially and numerically flexible. Part-time workers are classified by the thesis as a peripheral workforce and are employed primarily to attain numerical flexibility. Greater product market pressures which arise from intensified competition and more selective customer demands mean that firms would have to operate with more competitive prices. They would also be more concerned with cost minimization, among other measures, in order to maintain a certain level of profits and their long-term competitive viability. One of the ways through which cost minimization can be achieved is the reduction of wage and non-wage labour costs. Given the cost advantages of part-timers, we would, therefore, expect that firms which had experienced greater product market pressures and intensified competition would be more likely to have expanded their part-time workforce, as compared to firms which had not experienced greater product market pressures.

Table 3.3
Responses to changes in competition in the private sector

Areas in which increase were reported	% of establishments affected by increase in competition	% of establishments not affected by increase in competition
Range of product or services supplied	61	51
Effort put into developing new services	76	67
Attention paid to scheduling the work of staff	81	70
(Number of respondents)	418	545

A greater use of part-time workers can be achieved by an increase in the absolute intake and/or by replacing full-timers with part-time workers. For the private sector as a whole, while 16% of the establishments reported an increase in the number of part-timers employed over the last five years, 9% said they had been substituting full-timers by part-timers over the previous two years. The findings shown in Table 3.4a illustrate whether the different product market pressures are positively associated with an expansion of the establishment's part-time workforce through an increase in the absolute intake or the replacement of full-timers. The Table shows the percentages of establishments which had or had not experienced the various product market pressures by whether they had increased the number of part-timers employed or not, and by whether there had been replacements of full-timers by part-timers.

58

Table 3.4a

Changes in the level of part-time employment by product market changes
(% of establishments)

Product market changes	Change in number of part-timers		Replaced full-timers by part-timers	
	increase	decrease or no change*	yes	no
1. Buyers' selectivity				
in price				
increase				
no increase	18	79	10	90
	25	79	10	90
		(p=0.03)	(p=0.38)	
in quality				
increase	20	77	11	89
no increase	15	80	8	92
		(p=0.01)	(p=0.35)	
in design				
increase	19	78	9	91
no increase	22	74	13	87
		(p=0.05)	(p=0.15)	
in availability				
increase	21	76	11	89
no increase	13	82	8	92
		(p=0.00)	(p=0.26)	
2. British competition				
increase	18	77	10	90
no increase	20	78	10	90
		(p=0.71)	(p=0.66)	
3. Foreign competition				
increase	12	66	8	92
no increase	23	56	11	89
		(p=0.27)	(p=0.91)	
4. Demand for products & services				
increase	22	62	9	91
same	13	71	8	92
decrease	6	85	6	94
		(p=0.00)	(p=0.60)	

*some row percentages do not add up to 100 as some respondents did not know the nature and the extent of the change

From section 1 of Table 3.4a, we can see that the association between selectivities of customers and the increase in the number of part-timers differs according to the nature of the selectivity. Establishments which had experienced an increase in customers' selectivity in price were actually *less* likely to have employed more part-timers, as compared to establishments which had not experienced price pressure. A similar negative relation can also be observed for the selectivity about designs of the products or services. Establishments which had experienced increases in customers' selectivity about the availability and the quality of their products and services were more likely to have increased the number of part-timers, as compared to establishments which had not encountered these two kinds of pressures.

Table 3.4a also indicates that whether there had been replacement of full-timers by part-timers varies according to the nature of customers' selectivities. Establishments which had experienced an increase in price selectivity were as likely as those which had not to report replacements of full-timers by part-timers. Establishments which encountered increases in their customers' selectivities about the quality and the availability of their products and services were more likely to report replacements, as compared to establishments which did not experience greater selectivities of these two types. The relation is, however, insignificant. The selectivity about design is negatively and insignificantly associated with replacements of full-timers by part-timers.

Section 2 and 3 show that the intensification of competition, British and foreign alike, was actually less likely to be related to an increase in the number of part-timers employed, whether through an increase in absolute intake or replacing full-timers by part-timers. Firms which had experienced an increase in foreign or local competition were actually less likely to have employed more part-timers, as compared to firms which did not report an increase in market competition.

Section 4 indicates that establishments which had an increase in product demands were more likely to have raised the number of part-timers they employed, as compared to establishments which had experienced no change or a decrease in their product demands. A positive but insignificant relation can be observed between changes in the level of product demands and the likelihood of replacements of full-timers by part-timers.

While these findings lend some supports to the implications we drew from the flexible firm thesis about the relation between the growth of part-timers and product market changes, they also indicate that the claims of the flexible firm thesis may well be too broad to capture the effects of specific product market changes. Our findings show that the expansion of the firm's part-time workforce, whether through an increase in the absolute intake or the replacement of full-timers, depends on the type of product market changes which the firm has experienced. In our case, it is the pressures on quality and availability of the products or services and the increase in demands which matter. Neither the price and design pressure nor the intensification of competition were significantly related to the expansion of the establishment's part-time workforce. These product market pressures may well be met by other measures, instead of by a greater use of part-timers.

Technological changes

It has been suggested that optimizing the use of fixed capital investment is one of the major reasons for the use of part-timers. The benefits to employers arise from a higher level of output from a given stock of capital or a lower stock of capital necessary to achieve the desired level of output. Robinson and Wallace (1984) noted that the employment of part-timers enabled firms to maximize the utilization of capital equipment and to maintain continuous production. Wood and Smith (1989) noted in the 1987 ELUS that one of the reasons given by employers for using part-time staff was to prolong the production of goods. The use of part-timers would, therefore, be particularly beneficial to establishments which have introduced new technologies. We would expect that the introduction of new technologies would be positively related to an expansion of the establishment's part-time workforce.

In the baseline employers survey of SCELI, establishments were asked whether they had introduced word processing, new computer systems and machinery with micro-electronics in the previous two years. Of all private sector establishments, 36% had not introduced any one of these three types of technologies, 23% had introduced one of the three types, 25% had introduced two types and 15% had introduced all three types. Thus, a majority of the establishments in our sample had had some degree of technological upgrade. Table 3.4b shows for the different numbers of new technologies introduced, the percentages of firms which reported changes in the number of part-timers employed and the percentages which had or had not replaced full-timers by part-timers.

Table 3.4b indicates that contrary to the expectation about the relative cost advantages of employing part-timers to optimize capital utilization, the greater the number of advanced technologies introduced, the *less* likely that the establishment had raised its intake of part-timers or replaced full-timers with part-timers. The introduction of new technologies is not related differentially with the replacement of full-

61

timers by part-timers. Establishments which had introduced no new technologies were as likely as those which had introduced one type of new technology to have replaced full-timers with part-timers.

The negative relation between the expansion of the part-time workforce and the introduction of advanced technologies may be due to the higher training costs needed to train employees to cope with the new technologies. The shorter working hours of part-timers would mean a lower level of returns for the training invested. This explains why the expected positive relation between an expansion of the part-time workforce and the introduction of new technologies is not borne out by our findings. Employers may have adopted other measures to optimize the use of new technologies.

Table 3.4b
Changes in the level of part-time employment by technological changes
(% of establishments)

Number of new technologies introduced	Change in the no. of part-timers		Replaced full-timers by part-timers	
	increase	decrease or no change*	yes	no
None	19	60	9	91
One type	17	66	9	91
Two types	15	67	7	93
All three types	12	80	7	93
	(p=0.001)		(p=0.54)	

*some row percentages do not add up to 100 as some respondents did not know the nature and the extent of the change

Shift-working

Another change which would be closely related to the expansion of the part-time workforce is the increase in the use of shift-working. The flexible firm thesis claims that recruiting part-timers to cover shift-working helps firms maximize flexibility in meeting the fluctuations in their product markets while minimizing the organization's commitment to the job security and career development of the worker.

Previous studies have noted that employers recruited part-timers to cover shift-work. Blanchflower and Corry (1986) reported from the 1980 WIRS that an average of 29% of the establishment's part-timers were employed to do shift-work. A greater proportion of these part-timers were involved in morning shifts and evenings or twilight shifts, and fewer worked afternoon shifts. Horrell and Rubery (1991) noted that one-third of the establishments in their survey used part-timers to work on twilight shifts. Robinson and Wallace (1984) found that the use of part-timers to do shift work gave employers cost advantages and helped keep the total wage payment down. We would, therefore, expect that an increase in shift-work would be positively associated with an expansion of the establishment's part-time workforce. The results shown in Table 3.4c lend support to this proposition.

Table 3.4c
Change in the level of part-time employment by the increase in shift-working (% of establishments)

Increase in shiftwork	Change in the no. of part-timers		Replaced full-timers by part-timers	
	increase	decrease or no change*	yes	no
Yes	24	66	18	82
No	15	66	7	93
	(p=0.006)		(p=0.00)	

*some of the row percentages do not add up to 100 as some respondents did not know the nature and the extent of the change

An increase in shift-work is positively associated with an increase in the number of part-timers and with the replacement of full-timers by part-timers. This suggests that employers had been capitalizing on the

63

relative cost advantages of employing part-timers to cover shift-work as one of their labour cost minimization measures.

Other labour use measures

The increase in part-timers is not the only labour use measure which establishments had undertaken to cope with the various product market influences and organizational changes. The flexible firm thesis also suggests that there are other ways to attain a flexible labour force. Since our focus is on part-time employment, we shall only note briefly the incidence rates of other labour use measures.

In the survey, establishments were asked whether they had increased the numbers of other kinds of peripheral workers like contract staff, agency workers, temporary workers, casual workers and homeworkers (hereafter these will be referred to as a single category called marginal workers). Of all establishments with 20 or more employees, 16% reported an increase in the numbers of marginal workers over the previous two years. Replacements of regular workers by marginal workers were reported by less than 10% of all establishments.

While part-timers and marginal workers are both classified as peripheral workers by the flexible firm thesis, it is interesting to note that our sample shows that there are differences in the incidence rates of these two types of workforce. The use rate of part-timers is higher than that of marginal workers. While only 9% of the establishments said they had never used any part-timers, the comparable figure for marginal workers is 28%. Part-timers had a larger share of the establishment's current workforce as compared to that of marginal workers. The average proportion of the establishment's total workforce who were part-timers was 20%, while that of marginal workers was 10%.

Besides the differences in their use rates, the position of part-timers vis-à-vis core workers (who, according to the flexible firm thesis, are full-time permanent employees) is also different from that of marginal workers. Establishments were asked whether and how often they transferred part-timers to full-time jobs. A similar question was asked for marginal workers. The chance of being transferred to the main workforce was lower for part-timers than that of marginal workers. Of all the establishments which used some part-timers, only 6% said they frequently transferred part-timers to full-time jobs. For all those establishments which employed some marginal workers, 12% frequently transferred marginal workers to the regular workforce. While we do not have the relevant information about why part-timers received such a different treatment, our findings suggest that the core workforce is less penetratable for part-timers than it is for marginal workers.[4]

These differences between the part-time workforce and other types of employees suggest that among workers whom the flexible firm thesis classifies as peripheral workforces, there may well be substantial differences which make it untenable to treat employees who are not full-time permanent staff as forming a homogeneous group. The core/peripheral dichotomy which the thesis draws up may well overlook the heterogeneities among what it calls the peripheral workgroup. However, a detailed examination of the differences between part-time and other 'peripheral' employees is beyond the scope of this chapter.

Structural determinants of demands for part-time workers

Besides the changes which we examined in the last section, the level of part-time employment would also be affected by structural features of the establishment. These structural factors would make employers differ from each other in terms of the primacy of minimizing the wage and non-wage labour cost, the ability to capitalize the cost advantages of part-timers, and hence their levels of demand for part-timers. These factors need to be taken into account to assess the net effects of the changes which were examined in the last section. In this section, four structural determinants of demand for part-timers will be examined. They are : size, industry, union presence and the workforce composition. The focus is on the way they would affect the level of demand for part-timers.

Size

For two sets of reasons, it can be hypothesized that small establishments would have a higher level of demand for part-timers, as compared to large establishments.

The scale of operation of small establishments, unlike large ones, does not enable them to reap the benefits of economies of scale. Their unit cost of production would, therefore, be higher than that of large firms. In order to survive and make a profit, small firms would have to keep the price level of their products or services high enough to cover the fixed cost of production. They are, therefore, in a disadvantaged position to compete with large firms in the product market as the latter are likely to have a lower unit cost of production due to their economies of scale. Possible ways through which small firms can raise their profits are : to increase their revenue by extending their operating hours, and cost minimization by reducing the wage and non-wage labour cost. Small firms would, therefore, find the relative cost advantages of part-timers beneficial for their business operation.

Small firms are also more likely to operate on a thin profit margin and, thus, have greater financial constraints, as compared to large firms. Our data provide some empirical evidence for this difference between small and large firms. Establishments with more than 20 employees were asked whether there had been increases (1) in the amount of credit they were expected to give; and (2) in the time their customers took to pay their accounts. For the credit question, 43% of those establishments with 20 to 49 employees said there had been an increase; for establishments with 200 or more employees, 35% had had the same experience. For the account question, 44% of establishments with 20-49 workers said their customers had taken more time to settle their accounts. This is the case for 39% of large establishments with 200 or more workers. Although small establishments were not asked the same question, the difference between establishments with 20-49 workers and those with 200 or more workers suggests that small establishments would experience even tighter financial constraints in running their business.

The stringent financial position of small establishments would make it difficult for them to upgrade their technology. Moreover, their small scale of operation also means that they may not need advanced technology. A street-corner confectionery shop or a newsagent would find a computerized stock-taking system of little use, as compared to a large department store. Table 3.5a shows the proportion of establishments which had introduced each of these technological improvements in each size category.

It can be readily noted that smaller establishments were much less likely than larger establishments to have introduced any one of the three forms of new technology. The lack of new technology means that small establishments would be more likely to rely on labour in the operation of their business. They would, therefore, be more concerned with economizing their labour costs. With the cost advantages of part-timers, smaller establishments which were more concerned with saving labour costs would have a higher level of demand for part-timers.

The second reason that may explain why size can affect the demand for part-timers is the differential ability of employers to recruit the kind of workers they prefer. This difference arises from the disparate job prospects which they can offer to workers. In the employer survey, small establishments were much less likely than large ones to have promoted any section of their staff in the previous year. While only 16% of small establishments had filled some jobs by internal promotion in the previous year, this is the case for 59% of establishments with 100 -199 employees, and 74% of establishments with 200 or more employees.

Table 3.5a
Percentages of establishments which have introduced new technology by size

Types of Technology	Establishment size (number of employees)				
	<20	20-49	50-99	100-199	200+
Word-processing	17	22	38	40	62
New computer system	29	42	63	68	83
New machinery with micro-electronics	14	19	34	41	60

The size of small establishments makes them inherently unable to provide many positions for the job advancement of their employees. The poorer job prospects offered by smaller employers would make them less capable in attracting better qualified employees. Individuals who have higher levels of formal qualification are likely to target at larger establishments which can offer better job returns and promotion opportunities. Small firms would be less appealing to better qualified workers and new entrants to the labour market who are likely to have a high level of employment aspiration which cannot be met by the unfavourable employment conditions of small firms.[5] Their undesirable job prospects thus mean that small establishments cannot be selective in their staff recruitment. Our data about entry qualification requirements provide some evidence for this difference between small and large firms.

In the survey, establishments were asked whether they had a qualification requirement when they recruited people over the age of 18 to fill lower-skilled operative jobs, higher-skilled operative jobs and clerical positions. Section A of Table 3.5b shows the percentages of establishments in each size category which had some qualification requirement for each of these three job categories. It can be seen readily that large establishments were more likely to have some rather than no entry qualification requirements, as compared to small establishments. Section B of Table 3.5b shows the percentages of establishments in each size category which had a City and Guild qualification requirement for higher-skilled operative jobs, and an O-level or typing qualification for clerical jobs. While 30% of those establishments with 200 or more employees required a typing qualification or an O-level qualification when they recruited workers for clerical posts, this is only the case for 7% of small establishments. Likewise, while 74% of large establishments had a City and Guild qualification entry pre-requisite for higher-skilled operative jobs, only 7% of small establishments had this requirement.

Table 3.5b
Percentages of establishments which had qualification
requirements for three job groups by size

	Establishment size (no. of employees)				
	<20	20-49	50-99	100-199	200+
1. Whether any qualification is required for :					
Lower-skilled jobs	4	12	17	16	18
Higher-skilled jobs	17	48	60	64	74
Clerical jobs	16	42	64	69	74
2. Whether specific qualification is required for :					
Higher-skilled jobs City and Guild	7	23	19	25	44
Clerical jobs O-level	5	12	15	19	33
Typing	7	23	30	36	30

The disadvantageous position of small firms to compete for better qualified and young workers would mean that they may need to recruit workers from a different section of the labour force. As we shall see in Chapter eight, a majority of part-time workers are married women who are in their 30s and 40s and who have worked previously. Small and large firms may have different levels of demand for married women who would prefer part-time work. In large firms, employment relations are regulated in a bureaucratic way which involves much administration costs in the recruitment, training and record-keeping of workers. To avoid expenses on personnel administration, large employers would value stable workers and may be unwilling to employ married women whom they think would have high turnover rates or would take more time off from work for childcare duties. On the contrary, small firms may take advantage of the job skills and work experience of married women to compensate for their inability to attract workers with higher school-leaving qualification and their financial incapability to provide new employees with training.[6] Hence, small establishments may have a higher level of demand for part-timers, as compared to that of large establishments.

A possible way through which small firms can overcome their small scale problem in providing staff training would be by getting assistance from external organizations. In the survey, establishments were asked whether there were local professional groups or employers groups which provided them with information on staff recruitment, pay or training. While only 16% of those establishments with fewer than 20 workers said external assistance on personnel matters was available to them, this is the case for 42% of establishments with 100 to 199 employees and 63% of establishments with 200 or more employees. This suggests that small establishments were less likely to benefit from external assistance for their personnel matters.

For reasons related to small scale operation, greater financial pressure, recruitment and capability to provide training, we can hypothesize that small establishments would have a higher level of demand for part-timers, as compared to large establishments. In our sample, for establishments with fewer than 20 employees, 24% of their workforce were part-timers. The figure for establishments with 20 - 49 employees is 16%, 8% for establishments with 50 - 99 employees, 11% for establishments with 100 - 199 employees, and 9% for establishments with 200 or more employees.

Industry

Besides the size factor, another major structural determinant is industry. The studies of Blanchflower and Corry (1986) and McGregor and Sproull (1991) recorded that industry had a significant influence on the demand for part-timers. Part-timers would be relatively less attractive to highly capital intensive industries in which on-the-job training is often specific and requires considerable amount of time. Employers in these industries may consider that the training and the associated investment are underutilized with the shorter working hours of part-timers. The lower level of returns to human capital investment means that firms would not prefer part-timers. Industries like chemical and engineering are often capital intensive and the training which the employer has to undertake for employees is costly. Our data also reveal that the likelihood of the introduction of new technology varies between industries. Table 3.6a shows for each kind of new technologies covered by the survey, the percentage of establishments in each industry which reported that they had introduced it.

Table 3.6a
Percentages of establishments which have introduced new technology by industry

Industry	Types of new technology		
	Word-processing	New computer system	New machines with micro-electronics
Chemical	59	81	50
Engineering	48	64	50
Other manufacturing	38	60	46
Construction	33	51	20
Retail and services	19	45	16
Transport	41	69	26
Finance	36	53	23

Table 3.6a shows that establishments in the chemical and engineering industries were much more likely to have introduced any one of the three new technologies as compared to establishments in other industries. For establishments in the chemical industry, 81% had introduced a new computer system in the previous two years. This proportion is the highest compared to other industries. Engineering industry ranked second : 64% of the establishments in this industry had introduced a new computer system. These two industries were also more

likely than other industries to have introduced new machineries. Employers in these two industries would be more likely to provide their employees with training to upgrade their work skills so that they could cope with the new technologies. Recruiting part-timers who work fewer hours would yield a lower level of returns to the training invested. Thus, for this economic reason, employers in chemical and engineering industries would demand fewer part-timers.

In retail and other personal service industries, the demand varies over the work day (or work week). Lunch-hour and weekend shopping create peaks in the demand for services. Moreover, some services cannot be stored, such as meals served in restaurants and bar service. Some other services take a limited period of time to provide, like office cleaning which is done for a few hours outside the normal office hours. These industries would find part-timers attractive as they provide the manning level to match the variable demand pattern while enabling employers to capitalize on part-timers' cost advantages and the effective utilization of manpower. Hence, we can hypothesize that establishments in retail and personal services industries would have a particularly high level of demand for part-time workers.

In our sample, retail and service establishments had the highest percentage of their workforce employed as part-timers (33%). In the chemical industry, the average proportion of part-timers employed is 5%. The figure for engineering establishments is 3%, for transport and construction industry it is 6%, and for establishments in finance industry the figure is 13%.

Previous studies have suggested that the difficulty in recruiting skilled workers would prompt employers to offer part-time jobs to retain skilled employees who cannot work full-time. This explanation implies that the likelihood of encountering recruitment difficulty would be positively related to the use rate of part-timers. However, when we compare the recruitment experiences of industries which had a higher and a lower proportion of their workforce employed as part-timers, their part-timer use rates do not vary in the way as suggested by the recruitment difficulty argument. The recruitment experience of retail establishments, which, as we have just noted, had the highest use rate of part-timers, was compared to that of chemical and engineering establishments in which the proportion of part-timers employed was lower. Table 3.6b shows the percentages of establishments in each of these three industries which reported difficulty in recruiting workers to a particular job group.

Table 3.6b shows that establishments in the chemical and engineering industries were more likely to report difficulty in recruiting higher-skilled operative workers, technicians, technologists and lower

71

grade professionals, as compared to retail establishments. That they had a lower percentage of their workforce who were part-timers suggests skills shortage is unlikely to have prompted these establishments to take on more part-timers. While speculations can be made about the means which these employers have adopted to resolve their recruitment problems (for example, by increasing the workload of the current workforce), for our purpose here, the findings do not lend support to the argument that the difficulty in recruiting skilled workers is related to the demand for part-timers.

Table 3.6b
Percentages of establishments which reported recruitment difficulty for each job group in retail, chemical and engineering industry

Job group	Industry (%)		
	Retail	Chemical	Engineering
Lower-skilled operative	18	9	12
Higher-skilled operative	24	29	29
Technicians and lower grade professionals	6	21	19
Technologists and upper grade professionals	4	24	20
Clerical	8	9	5
Lower grade administrative	6	12	8
Upper grade administrative	6	14	8
(No. of respondents	277	41	178)

Union representation

Besides size and industry, the presence of union in the establishment is another major structural determinant which need to be considered. It was pointed out in the discussion on size effect that in addition to wages, labour costs also include administrative costs of recruiting and training new employees; supervising and maintaining personnel records for each worker. These costs vary on a per-worker basis, rather than with the number of hours worked (Oi, 1962). Replacing one full-timer by two part-timers means higher administrative costs.

Unions may incur higher administrative costs due to their formalized rules and procedures which influence the hiring, transferring, disciplining and laying off of employees by the management. Unionists may regard part-timers, being predominantly women, as less attached to the labour market and more difficult to recruit and organize. Unions would also oppose to a high use rate of part-timers whom they fear would drive the general wage level down. Thus, for their own interests, unions would make it costly for employers to employ part-timers. Unionized establishments would therefore employ fewer part-timers to minimize administrative labour cost.[7] In our sample, unionized establishments had, on average, 11% of their workforce who were part-timers, while for non-unionized establishments the figure is 22%.

Composition of the workforce

Besides the presence of union, fixed labour costs for a firm are also associated with its workforce composition which, in turn, would affect the level of demand for part-timers. Training costs vary between jobs which have different skill levels. The amount of training which firms need to give to new recruits of lower-skilled operative job positions is likely to be less costly than what is needed for higher-skilled operative jobs.

Job positions also vary in terms of their recruitment cost. The turnover of employees in lower-skilled operative positions is less disruptive to the organization's routine than that of administrative and managerial employees. Frequent turnover of the latter would incur high recruitment and other administrative costs. Thus, employers would devote more resources and make more extensive search in recruiting people for administrative and management jobs than for lower-skilled operative jobs. For example, advertisements in national newspapers are likely to reach potential applicants outside the local labour market, as compared to advertisements in local job centres or local newspapers. The extent of extensiveness of search can be indicated by the different recruitment methods which employers use for different job positions.

In our sample, 55% of those establishments with more than 20 employees rated job centres as the most important recruitment method for lower-skilled operative jobs, and 39% said they were most important for recruiting people to fill routine clerical positions. The second commonest method for the recruitment of these two job categories was local newspapers. While 60% regarded local newspapers as important for clerical jobs, 43% said it was important for lower-skilled operative jobs. Less than 10% rated national press as an important recruitment method, whether for lower-skilled operative jobs or for clerical jobs. On the contrary, for the recruitment of workers to fill upper administrative and management job positions, only 4% said job centres were the most important method while 49% said national newspapers were the most important channel. Placing job advertisements in national newspapers is likely to be more expensive than in local job centres and newspapers. This, in turn, implies that the recruitment costs for administrative and managerial positions would be doubled if two part-timers are recruited to fill up one full-time position. This is less likely to be the case for the recruitment of lower-skilled operative jobs. Thus, firms with a high proportion of lower-skilled operative jobs would find part-timers more attractive as they can then economize both the wage cost and the recruitment and training costs. In our sample, the proportion of an establishment's workforce which were lower-skilled operative jobs was positively correlated with the share of part-timers in its total workforce (the correlation coefficient is 0.23).

The picture is, however, different for clerical jobs. The commonest recruitment method for this type of jobs, as we have noted, was through local newspapers, followed by the local job centre. We might expect that firms which had a higher percentage of their workforce who were clerical workers would recruit more part-timers to lower recruitment costs. However, on the contrary, our data indicate that the proportion of clerical workers employed was negatively correlated with the percentage of the workforce employed as part-timers (the correlation coefficient is -0.15).

The negative relation between the level of part-timers employed and the share of clerical jobs in the total workforce may be explained by technological change and the subsequent upskilling of jobs and the need for staff (re)training. Establishments which had adopted new technology like word processing, micro-electronics and new computer systems were asked for each of the seven pre-defined job groups, whether employees had to work at a higher skill level and whether they needed further training and re-training as a result of these changes. The clerical job group was the most frequently cited one in which there was a need for skills improvement and further training of the staff : 31% of the establishments said clerical workers had to work at a higher skill level, and 51% said they had to undergo re-training or further training.

The upskilling and the new training which employers needed to provide for their clerical workers mean that these positions are less likely to be filled by part-timers who will yield a lower level of returns for employers' investment in staff training. If we take word processing as the most relevant new technology to clerical work, the negative association between new technology and the establishment's employment of part-timers is most obvious. In our sample, for establishments which had introduced word processing, 9% of their clerical employees were part-timers, whereas for establishments which had not introduced word processing, the comparable figure is 18%. The higher training cost is likely to offset the advantage of the lower recruitment cost of part-time clerical workers. This may explain the negative relation between clerical jobs as a proportion of the establishment's total workforce and the level of part-timers it employed.

With regard to the composition of the workforce, we would expect the proportion of part-timers to be positively related to the proportion of lower-skilled workers but negatively related to the proportion of clerical workers.

Multivariate analysis

A multivariate analysis is conducted to ascertain the net effect of the structural factors, product market pressures, the use of new technology and the use of shift-working. In conducting the multivariate analysis, there are two complications which arise from the data structure. Firstly, about 25% of the private sector establishments did not employ any part-timers. This makes ordinary least squares regression an inappropriate estimation method as the linearity assumption of the least squares method is violated by the truncation at the lower end of the normal distribution curve.[8] Tobit modelling is more appropriate as this method takes into account cases which have a zero value on the dependent variable to estimate the parameters.[9]

The second problem is related to the shorter interview schedule administered to establishments with fewer than 20 workers. For issues related to product market pressures, these establishments were asked the question about the change in the demand for their products and services. They were not asked questions about the different kinds of demand selectivities of customers and the increase in competition. Hence, in the multivariate analysis, the independent variables which we are able to include are the four structural factors, changes in product demands, technological changes and shift-working but not the different kinds of selectivities of buyers or the competition questions. The results are given in Table 3.7. The dependent variable takes the form of part-timers as a percentage of the establishment's workforce.

The results lend support to the hypothesis about the effect of establishment size. Small establishments employed a significantly higher proportion of part-timers, as compared to establishments with

200 or more employees (the reference category).[10] Moreover, the coefficients of the various size categories show that the size effect is a non-linear one.

The effects of industry lend support to the hypotheses discussed in the previous section. Retail and personal services establishments employed more part-timers than all other industries. The gap is widest for primary industries (agriculture and extractive), chemical and engineering industries, and smallest for finance industry.

The effect of union is insignificant, although its direction is in line with the earlier discussion. The insignificance of the union factor may be explained in two ways. In our sample, small establishments were much less likely than large establishments to have unions. While 75% of small establishments (fewer than 20 employees) did not have union representation, this is the case for only 22% of large establishments (200 or more workers). The union effect is spurious when the size factor is included. The second possible explanation is related to the concern of union with regard to the management's manpower use. For those establishments which had trade unions, only 10% had negotiated with trade unions over the use of part-time employees. Unions seemed to be more concerned with the absolute level of employment, as 35% of unionized establishments had negotiated with unions over changes in the number of workers employed in the previous two years.[11] In times of general recession, it may well be that unions were more concerned with the general employment level rather than with the employment of a specific workforce. Hence, the effect they had on the establishment's part-time employment policy was not significant.

Lower-skilled operative jobs as a proportion of the establishment's total workforce is positively associated with its level of part-time employment. This suggests that employers had been capitalizing on the lower training and recruitment costs of part-timers to fill this type of job positions. The hypothesized negative effect of the proportion of clerical workers employed is borne out by the findings.

Table 3.7
Tobit modelling of part-timers as a % of the establishment's workforce
(private sector establishments)

Variable	Coefficient	S.E.	T-ratio
Constant	18.96	3.63	5.22
Size of the establishments			
fewer than 20	8.78	2.72	3.23**
20-49 workers	1.62	2.92	0.55
50-99 workers	-1.86	2.87	-0.65
100 - 199 workers	1.40	2.89	0.48
200 or more workers	-	-	-
Industry			
Agriculture and Extractive	-36.76	5.13	-7.16**
Chemical and Engineering	-34.78	2.46	-14.15**
Other manufacturing	-26.93	2.61	-10.31**
Construction	-30.66	3.88	-7.89**
Transport	-26.30	4.85	-5.42**
Finance	-15.81	3.07	-5.16**
Retail	-	-	-
Union Representation			
Presence	-2.35	1.89	-1.24
Absence	-	-	-
Composition of the workforce			
Lower-skilled workers as a % of the workforce	0.17	0.068	4.83**
Clerical workers as a % of the workforce	-0.21	0.063	-3.28**
Change in demand for product or services			
Increase	4.38	2.26	1.94*
No change	6.80	2.81	2.42**
Decrease	-	-	-
Increase in shift-working			
Yes	6.76	2.41	2.80**
No	-	-	-
Number of technologies introduced	-0.41	0.36	-1.13
s	25.73	0.74	34.67

Log-likelihood = -2988.8; Number of valid cases = 906;
**denotes significant at the 0.05 level; *denotes significant at 0.1 level.

Establishments which had experienced an increase in the demand for their products and services employed a higher level of part-timers, as compared to establishments which had experienced a decrease. This suggests that during the general economic recession in the 80s, employers might well be uncertain about the extent to which a revival of business conditions could be sustained. To take precautions against sudden future business downturn, the expansion of manpower was accomplished by expanding workforces which would not incur high wage and non-wage costs (for example, national insurance contribution, various employment rights payments). This may well explain the greater use of part-timers to meet the manpower requirement associated with the growth in demand. Establishments whose product demands remained stagnant also had a significantly higher level of part-timers, as compared to those which experienced a decrease. This suggests that the stagnation of product demands had also imposed a pressing need on establishments to minimize labour costs by more employing part-time workers.

An increase in shift-working was significantly and positively related to the proportion of part-timers employed. Employers had taken advantage of the relative cost advantages of part-timers and recruited them to cover the higher level of shift-working.

In line with the result of the earlier bivariate analysis, the greater the number of new technologies, the lower was the use rate of part-timers. But the result is an insignificant one when other factors are taken into account. The negative relation between the level of part-time employment and technological advancement may be explained by the additional skills requirements and training needs brought about by the introduction of new technologies, as the earlier discussion has suggested. Establishments might have resorted to other measures to cope with the manpower requirements which arose from the introduction of new technologies.

Our analysis thus far has focused on the private sector. In the next section, part-time employment in the public sector will be examined.

Part-time employment in the public sector

The flexible firm thesis is primarily about changes in the private sector in which. the fundamental concern is profit maximization. This is not the case for the service provision in the public sector which, as we shall see in the next chapter, takes up a considerable proportion of the part-time workforce. Due to the nature of the goods and services it provides, the public sector is less likely to face competition, as compared to the private sector. In our sample, while 48% of the private sector establishments were affected by more intense local competition, this is the case for 28% of all public sector establishments. However, this does not mean that the public sector can operate without any pressures on their cost expenditures. A major constraint which they face comes from the fiscal policy of the government.

The viability of service provisions by establishments in the public sector depends primarily on the financial support which they receive from the central government. Changes in the fiscal policy of the British government under the Thatcherite rule, which aimed at reducing the government's role in the market, have imposed various spending constraints on different sections of the public sector. Fleming (1989) recorded a drop in the employment of the public sector, taken as a whole, between 1979 and 1989. Walker (1988) recorded that there had been cutbacks of government expenditures, especially in the provision of education and housing between 1974 and 1983. The reduction of the total expenditure has also affected the grants which central government gave to local authorities. Sheldrake (1990) recorded that the central government's contribution to local authority spendings fell from 61% to 46.5% between 1979 and 1987. Walker and Moore (1987) pointed out that the 1980 Local Government Act introduced a new set of regulations. The effect of these regulations was to require local authorities to operate as private companies. In our sample, 87% of the public sector establishments reported that they had been affected by changes in the financial practices of the government. Thus, the financial constraints which arose from the reduction in the fundings they received from the central government would have prompted public sector establishments to seek for or make greater use of cost reduction measures.

Alongside with the reduction in financial support from the government, a majority of the public establishments had been affected by changes in the public's demand for their services. In our sample, 64% of the establishments reported an increase in the demand for their services. A rise in the public's demand together with a reduction in funding may well lead to the need to restructure the workforce in order to minimize labour costs as a measure to cut down expenditure. The employment of part-timers with their relative cost advantages would, therefore, be expanded as a means to be more cost effective in meeting the public's demand for services. There is evidence which suggests that the financial constraints experienced by the public sector were associated with a higher use rate of part-timers. Walker (1988) analysed the employment change of the public sector between 1979 and 1984. She noted that female full-time employment has fallen more rapidly than that of female part-timers. In her study of the National Health Services in Scotland, Pulkingham (1992) recorded that the cost reduction requirements introduced through a series of 'efficiency initiative' led to a reduction in the full-time workforce and a rise in part-time employment between 1979 and 1988.

To assess the net effect of the increase in the demand for public goods and services on the proportion of part-timers employed, we shall take into account the type of services which the establishment provided. The public sector in our sample consisted of establishments which provided two broad types of service : professional services like healthcare and teaching; more routine services like policing, fire brigade, cleaning and recreation services. Establishments which provided the first type of services employed an average of 36% of their workforce as part-timers, the comparable figure for those establishments which provided the second type of services is 8%. The substitution of full-timers by part-timers was also more prevalent among the former type of establishments than among the latter type. While 20% of those establishments which provided professional services had replaced full-timers by part-timers, this is the case for 11% of those establishments which provided more routine services.

The extent to which the cost advantages of part-timers can be capitalized would also vary according to structural features and other changes which the establishment had experienced. As in the analysis for the private sector, we shall consider the structural determinants size, presence of union and the composition of the workforce, in addition to the type of service which the establishment provided.

Contrary to that of the private sector, the effect of size would be insignificant in the public sector. The Baseline Employers Survey of SCELI was conducted at a time when privatization policies of the Thatcherite government have not been implemented in full-scale. Policies which affected labour uses at the establishment level were more likely to be formulated at the central level. Local units were unlikely to be the loci of decision-making about labour uses. This is evident in the kind of factor which the establishment considered as important in influencing the level of pay they offered. Among the public sector establishments in our sample, 96% said national agreements were crucial and only 17% said their own internal policies were important in influencing the level of pay they offered. The scale problem of small establishments could be overcome. Thus, we would expect establishment size to be insignificant in affecting the use rate of part-timers in the public sector.

Table 3.8

OLS regression of part-timers as a % of the establishment's workforce (public sector establishments)

Variable	Unstandardized coefficients	S.E.	T-ratio
Constant	25.36	5.31	4.78
Size			
1-19 workers	4.40	4.04	1.13
20-49 workers	5.04	3.26	1.54
50-99 workers	0.04	3.69	0.01
100-199 workers	-1.93	3.52	-0.55
200 or more workers	-	-	-
Type of Service			
Cleaning, recreation, policing, etc.	-22.06	2.68	-8.24**
Healthcare & teaching	-	-	-
Union Representation			
Yes	5.03	5.67	0.88
No	-	-	-
Workforce Composition			
Lower-skilled as a % of the workforce	0.29	0.06	4.97**
Clerical workers as a % of the workforce	-0.007	0.079	-0.08
Change in demand			
Increase in demand	0.16	3.00	0.05
No change	3.004	3.52	0.85
Decrease	-	-	-
Increase in shift-working			
Yes	1.14	4.83	0.24
No	-	-	-
Number of new technologies introduced	-0.41	1.11	-0.37

R-square = 0.36
Number of valid cases = 323
**denotes <0.05 significance level

With respect to union pressures, since only 4% of the establishments were without union representation, the effect of union would be insignificant. The greater the number of lower-skilled operative jobs, the more likely the establishment would find the use of part-timers economical, as the establishment can then capitalize on their lower training and recruitment costs. Establishments which had introduced modern technologies would not like to underutilize the training investment they provided for their employees and, therefore, would have a lower use rate of part-timers. An increase in the use of shift-work would be positively related to the use rate of part-timers as they gave the establishment the advantage of flexible manning level. The net effect of changes in the demands for public goods and services on the proportion of part-timers employed were assessed together with these factors. Ordinary least squares (OLS) regression method was used as very few public sector establishments did not employ any part-timers. The results are given in Table 3.8.

The results indicate that only the type of service and the proportion of lower-skilled workers employed are significant. Establishments which provided policing, fire, cleaning and recreation services employed a lower proportion of part-timers, as compared to establishments which provided healthcare and teaching services. The higher the proportion of lower-skilled workers, the higher the proportion of part-timers employed.

The other factors are insignificant, although the directions of the effects are in line with our earlier discussion, except for the proportion of clerical workers employed. Size did not have a significant effect on the proportion of part-timers employed. The share of clerical workers had an insignificant and negative effect. The effect of union is also insignificant. Changes in demand and increase in shift-working were positively related to the proportion of part-timers employed, while the effect of a greater number of new technologies was negative. However, these factors were insignificant when other factors were taken into consideration. This suggests that the public sector establishments may have adopted other measures to cope with increases in the public's demand in the context of more stringent financial situations, instead of a significantly higher use rate of part-timers.

Conclusion

In this chapter, the major cost advantages for employers to employ part-time workers were first noted. The discussion also pointed out that the demand for part-timers could vary, on the one hand, between establishments which had been affected differently by product market changes and technological advancements, and on other hand, according to disparate organizational features of the establishment. The public and private sector were examined separately. The effects of the product market and technological influences were then evaluated together with other features of the organization in two multivariate analyses.

The analysis for the private sector indicates that heavy users of part-timers were (1) small establishments; (2) retail and personal services establishments; (3) those which had a high proportion of lower-skilled job positions; (4) those which had made greater use of shift-work and (5) establishments which had experienced an increase or a stagnation of products demands.

The analysis of the public sector show different findings. When the type of services and the proportion of lower-skilled workers employed were taken into account, the various changes which the establishment had experienced did not have significant effects on its use rate of part-timers. The analyses also show that establishments in the public and the private sector had responded differently to changes in their product demands. While fluctuations in product demands led to a greater use rate of part-timers in the private sector, this is not the case in the public sector. The pursuit of flexibility through the use of part-time workers differ between the two sectors. In fact, as its focus is on privates firms, the flexible firm thesis cannot deal with the difference between public and private sectors. The previous section represents a preliminary attempt to gauge some of the differences between the public and the private sector. Further studies are needed to examine in greater details the public/private distinction.

This chapter outlines the organizational context of part-time employment. It will serve as a backcloth for the discussion of the job structure of part-time work in the next chapters when part-time jobs are compared to full-time jobs.

Notes

1   For such an attempt using the same dataset see Wilkinson and White (1994), Gallie and White (1994).

2   A contentious issue of the thesis is whether the use and the mixing of different labour use policies are outcomes of strategic calculation and long-term planning by the management, or whether they are just ad hoc decisions taken in response to short term events. See McGregor and Sproull (1991) for an attempt to deal with this issue.

3   The concentration of part-timers in workplaces with fewer than 20 employees has also been recorded in the former West Germany (Buchtemann, 1989) and in France (Marshall, 1989).

4   In her comparative study of the retail banking sector in France and in Britain, O'Reilly (1994) found that newly recruited employees first worked on a probationary period as temporary workers before they were given a more permanent status. This suggests that temporary workers may well be a transient status only.

5   We shall see in Chapter four from the employees that workers in small workplaces were less likely to have promotion opportunities and were offered a lower wage level. Vainiomaki and Wadhwani (1991) used the panel data of about 1,000 British manufacturing companies and found that their 'product market power' was positively related to the wage rates of their employees.

6   In a study of American firms, Knoke and Kalleberg (1994) noted that small firms were less likely to have formal staff training provision, as compared to large firms.

7   Blanchflower and Corry (1986) explored the effect of industrial relations on the demand for part-timers. They suggested that if employers preferred non-union employees, and since part-timers are much less likely to be union members, the use of part-timers would be related to informal rather than formal methods of industrial relations. The result of their analysis shows the presence of a manual union had a negative effect on the part-time use rate of the establishment whereas the presence of a non-manual closed shop union had a positive effect.

8   Two previous studies have also conducted multivariate analyses on the demand for part-timers at the establishment level. Sproull (1989) and Mcgregor and Sproull (1991) used ordinary least square regression which does not handle correctly cases which did not employ part-timers. Blanchflower and Corry (1984) used probit model to estimate the probability of an establishment being classified as 'part-time using'. It was pointed out in chapter one that the notion of 'part-time using' establishment is delineated in quite an arbitrary way.

9   The estimation is done by using the software LIMDEP. For a review

of tobit model, see Amemiya (1984). In fact, multinomial logit modelling was also attempted to deal with cases that do not have any part-timers. However, information was lost by collapsing the dependent variable into categories. Hence, this method was not used in the final analysis.

10 Using American data, Montgomery (1988) estimated a range of determinants of employers' demand for part-timers. He found that size was positively associated with the level of part-timers employed.

11 Findings from the 30 establishments survey show that prime concern of trade union, as reported by the management, was with pay level. Part-time employment was mentioned by no more than 1% of all establishments as the second main concern of their unions.

4 The market situation of part-time work

In the last chapter, we identified the type of employers who had a higher demand for part-timers. It was found that size, industry and the composition of the workforce of the firm and recent product market changes experienced were significantly associated with the level of demand for part-timers. In this and the next chapter, the analysis will move from the organizational level of part-time work to the job-level. We shall examine the employment structure of part-time job in terms of two major aspects, namely, market situation and work situation. The focus of this chapter is two-fold. First, we shall assess the extent to which part-time work can be regarded as a secondary form of employment vis-a-vis full-time work in terms of several major dimensions of market situation. The second aim is to see whether there are significant variations among different part-time jobs.

This chapter is divided into four sections. In the first section, the definition of part-time work which is commonly used in the literature will be discussed. The different legal statuses of workers who work different weekly hours will be examined. The second section describes the industrial distribution as well as the distribution of full-time and part-time jobs by three structural features which will have significant impacts on major market and work situations. The third section deals with one crucial determinant of the market situation, namely, the skill level of part-time jobs as compared to that of full-time jobs. The last section examines the full-time/part-time distinction in terms of four major aspects of market situation : job security, wage rate, promotion prospects, and fringe benefits.

The legal status and the definition of part-time work

Part-time work is commonly defined as that which involves fewer than 30 hours a week. This delineation is adopted in the official labour force statistics and in most other studies in the literature. In Britain's Labour Force Survey, part-time and full-time employment status are enumerated on a self-definition basis. In the main survey of Social Life and Economic Initiative (SCELI), respondents were asked for their economic status in the reference week of the survey. For those who were employed, they were asked to define themselves either as working full-time or part-time, with 30 hours as the dividing line.[1] On this basis, about 20% of all employees worked part-time. This proportion is similar to the 1986 Labour Force Survey which recorded that 25% of those in employment were part-timers.Underlying the 30-hour cut-off point are the different ranges of legal employment rights to which workers who work full-time and part-time are entitled. However, a closer look at these rights reveals that the 30-hour delineation obscures the different legal statuses of part-time workers who work different numbers of hours per week. The principle current legislation which provides the framework for employment protection is the Employment Protection (Consolidation) Act 1978. This Act stipulates a range of employment rights for all workers. Irrespective of the number of working hours per week and the duration of continuous employment for their current employers, all workers are entitled to basic employment protection rights; these include protection against race and sex discrimination and against unfair dismissal for trade union reasons, equal pay, time off for ante-natal care and for safety representativeness. However, other types of rights to which a part-time worker is entitled vary according to the number of his or her weekly working hours, and the duration of continuous service for his or her employer.

Part-timers who work less than eight hours per week are not entitled to redundancy payments and written particulars. Those who work more than eight hours and fewer than 16 hours a week are entitled to time off for trade union activities and duties and an itemized pay statement, irrespective of how long they have worked continuously for their current employers. However, a minimal of five years' continuous service is needed for these part-time workers to be entitled to protection against unfair dismissal, medical suspension pay, guarantee payments, statutory notices, written particulars of employment, maternity pay and maternity job-back rights and redundancy payment.[2] For workers who work 16 hours or more per week, there are different qualifying periods of continuous employment for entitlement to different rights. For redundancy payment, protection against unfair dismissal, maternity pay and maternity job-back rights,

88

the qualifying period is two years; for protection against unfair dismissal, the qualifying period is one year. Six months of continuous employment are needed for entitlement to written reasons for dismissal; 13 weeks for written particulars of employment etc.[3]

On this legal basis, we can actually differentiate, in a cross-sectional manner, part-timers according to their weekly working hours. Part-time workers who work fewer than 16 hours per week are the group who is minimally protected under the existing legal framework, as compared to part-timers who work 16 hours or more.[4] The different extent of employment security implied in the legal protection may, therefore, make it inappropriate to treat all part-timers who work fewer than 30 hours a week indiscriminately as a homogeneous workforce and contrast them to those who work full-time.[5] This calls into question the distinctiveness of 30 hours as the defining boundary between full-time and part-time work. Are those part-timers working fewer than 16 hours more marginalized than those who work 17 to 29 hours a week in terms of their job security? To what extent are the relative legal (dis)advantages exacerbated or ameliorated by (un)favourable job returns? These questions need to be addressed before one can take the 30-hour cut-off point as the defining boundary for full-time/part-time employment.[6]

In the survey, respondents who were in paid work during the reference week of the survey were asked how many hours per week they worked in their jobs (excluding meal intervals and unpaid overtime) for their most recent pay. This information on weekly working hours enables us to differentiate part-time workers on the legal basis. Using this information, part-timers are divided into two categories : those who worked 16 hours or fewer a week and those who worked 17 to 29 hours a week. For ease of reference, the former will be called short-hour part-timers and the latter long-hour part-timers.[7] These two groups will be compared to full-timers.

The distribution of part-timers between the two sexes was highly uneven. Less than 1% of the part-timers were male employees. Because of their small number, male part-timers will be excluded in the subsequent analysis. In other words, we have four categories of employees for comparison : female employees divided into short-hour part-time, long-hour part-time and full-time workers, and male full-time workers. In terms of the working-hour status, 60% of all working women in our sample were full-timers, 18% were short-hour part-timers, and 22% were long-hour part-timers.[8]

Distribution of part-timers by industry, firm size, class and unionization

There are several workplace and job features which are likely to affect job rewards. To the extent that working-hour status is closely associated with them, the differential market situation may just be an artefact of these factors, rather than the effect of the working-hour status *per se*. To facilitate the subsequent discussion and analysis, an account of the distribution of part-time and full-time jobs in terms of these features will be given. Three of them are considered here, namely, class, workplace size, and unionization. First, we shall examine the industrial distribution of full-time and part-time jobs.

Industrial distribution

In line with other studies and the findings in Chapter three, part-timers were concentrated in the service sector.[9] Table 4.1 shows that a majority of the two categories of part-timers were in service industries like education and health; retail, hotel and catering industries and other service industries like recreation, personal and social welfare services. Chemical, engineering and other manufacturing industries which included clothing, food and drinks together took up about 8% of short-hour part-timers and 11% of long-hour part-timers.

Class distribution

The four types of market situation which will be examined in the next section are closely associated with the class position of the job. In order to assess the net effect of working-hour status per se, we need to consider the class distribution differences of the three working-hour statuses. The class schema which we shall adopt (and for the rest of the thesis) is the one devised by Goldthorpe (1980).[10] This schema was originally designed to put together occupational categories the members of which are comparable in terms of the kind and level of market and work situation they enjoy.[11] Market situation refers to the level of income and other conditions of employment, the degree of employment security and chances of economic advancement. Work situation means the location within the systems of authority and control governing the process of production.

The schema was later re-defined. Positions within the labour markets and production units are differentiated in terms of the employment relations that they entail. The emphasis is on the positions as defined by the social relations of production, rather than on the incumbents of these positions. Occupations are first differentiated according to the employment status, that is, employer, employees or self-employed.

Table 4.1
Distribution of working-hour status by industry (Standard Industrial Classification, 1980)

Industry	Working-hour status (%)			
	Short-hour part-timers	Long-hour part-timers	Female full-timers	Male full-timers
Energy & water supply	0	0	3	6
Chemical & Engineering	4	5	12	27
Other manufacturing	4	6	12	12
Construction	2	0.4	0.7	6
Wholesale	1	2	3	4
Retail, hotel, catering	31	25	14	7
Transport	2	3	4	11
Banking & insurance	6	8	10	8
Public administration	7	4	7	7
Health & education	31	34	27	9
Other services	12	11	7	2
Total	100	100	100	100
N	303	369	1,002	2,133

For employees, they are further differentiated according to whether their employment conditions are regulated by a labour contract or by service relations. Erikson and Goldthorpe (1993:41) described the differences between these two types of employment relations as such :

> Employment relationships regulated by a labour contract entail a relatively short-term and specific exchange of money for effort. Employees supply more-or-less discrete amount of labour, under the supervision of the employer or of the employer's agents, in return for wages which are calculated on a 'piece' or time basis. (Erikson and Goldthorpe, 1993, p. 41)

In contrast, employment relations formulated in terms of a service relationship involves :

> not only [of] reward for work done, through a salary and various perquisites, but also comprises important prospective elements - for example, salary increments on an established scale, assurances of security both in employment and, through pensions rights, after retirement, and above all, well-defined career opportunities. (Erikson and Goldthorpe, 1993, p. 41)

The class schema thus devised is made up of seven classes. These are : I -higher-grade service class which comprises higher-grade professional and managerial occupations; II -lower-grade service class which includes lower-grade professionals and administrators, higher grade technicians and supervisors of non-manual employees; III - routine non-manual employees - largely clerical - in administration, commerce and rank-and-file employees in service industries; IV - small proprietors and self-employed artisans; V - lower-grade technicians and supervisors of manual workers; VI - skilled manual wage-workers; VII - semi-skilled or unskilled manual wage-workers.[12] Since our focus is on wage work, the small proprietors category will not be considered.

Following the practice of Goldthorpe and his associates in his analysis of women's social mobility through their own employment (Goldthorpe, 1980:280), the routine non-manual class is sub-divided into clerical occupations and rank-and-file employees in personal service industries. The latter includes mainly occupations like shop assistants, cashiers, check-out and wrap operators. It has been found that the employment conditions of these occupations were similar to those of semi-/unskilled manual employees and are included in the semi-/unskilled manual working class.[13] The class distribution of the three working-hour statuses is shown in Table 4.2.

Table 4.2
Distribution of working-hour status by class

Class	Working-hour status (%)			
	Short-hour part-timers	Long-hour part-timers	Female full-timers	Male full-timers
Higher-grade service	1	0.5	5	17
Lower-grade service	8	14.5	27	15
Routine non-manual	35	41	36	8
Technicians & foremen	2	3	4	13
Skilled manual class	4	5	6	22
Semi-/unskilled manual	50	36	17	25
Total	100	100	100	100
N	304	369	1,006	2,135

It can be seen that few short-hour part-timers were in either higher-grade or lower-grade service class, as compared to long-hour part-timers or full-time employees. Both types of part-timers were rarely in supervisory positions of manual workers or in the skilled working class. A majority of them were in the routine non-manual class. The greatest proportion was in the semi-/unskilled manual class. Employees who were in full-time jobs were more likely to be in the service class and less likely to be in the semi-/unskilled manual working class, as compared to the two types of part-timers.

In the analysis of the job returns differences between jobs of different working-hour statuses, we shall take into account the concentration of part-time jobs in routine non-manual class and in semi-/unskilled manual occupations.

93

Size of the firm can be expected to affect the market situation of the job. This is likely to be the case for the regulation of the employment conditions. Larger firms are more likely than small firms to have a higher degree of institutionalization of rules and regulations which govern employment relations. The allocation of jobs and the pricing of labour will follow rules of the firm rather than being determined by the going market rate. Employment conditions are thus likely to be better well-structured and bureaucratically regulated. Besides the regulation of employment conditions, promotion prospects and wage rate would vary between firms of different sizes. Due to their limited number of job positions, small firms would be less likely to be able to offer promotion prospects to their employees, as compared to large firms. Small firms tend to operate in a competitive product market where there are a lot of suppliers. Keen competition and lower product market power mean that small firms are less capable of offering wage rates which are above the market rates.

In the survey, the firm size was enumerated as the number of workers at the place where the respondent worked. Strictly speaking, this measures the size of the workplace and is not the equivalence of firm size. Nevertheless, the workplace size would enable us to capture effects of the firm size as the two are closely and positively related to each other. Table 4.3 shows the distribution of workers in the three working-hour statuses between workplaces of different sizes. Most part-timers worked in small workplaces with 25 or fewer workers. A greater proportion of full-timers were employed in medium and large firms, although female full-timers were less likely than their male counterparts to work in large workplaces. With regard to the difference among part-timers, Table 4.3 also shows that short-hour part-timers were more likely to work in small workplaces rather than medium or large-sized workplaces, as compared to long-hour part-timers.

Unionization

The third structural feature which will affect market situation is unionization. We noted in Chapter one that unionization was suggested as one explanation for the segmentation of the labour market. Unions help enhance workers' employment conditions. The roles which unions play in regulating industrial relations, in job recruitment and allocation and in the introduction of new technology at the workplace buffer workers against managerial prerogatives. Labour supply can also be regulated by unions, thereby preventing market forces from operating in an unfettered way. The classic example is closed shop unions. Thus, workers in the unionized sector enjoy better employment protection and their work conditions would be duly regulated through union-management negotiation and bargaining, as compared to workers in the non-unionized sector.

Table 4.3
Distribution of working-hour status by workplace size

Workplace size	Working-hour status (%)			
	Short-hour part-timers	Long-hour part-timers	Female full-timers	Male full-timers
1 - 24 workers	67	49	34	26
25 - 99 workers	17	23	22	22
100 - 499 workers	11	17	24	24
500 or more workers	4	11	20	28
Total	100	100	100	100
N	297	363	983	2,100

In the survey, employees were asked whether there were any trade unions representing people who did their kind of work at their workplace. They were also asked whether they were currently members of any trade unions or similar organizations. Part-timers were less likely than full-timers to be represented by trade unions. While 37% of short-hour part-timers and 52% of long-hour part-timers said there were unions which represented them, this is the case for 60% of both female full-timers and male full-timers. In terms of membership rates, the shorter the weekly working hours, the lower is the membership rate. Only 16% of short-hour part-timers and 35% of long-hour part-timers were currently union members, as compared to 46% of female full-timers and 52% of male full-time employees.[14]

The membership rate among part-timers was still lower than that of full-timers, even after the presence of the union representation at the workplace was taken into account. Short-hour part-timers were less likely to be union members even though a union was present at their workplaces, as compared to workers in the other two working-hour status categories. Among those short-hour part-timers who had union representation at their workplace, 45% were members. This is the case for 67% of the long-hour part-timers, 74% of female full-timers and 82% of male full-timers. Thus, where unions were present, part-timers, especially those who worked fewer hours per week, were still less likely to be union members.[15]

In this section, we noted that part-time jobs were concentrated in various types of service industries. They were mostly occupations which belonged to the routine non-manual class and the semi-/unskilled class, and they were more likely to be in small workplaces, and workplaces without union representation. Most part-timers were women, and a majority of them were not union members. There were differences among part-timers. Short-hour part-timers were particularly unlikely to be trade union members or to have union representation at their workplaces. Fewer short-hour part-timers were in the lower-grade service class, as compared to long-hour part-timers and full-time workers. Short-hour part-timers were also more likely to be in semi-/unskilled manual class.

In the next section, the issue of job skills will be discussed. Several indicators of skills will be used to compare part-time to full-time work. In the comparison, we shall take into account the concentration of part-time jobs into two class positions, namely, routine non-manual and semi-/unskilled manual working class.

Skills : levels and transferability

We have noted in Chapter one that segmentation theory posits that secondary jobs involve low-skilled work, or work that utilizes only the most basic working skills. Besides the level of skills, there is another aspect, namely, the degree of transferability from one employing organization to another. These two aspects of skills have been suggested by segmentation theory as distinguishing secondary from primary jobs. The level of skills will be dealt with first.

Skill levels

According to segmentation theory, jobs in the primary labour market are more likely to be skilled work than jobs in the secondary segment. Employers are either unwilling or unable to provide secondary job-holders with training investment, or the nature of their work does not make it worthwhile for employers to upgrade the skill level of workers.

There is no commonly acknowledged definition of skills in the literature. Marshall and his associates (1988:116) pointed out that there are at least four usages of the term 'skills' - skills as autonomy, as techniques, as credentials, and as social status. Here, we are concerned with the second usage which is closely related to the level of job complexity. We are not concerned with the skill levels of workers or of pay grades which are the other two common applications of the term.[16] Jobs are designed to suit the production requirements of the employer. The skill level of a job can be quite independent of that of the worker. Pay grades are closely related to the worker's working experiences, rather than reflecting purely the skills requirement of the job. This renders pay scales unsuitable as a measurement of skill levels. In the ensuing analysis, we shall use various indicators to measure skill levels.

In the main survey of SCELI, three indicators were used to measure the skill level of the job : the qualification currently needed to apply for the job; the amount of time needed to learn to do the job well; the amount of time the respondent had been trained or would be trained for the type of work he or she had been doing since completing full-time education. When measured against these three indicators of skill levels, our findings show that part-time jobs were worse than full-time ones. Table 4.4a shows that over half of both short-hour and long-hour part-timers said that no qualification was needed to apply for their job. This is the case for about one-third of female and male full-time jobs. Moreover, while only 9% of short-hour part-time jobs required a formal qualification of above A level, 12% of long-hour part-timers, 23% of the female full-time jobs and 27% of male full-time jobs do not need such qualifications.

It can also be seen from Table 4.4a that short-hour part-time jobs were mostly likely to be jobs which did not have any formal qualification requirements, as compared to the other two working-hour statuses. They were also least likely to be jobs which required degree or non-degree higher-education qualifications. Table 4.4a also shows that while the major gap is between full-time and part-time status, there are differences between the two part-time working-hour statuses. Long-hour part-time jobs were more likely to require an O level qualification and less likely to be without any qualification requirement, as compared to short-hour part-time jobs.

The difference between the three working-hour statuses remains considerable when class is taken into account. Within the routine non-manual class, 63% of the short-hour part-timers said their jobs did not have any formal qualification requirements; this is the case for 50% of the long-hour part-timers, 19% of the female full-timers, and 25% of male full-timers. Within the semi-/unskilled manual working class, 91% of the short-hour part-timers said there were no formal qualification requirements for their jobs; the comparable figures for long-hour part-timers, female and male full-timers are 94%, 82% and 77% respectively.

Table 4.4a
Distribution of working-hour status by job qualification

Job qualification	Working-hour status (%)			
	Short-hour part-timers	Long-hour part-timers	Female full-timers	Male full-timers
None	77	64	36	31
Vocational	5	7	9	9
O-level	7	15	24	22
A-level	1	2	9	9
Non-degree higher education	5	7	11	12
University degree	4	5	12	16
Total	100	100	100	100
N	289	354	943	1,916

<Question : "If they were applying today, what qualifications, if any, would someone need to get the type of job you have now?">

The second indicator of skill level is the amount of time the worker takes to master his or her current job. Work which requires a higher level of skills will take the worker a longer period of time to master, and vice versa. Table 4.4b shows that a majority of short-hour part-time jobs and nearly half of long-hour part-time jobs took the worker less than one month to learn to do the job well. This is only the case for one-quarter of female full-time jobs and 17% of male full-time jobs. At the other extreme, less than 10% of both categories of part-time jobs took the workers two years or more to learn to do their jobs well, while the figures for female and male full-time jobs are 15% and 37% respectively. It can also be noted from Table 4.4b that short-hour part-time jobs were more likely to involve unskilled work, as compared to long-hour part-time jobs. While 70% of short-hour part-time jobs required the worker less than one month to master the job, this is the case for 48% of long-hour part-time jobs.

Table 4.4b

Distribution of working-hour status by duration of on-the-job learning

Duration of on-the-job learning	Working-hour status (%)			
	short-hour part-timers	long-hour part-timers	female full-timers	male full-timers
Less than one month	70	48	25	17
1 - 3 months	16	22	21	15
4 - 6 months	3	11	15	12
7 - 12 months	3	5	14	10
1-2 years	3	5	10	11
More than 2 years	5	8	15	37
Total	100	100	100	100
N	289	354	943	1,916

<Question : "How long did it take you after you first started doing this type of job to learn to do it well?">

The disparity between the three working-hour statuses is still evident after the class position to which the job belonged is held constant. Within the routine non-manual class, while 62% of the short-hour part-time jobs took less than one month to master, this is the case for 37% of long-hour part-time jobs, 20% of female full-time jobs, and 16% of male full-time jobs. Among jobs in the semi-/unskilled manual working class, 84% of short-hour part-time jobs needed less than one month to master; this is the case for 74% of long-hour part-time, 51% of female full-time, and 35% of male full-time jobs.

The third indicator of skill level is the amount of training for the work. For jobs which have a higher skill level, it is reasonable to expect that workers will be given training or have been trained before for the work they are doing. Moreover, the higher the level of skills, the longer the duration of training. Table 4.4c gives the result for the three working-hour statuses. A majority of short-hour and long-hour part-timers had not received or would not receive any training for the type of work they were doing. Even if training had been or would be undertaken, the duration was, generally, shorter than that of full-time male and female work, especially for training that would last for more than two years. While the major gap was between full-timers and part-timers, the two part-time statuses also differed from each other. Short-hour part-time jobs were more likely than long-hour part-time jobs to be unskilled work. A greater proportion of the former did not or would not receive any job training as compared to the latter.

Table 4.4c
Working-hour status by amount of job training

Duration of training	Working-hour status (%)			
	Short-hour part-timers	Long-hour part-timers	Female full-timers	Male full-timers
None	84	74	52	44
Less than 1 month	5	8	10	8
1 - 3 months	2	4	7	6
4 - 6 months	1	2	3	3
7 - 12 months	2	2	5	4
1-2 years	3	4	7	5
More than 2 years	6	5	16	30
Total	100	100	100	100
N	289	354	943	1,916

When the class position to which the job belonged were taken into account, workers who were in part-time jobs were still worse off than full-timers. Within the routine non-manual class, 78% of short-hour part-timers were not or would not be provided with job training; this is the case for 75% of part-timers who worked longer hours, 53% of female full-timers and 33% of male full-timers. Among workers who were in the semi-/unskilled manual working class, while 95% of short-hour part-timers were not or would not be provided with training, 90% of long-hour part-timers, 74% of female full-timers and 66% of male full-timers had no training for their jobs.

The main point which we can conclude from the above analyses of the three indicators of skills is that the skill level of part-time work was lower than that of full-time work. The disparities remain even after we have taken into consideration the class into which part-time jobs were concentrated. The major gap was in terms of the full-time/part-time distinction, while there were also differences among part-timers. The jobs of those part-timers who were least protected by the existing employment legislations were more likely to be unskilled work.

The delineation of skill levels by using these criteria is very much in line with the respondent's own assessment of whether his or her work was skilled or not skilled. When the respondents were asked whether they considered their current jobs to be skilled or not, the shorter the working hours, the greater the proportion of workers who perceived their work to be unskilled. While 70% of short-hour part-timers did not regard their jobs as skilled, the figure for long-hour part-timers is 56%; 30% for female full-time and 21% for male full-time workers.

The difference remains when the working-hour status was disaggregated according to the two class categories into which part-time jobs were concentrated. Within the routine non-manual class, while 52% of short-hour part-timers considered their jobs to be skilled, this is the case for 54%, 75% and 69% of long-hour part-timers, female and male full-timers respectively. Among workers who were in the semi/unskilled manual class, while only 15% of short-hour and 20% of long-hour part-timers considered their jobs to be skilled, the comparable figures for female and male full-timers are 44% and 54% respectively.

The use of advanced technology and skill levels

Segmentation theory suggests that the use of modern technology is a reason why employers differentiate primary and secondary employment. While the work of primary jobs involves the use of modern technology, this is unlikely to be the case for secondary workers whom employers believe to have a high turnover rate. In terms of the likelihood of using modern technology in their work, our findings show that part-timers were more disadvantaged than full-timers. In the survey, respondents were asked whether their jobs involved the use of computerized or automated equipment. While only 16% of short-hour part-timers and 25% of long-hour part-timers gave a positive response, this is the case for 43% and 47% of female and male full-time workers respectively.

We noted in the last chapter that small establishments were much less likely to have upgraded their technology. In the last section, we also saw that part-time jobs were more likely to be in small rather than large workplaces, as compared to full-time jobs. Thus, to assess the net effect of working-hour status *per se*, size of the workplace has to be taken into account. Table 4.5a gives the percentages of workers in each of the three

101

working-hour statuses who said their work involved the use of automated or computerized equipment by the size of their workplaces.

Table 4.5a

Percentages of full-timers and part-timers whose work involved the use of computerized or automated equipments by size of the workplace

Size of the workplace	Working-hour status (%)			
	Short-hour part-timers	Long-hour part-timers	Female full-timers	Male full-timers
Less than 25 workers	11	19	35	37
25 - 99 workers	24	20	43	40
100 or more workers	29	26	48	55

It can be seen that after taking into account the size of their workplaces, part-timers, as compared to their full-time counterparts, were still less likely to use advanced technology. In workplaces with fewer than 25 workers, only 11% of short-hour part-timers said their work involved the use of modern technology, while this is the case for 19% of long-hour part-timers and about one-third of both female and male full-timers. Part-timers who worked in large workplaces also fared worse than their full-time counterparts. In each of the workplace size category, the gap between full-time and part-time jobs is considerable while that among the two part-time categories is relatively minor.

The use of advanced technology is closely related to the level of job complexity and hence, in turn, would be associated with the level of skills. Jobs which involve the use of advanced technology would be less likely to be unskilled. The association between the use of advanced technology and skill levels is illustrated in Table 4.5b. For the sake of simple presentation, only the percentages for the lowest end of each indicator are given here.

Table 4.5b
**Percentages of workers whose job involved or did not involve
the use of computerized or automated equipment by the three
indicators of skill levels**

	Whether the job involved the use of computerized or automated equipment	

Indicators of skill levels
1. no formal qualification required

	yes	*no*
short-hour part-timers	60	81
long-hour part-timers	34	72
female full-timers	14	51
male full-timers	17	44
all workers	19	54

**2. No training was provided/
would be provided**

	yes	*no*
short-hour part-timers	71	87
long-hour part-timers	59	79
female full-timers	44	58
male full-timers	33	54
all workers	38	62

3. Job took less than one month to master

	yes	*no*
short-hour part-timers	57	72
long-hour part-timers	38	51
female full-timers	15	32
male full-timers	11	23
all workers	15	34

Among workers whose jobs involved the use of advanced technology, only 19% said their jobs had no formal qualification requirements while this is the case for 54% of those whose jobs did not involve the use of computerized or advanced technology. A similar gap can be noted in terms of the other two indicators of skill levels. Among workers whose job involved the use of computerized or automated equipment, only 38% said they were not or would not be provided with training and only 15% said it took them less them one month to master their job. The comparable figures for workers whose job did not involve the use of such advanced technology are 62% and 34% respectively. The difference is also evident for workers in each working-hour status. Workers whose jobs did not involve the use of computerized or automated equipment were more likely to say their job had no formal qualification requirements, that they were not or would not be provided with training, and that their jobs took less than one month to master, as compared to workers whose jobs involved the use of automated or computerized equipment.

Transferability of skills

Most previous studies on the skills of part-time jobs do not distinguish the transferability of skills from the level dimension. A majority of them focus only on the question of level (Horrell et al.,1989; Gallie, 1991; Beechey and Perkins, 1987; Rubery et al. 1994). In fact, the issue of transferability is more pivotal to segmentation theory as it underlies the minimal movement of workers between primary and secondary labour market segments, especially outward movements from a firm internal labour market. Skills in the firm internal labour market, it is argued, tend to be specific to meet the production requirement of the firm. Workers trained with firm-specific skills are given preferential employment conditions. These help foster in them a high level of attachment to the organization, thereby stabilizing the employment relationship, and ensure that returns to the human resources investment made by employers is maximized. Primary workers with firm-specific skills are 'trapped' in their employing companies as the skills they accumulate with their current employers cannot be readily applied to work in another company. Changing employers would entail losing the higher level of job rewards which their current employing organization offers them for their specific skills. In other words, their job prospects are with their current employers rather than in changing to another one.

In contrast to primary jobs, secondary jobs are not invested with firm-specific skills. Workers who are on secondary jobs accumulate only general and basic work skills. They are, therefore, not tied down to a specific employing organization. Unlike primary workers, secondary workers do not incur any loss to their job rewards when they move between different workers. In other words, their job prospects do not vary with whether they stay with their current employer or change to another employer.

The concept of transferability is not easy to operationalize. Given the information available in the survey, the following attempt can best be regarded as an exploration, rather than a definitive statement, of the extent to which part-time work involves general, non firm-specific skills. The preceding discussion implies that the degree of transferability is closely related to the *relative* advantage of staying with the current employer versus switching to another employer for getting better job opportunities. The question that we want to address is, therefore, : does part-time work require primarily general skills, and hence to stay with his or her current employer or to change employer offer equal job prospects?

In the survey, respondents were asked, generally speaking, which option would offer them best job opportunities - staying with their current employer or changing employer - if they were trying to get a better job. The response distribution for part-timers and full-timers is given in Table 4.6.

Table 4.6
Working-hour status by job opportunities

Working-hour status (%)	Best job opportunities			
	Stay with current employers	Change employer	Total	N
Short-hour part-time	43	57	100	(276)
Long-hour part-time	57	43	100	(341)
Female full-time	61	39	100	(940)
Male full-time	60	40	100	(1,995)

<Question : "If you were trying to get a better job, generally speaking, which would offer you the best job opportunities?">

It can be seen that the proportion of short-hour part-timers who said their best job opportunity was with their current employer rather than changing employers is smaller than that for both long-hour part-timers and full-timers. This suggests that the current employing organization of part-timers was not offering them additional advantages over other employers, as compared to the situation for long-hour part-timers and full-timers. Compared to the other two working-hour statuses, part-time workers working 16 hours or fewer a week were less likely to be attached to the internal labour market of their employing organization. We shall return to this question concerning the disadvantaged position of part-time workers in their employing establishments when dealing with the question of promotion prospects in a more comprehensive manner.

In this section, we have noted that part-time jobs were more likely to be unskilled work. A majority did not require either any job-entry qualification or a long period of on-the-job learning. A large proportion of them did not or would not offer the incumbents job training. They were also less likely to involve firm-specific work skills. The skill level of a job is one of the most crucial factors in determining job returns. A higher skill level is associated with a higher level of job rewards. For segmentation theory, the specificity of skills also determines to which segment a worker belongs and whether he or she enjoys a wider range of job rewards. In the next section, four major kinds of job rewards will be analysed, and the way differences in job-skills are translated into disparate job rewards between full-time and part-time workers will be examined.

Job returns differences between full-time and part-time work

In this section, four major types of job returns, namely, job security, promotion prospects, wage level and the entitlement to fringe benefits of part-timers will be compared to those of full-time workers.

Job security

Segmentation theory suggests that secondary employment is characterized by a low level of job security. Jobs in the secondary segment are precarious. They are created and dispensed with according to the business conditions of their employing organizations. The flexible firm thesis claims that the part-time workforce, as a component of the peripheral workforce, is more exposed to market fluctuations than workers who belong to the core full-time permanent workforce. Rodgers (1989) suggested that precarious jobs were characterized by a short time horizon. They are created to meet short-term needs of production, and therefore their employment contracts last for a shorter period of time than that of non-precarious jobs. Are part-time jobs more precarious and workers are more likely to bear the brunt of manpower cut?

In terms of the time horizon of the employment contract, our data show that part-time jobs were actually not short-term contract jobs. Very few part-timers were on a temporary contract which lasted less than 12 months or between one and three years. Over 80% of part-time jobs, whether short-hour or long-hour, were on a permanent contract basis. Similarly, over 80% of male and female full-timers were also on a permanent contract.

The formal employment contract may or may not reflect the actual extent of job insecurity faced by the employee. A permanent job may still be a precarious one if there is a great likelihood of job loss. For this reason, the second indicator of job security, namely, the likelihood of job loss, was also examined. In the survey, respondents were asked whether there was any chance at all that they would lose their jobs and become unemployed in the next twelve months. The findings show that, contrary to the secondary labour market hypothesis, part-timers did not differ significantly from full-timers in terms of their likelihood of job loss. While 85% of short-hour part-timers said they would not lose their jobs in the next twelve months, the figures for long-hour part-timers and female full-timers and male full-timers are 81%, 84% and 77% respectively. If there is any difference, it was the male workers who sensed a greater risk of losing their jobs.

The chance of job loss may well be particularly high in certain occupational groups. With the shrinking of manufacturing industries, we may expect that semi-/unskilled manual workers would be particularly vulnerable to job loss. Do part-timers who are in these occupations have a greater risk of job loss than their full-time counterparts? Our findings do not support this. For employees who were in the semi-/unskilled manual occupational group, 25% of the full-time working women and 31% of male full-timers said there was a chance that they would lose their jobs, as compared with 13% of short-hour part-timers and 15% of long-hour part-timers. Full-time male workers, rather than female part-timers, were more likely to say they would lose their jobs.

Besides the likelihood of job loss, respondents were also asked directly to assess the degree of job security offered by their current jobs. About 90% of workers in all three working-hour statuses rated their jobs as either very secure or fairly secure. Thus, our findings indicate that the unfavourable job security of the two categories of part-timers, as implied in their legal employment protection, is not reflected in their experience on their jobs. If there is any difference, those women and men working full-time were the most likely to say that they would lose their jobs, rather than the part-timers.

While the analysis here is based on the self-assessment of workers about the *potential* job security associated with their current jobs, another way to examine the employment insecurity of part-time employment is the extent to which it is associated with the *actual* unemployment experience of the individual. In Chapter one, it was noted that a high level of unemployment is suggested by segmentation theory as one of the hallmarks of the secondary labour market. Longitudinal data which covers the previous (un)employment experience of an individual are needed to evaluate this hypothesis. We shall return to this aspect of job insecurity of part-time work in Chapter eight when the work history of women is examined.

Promotion prospects

If part-time work is not particularly insecure, does it offer any job prospects to the job-holder? Another major employment condition which distinguishes primary from secondary employment is the presence or absence of promotion prospects. Segmentation theory suggests that secondary jobs are dead-end when compared with primary jobs; they do not carry promotion opportunities. In the earlier discussion of skills transferability, our findings suggest that short-hour part-time workers were less likely to possess firm-specific skills. Hence, staying with their current employers did not give them an advantage over moving to another employer in terms of securing better job prospects.

The non-specificity of work skills can also contribute to a worker's poorer promotion opportunities within his or her employing organization. Employers are more likely to offer promotion prospects to workers with firm-specific skills in order to retain them in the organization, since the training needed to build up those skills is costly for the employer. What then is the likelihood of part-timers having promotion chances as compared to full-timers? In our sample, while only 17% of short-hour part-timers said their jobs offered them promotion prospects, this is the case for 27% of long-hour part-timers, 52% and 63% of female and male full-timers respectively.[17]

However, the effect of working-hour status *per se* on the presence or absence of promotion prospects may be confounded by other pertinent determinants. We have noted that part-time jobs were concentrated in smaller workplaces. A small workplace inherently restricts the number of higher-ranking positions which workers from lower-ranking positions can move into. On the contrary, jobs in large firms are likely to be graded and organized into hierarchies with clear lines of progression. Workers in large firms are, therefore, more likely to have promotion chances than those who are employed in small firms. In Chapter three, it was noted that, in the private sector, larger firms were much more likely than small firms to have promoted some of their staff members. This association between firm size and staff promotion does not tell us the way the chance of promotion varies between individual employees. We need an analysis of the association at the job level. The results from the employee survey show that, at the job level, the likelihood of having promotion prospects increases with the size of the workplace. For all working women, while 42% of those employed in workplaces with fewer than 25 employees were offered advancement prospects, this is the case for 67% of those who worked in workplaces with 500 or more employees. Hence, the effect of workplace size needs to be considered to assess the net effect of working-hour status.

As part-timers were more likely to be in positions which were below the professional and managerial positions, class is another crucial control variable which needs to be considered. For female employees, while 61% of those who were in the two service classes had promotion prospects, this is the case for 45% of routine non-manual workers and 21% for semi-unskilled manual workers. For male employees, 70% of those who were in the service class were offered promotion prospects on their jobs; this is the case for 45% of skilled manual workers and 48% of semi-/unskilled manual workers. These figures suggest that promotion opportunity differs according to the class position to which the job belongs to.

Besides workplace size and class, promotion chances would also differ between employment in the public and the private sector. Employment in the public sector is likely to be well structured with clearly defined hierarchies of job positions. Employees in the public sector would, therefore, have a greater chance of moving up the job ladder. In our sample, for all working women, 50% of those who were employees in the public sector had promotion opportunities, as compared to 34% of those who were employed in the private sector. The comparable figures for men are 70% and 59% respectively.

In addition to these labour market features, two personal characteristics of the must also be taken into account, namely, the level of formal qualification and age. Existing theories suggest that the level of formal qualification can affect promotion prospects. It has been suggested that employers are more likely to regard workers with higher levels of formal qualifications as trainable and promotable (Wilensky and Lawrence, 1979). This is because more schooling enhances cognitive and general skills which in turn facilitate the acquisition of specific skills at the workplace.[19] Thus, we can expect the higher the level of a worker's formal qualification, the greater the probability that he or she will be allocated a job with promotion prospects.

Age would also be closely related to the chance of promotion prospects. A young person in the early stage of his or her working life is more likely to be given advancement prospects than an older person near retirement age. Employers would find it more worthwhile to retain young rather than old employees by offering them job prospects. Moreover, an older worker may well have reached the top position of their career or job ladder from which further promotion is inherently not possible. Hence, it is reasonable to expect that younger persons, rather than older ones, would hold jobs offering promotion chances.

To examine the independent effect of working-hour status on promotion prospects, a multivariate analysis is conducted. Since our dependent variable is a yes/no dichotomous one, the parameters were estimated by means of a binary logistic regression. The focus is on whether working-hour status still has a significant effect on the odds of having promotion prospects rather than not having them, after other factors were controlled for. As the comparison between part-timers and full-timers is the main focus, the regression was conducted for working women only. The results are given in Table 4.7. In the regression, degree and non-degree higher-education qualification were combined into one category as higher-education.

The estimates shown in Table 4.7 are the exponentiated log-odds. The size of the workplace significantly affected the presence of promotion prospects. Large workplaces raised the odds of having promotion prospects rather than not by almost two times, as compared to small workplaces. Table 4.7 also shows that being in a semi-/unskilled manual occupation and in a sales occupation reduced the odds of having promotion prospects by a factor of 0.34, as compared to those who were in the professional and managerial classes. Employees in the private sector have a poorer chance of having promotion prospects, as compared to workers in the public sector. The level of formal qualifications also affected the employee's likelihood of having promotion chances. Degree or non-degree education qualifications raised the odds of having promotion chances rather than not by a factor of 1.98, as compared to those who had no formal qualifications. Age had the expected negative effect on the odds of promotion chances.

After these factors were controlled for, the working-hour status of an employee still has a significant effect on the odds of having promotion prospects or not. Part-time status reduced the odds of having promotion opportunities, with short-hour part-time status being the least likely out of the three statuses.

Thus, in terms of promotion prospects, the preceding analysis shows that part-time workers were significantly more likely than full-timers to be in dead-end jobs, particularly for short-hour part-time workers who were least well protected under the existing legislations.[19]

Table 4.7
Logistic regression for the presence of promotion prospects for female employees

Variables	Multiplicative estimates	Standard error
Constant	0.56	(0.35)
Working-hour status		
short-hour PT	1	
long-hour PT	1.87**	(0.24)
full-time	3.76**	(0.22)
Workplace size		
1-24 workers	1	
25-99 workers	1.52**	(0.17)
100 or more	1.97**	(0.16)
Class		
higher-grade service	1	
lower-grade service	0.52**	(0.25)
routine non-manual	0.69	(0.21)
technicians	0.45**	(0.29)
and skilled manual		
semi-/unskilled	0.34**	(0.21)
manual		
Sector		
public Sector	1	
private Sector	0.50**	(0.15)
Formal qualification		
no Qualification	1	
vocational	0.68	(0.33)
O-level	1.05	(0.18)
A-level	1.21	(0.28)
higher-education	1.98**	(0.22)
Age group		
20-29 years	1	
30-39 years	0.79	(0.19)
40-49 years	0.54**	(0.20)
50-59 years	0.45**	(0.23)

**denotes significant at <0.05 level
Scale deviance = 602, Degree of Freedom = 500; Number of cases = 1,191

Many studies point out that part-time jobs are often low-paid (Duffy and Pupo, 1992; Hurstfield, 1978; Leeds, 1990; Jones and Long, 1979; Simpson, 1986). In our present sample, the average gross hourly wage for the two categories of part-timers is 2.9 and 3.3 pounds, as compared to 4.1 and 4.7 pounds for female and male full-timers respectively. But like promotion prospects, wage rates are also affected by the worker's individual features as well as factors which are related to the job and the workplace. In this section, as in the last, a multivariate analysis is used to assess the net effect of working-hour status on the wage rate after taking into account other factors.

According to human capital theory, earnings are determined primarily by the amount of human capital a worker has. In this section, the effect of one major kind of human capital, namely, school-leaving qualifications will be considered. This analysis will be extended in Chapter six to include the effects of previous work and non-work experiences.

Segmentation theory suggests that there are factors which impede market forces from equalizing the wage rate of workers who have similar qualifications and work experiences. Existing studies have repeatedly shown that unionization and firm size are two crucial institutional forces which bring about persistent wage gaps. A number of researches found that unionization, whether at the organization or the individual level, had a mark-up effect on the wage rate (Stewart, 1983; Yaron, 1991; Sloane and Murphy, 1989; Mastekaasa, 1993; Blanchflower, 1984).

It has been found that firm size is positively related to the wage level which workers receive. In several studies, national and cross-national alike, it was noted that workers in larger firms received a higher wage rate than workers in small firms, after the presence of union and job position were taken into account (Kalleberg and van Buren, 1992; Mellow, 1982; Brown and Medoff, 1989; Oi, 1991).

The class position to which the job belongs is another crucial factor that needs to be taken into account. These factors were regressed onto the natural logarithm of gross hourly wage together with the working-hour status and formal qualification, using ordinary least square (OLS) regression.

In the equation, the level of formal school qualification is treated as a series of dummy variables with university degree as the reference category. The class position of the job is also treated as a series of dummy variables with higher grade service class as the reference category. Workplace size and union representation are included as control variables. Working-hour status is treated as dummy variables with the short-hour part-time status as the reference category. The results are shown in Table 4.8a. Since the focus is the full-time/part-time comparison, the analysis is conducted for working women only.

Table 4.8a
OLS regression on log hourly wage for working women

Variable	Unstandardized coefficient	S.E.	T-value
Level of formal qualification			
no qualification	-0.454	0.04	-10.82**
vocational Level	-0.418	0.06	-7.32**
Advanced Level	-0.402	0.04	-9.46**
non-degree Higher Education	-0.206	0.04	-4.54**
degree	-	-	-
Class			
semi-/unskilled manual	-0.439	0.06	-7.89**
technicians and skilled	-0.284	0.06	-4.47**
retail and sales	-0.387	0.05	-7.14**
routine non-manual	-0.334	0.05	-6.25**
lower-service class	-0.164	0.05	-3.20**
higher-service class	-	-	-
Union representation			
present	-0.111	0.02	5.05**
not present	-	-	-
Workplace size			
less than 25 workers	-0.147	0.02	-6.59**
25 workers or more	-	-	-
Working-hour status			
short-hour part-time	-	-	-
long-hour part-time	0.027	0.03	0.854
full-time	0.012	0.01	1.204
Constant	1.658	0.06	28.79

Adjusted R-square = 0.337; R-square = 0.344N = 1,325;
**denotes significant at <0.05 level
S.E. stands for standard error

The results show that the effect of formal school qualifications is in line with the hypothesis of human capital theory. The higher the level of qualification, the lower the wage rate. Class has the expected effect. Jobs which were in semi-/unskilled manual occupations and retail and service occupations had a lower wage rate than jobs which were in the higher-grade service class. The effect of workplace size was in line with other empirical studies. Workers in small workplaces had a lower wage rate, as compared to workers in large workplaces. The presence of union representation at the workplace had a significant mark-up effect on the wage rate.

Finally, long-hour part-timers and full-timers had higher wage rates than short-hour part-timers. However, the differences were insignificant. When the same wage equation was repeated without distinguishing part-time workers into two categories, that is, with the working-hour status as a dummy, the result shows that the part-time status gives the worker a significantly lower wage rate, when the same set of factors are held constant. This second set of results is shown in Table 4.8b.

Table 4.8b
OLS regression on log hourly wage for working women

Variable	Unstandardized coefficient	S.E.	T-value
Level of formal qualification			
none	-0.431	0.04	-10,4**
vocational	-0.411	0.06	-7.32**
O-level	-0.394	0.04	-9.41**
A-level	-0.311	0.04	-6.38**
non-degree higher education	-0.189	0.04	-4.21**
degree	-	-	-
Class			
semi-/unskilled manual	-0.397	0.05	-7.26**
technicians and skilled manual	-0.287	0.06	-4.58**
retail and sales	-0.343	0.05	-6.46**
routine non-manual	-0.302	0.05	-5.75**
lower-grade service	-0.161	0.05	-3.20**
higher-grade service	-	-	-

(continued)

114

Table 4.8b (continued)

Variable	Unstandardized coefficient	S.E.	T-value
Union representation			
present	0.107	0.02	4.91**
absent	-	-	-
Workplace size			
fewer than 25 workers	-0.121	0.02	-5.49**
25 or more workers	-	-	-
Working-hour status			
full-time	0.143	0.02	6.28**
part-time	-	-	-

R-Square = 0.363; Adjusted R-Square = 0.357; N = 1,325
**denote significant at <0.05 level, s.e. stands for standard error

Comparing the two sets of results, there are two main points to note : (1) full-timers enjoyed an advantage over part-timers, even after the human capital factor and the salient features of the job and of the workplace were taken into account; (2) the distinction between part-timers in terms of their legal status is not significant.

Fringe benefits

Another component of job rewards suggested as a means used by employers to differentiate primary from secondary employment is the provision of fringe benefits. Segmentation theory suggests that employers provide primary workers with fringe benefits as an important part of the package of job rewards. Secondary workers are less likely to enjoy fringe benefits. As questions about fringe benefits were asked in only three of the six localities in SCELI, the following discussion is an exploration of the way working-hour status affects the entitlement to different types of fringe benefits.

As shown in Tables 4.9a to 4.9c, part-timers, whether of the long-hour or short-hour type, were less likely to be entitled to different kinds of fringe benefits. In Northampton, short-hour part-timers were the group which were least likely to be entitled to membership in a pension scheme, sick pay, unpaid leave for domestic problems, subsidized/free meals and recreation or sports facilities. In Coventry, they were particularly unlikely to be included in a pension scheme, to be given sick pay and additional maternity pay, and provided with recreation and sports facilities, as compared to the other two working-hour statuses.[20]

Table 4.9a
Percentage of workers who said that their jobs were provided with benefits (for Northampton)

Fringe benefits	Working-hour status (%)			
	Short-hour part-timers	Long-hour part-timers	Female full-timers	Male full-timers
Pension scheme	18	40	68	74
Sick pay	12	38	62	69
Paid leave for domestic problems	12	44	57	67
Unpaid leave for domestic problems	61	64	66	59
Use of company car	4	3	11	30
Free transport	17	18	23	31
Discount of goods	25	33	41	47
Subsidised/free meals	12	35	47	39
Finance/loans	5	21	19	22
Accommodation/ housing	2	8	16	14
Life assurance	-	8	18	40
Private health scheme	4	17	21	32
Recreation/sports facilitates	17	36	34	41
Additional maternity pay	8	30	38	24
Childcare facilities	13	9	13	1

Table 4.9b
Percentage of workers who said that their jobs were provided with benefits (for Coventry)

Fringe benefits	Working-hour status (%)			
	Short-hour part-timers	Long-hour part-timers	Female full-timers	Male full-timers
Pension scheme	9	38	56	80
Sick pay	21	44	55	78
Paid leave for domestic problems	20	39	49	75
Unpaid leave for domestic problems	75	89	64	66
Use of company car	2	3	10	26
Free transport	7	12	19	24
Discount of goods	29	17	40	58
Subsidised/free meals	22	28	23	38
Finance/loans	2	6	11	20
Accommodation/housing	0	1	5	10
Life assurance	2	11	12	40
Private health scheme	5	7	13	28
Recreation/sports facilities	7	23	34	48
Additional maternity pay	5	20	32	17
Childcare facilities	4	5	5	4

Table 4.9c
Percentage of workers who said that their employment provided benefits
(for Swindon)

Fringe benefits	Working-hour status (%)			
	Short-hour part-timers	Long-hour part-timers	Female full-timers	Male full-timers
Free meal	26	24	34	43
Finance of loans	8	4	17	20
Accommodation	2	9	13	14
Travel cost	15	20	22	37
Childcare	0	0	0	1
Private health scheme	3	2	24	31

Thus, in addition to the lack of advancement opportunities on their jobs and the lower wage rate, part-time workers were also disadvantaged by the lack of entitlement to a range of fringe benefits.

Conclusion and discussion

In this chapter, the differences between part-time and full-time work were examined. The discussion began with the legal status of part-time workers as compared to full-timers. According to the current legislation, the extent of legal employment protection to which part-time workers are entitled depends on the number of hours they work per week.

The main part of this chapter then focused on the ways that the disadvantageous legal position of part-time workers relative to full-time workers is reflected in four major kinds of employment conditions. Our analysis shows that the skill level of part-time jobs is lower than that for full-time jobs. The work of part-timers is less likely to involve the use of modern technology. Contrary to the implication which we can draw from the secondary labour market theory about the relation between part-time work and employment insecurity, our findings show that the job security level of part-time work is similar to that of full-time work.

The hypothesized relation between employment insecurity and the full-time/part-time distinction is not borne out by our findings, the analyses of promotion prospects and wage rate lend empirical support to segmentation theory. The findings suggest that the full-time/part-time boundary contributed to the wage gap and the differential promotion prospects for employees who were comparable in terms of their levels of formal qualification, the class position to which their occupations belong and the features of the workplace in which they work. Part-time jobs, as compared to full-time jobs, are less likely to offer their incumbents promotion prospects, as compared to full-time jobs. The wage rate of part-time jobs is lower than that of full-time jobs. Part-time workers are entitled to fewer fringe benefits.

While the main gap is between full-time and part-time work, our findings also indicate that there are differences among the part-timers. Those who are less well protected by the existing legislations are particularly less likely to enjoy promotion prospects. They are also less likely to be entitled to a range of fringe benefits.

These findings suggest that employers have been capitalizing on the lower wage and non-wage labour costs (in terms of payments for employment protection rights) of part-timers to enable them to cope with their stringent financial situations and fluctuations in their workload. This is especially the case for small firms and establishments in the retail and personal services industries which, as we have seen in the last chapter, had a particularly heavy demand for part-timers. With their reduced number of working hours, part-timers are not invested with on-the-job training to upgrade their work skills. In this way, the total labour costs can be kept down while the manning level is made flexible enough to meet the peaks and troughs in product or services demands. The differentiation of the various aspects of market situation of full-time and part-time work thus enables employer to make effective deployment of person-hour work, while minimizing their wage bills and fixed labour costs.

The market situation is one dimension which labour market theories suggest for distinguishing one form of employment from another. The other aspect is the work situation, which is argued by one particular version of segmentation theory to be another way by which the labour market is segmented. This is the focus of the next chapter.

Notes

1   It is possible that the self-definition may differ from the actual number of working hours in certain occupations. For example, in the case of full-time teachers, the normal working hours considered as

full-time is below 30 hours. Martin and Roberts (1984) argued that the self-definition was preferred to the actual working hours as women who worked less than the normal working week for their particular job generally considered themselves to be part-time and were treated as such by their employers. In their wage analysis, Ermisch and Wright (1993) noted that using self-definition made it necessary to alter the method they used to estimate the hourly earnings function. However, in our case, the discrepancy between the two methods of enumerating part-time status is quite small. In the SCELI sample, for all those working women who defined themselves as part-timers, 7% worked more than 30 hours in their most recent pay period; and for those who defined themselves as working full-time, 3% worked less than 30 hours per week. In view of this small discrepancy, the self-definition will be adopted here, as our interest is not with the actual number of working hours supplied but with the working-hour status of the worker.

2   At the time of writing this thesis, a new legislation is about to come into effect which will provide all working women with maternity leave, regardless of length of service with an employer or the number of hours worked. The change is the result of introducing the Pregnant Workers Directive of the Council of Europe into Britain. Another prospective changes under consideration by the British government is the abolition of the different qualifying periods.

3   Prior to the current legislation, the qualifying periods and the hours threshold have been changed with various amendments made to the Employment Protection Act. See Disney and Szyszczak (1984) for a discussion of these various changes. See Income Data Services (1985) for some legal cases of part-timers' employment rights.

4   Of all the employees in SCELI, 2% were part-timers who worked fewer than eight hours per week. They were combined into one category together with those part-timers who worked nine to 15 hours per week.

5   For a discussion of the proportions of full-time and part-time workers who are covered by employment protection rights using different working-hour thresholds, see Hakim (1989).

6   The situation in former West Germany also suggests that the part-time workforce is rather heterogeneous. It was found that part-

timers who had different ranges of weekly working hours moved in and out of different employment statuses in different ways. See Buchtemann (1989) for a discussion of the transition patterns for what are called 'marginal' part-time workers and 'regular' part-timers in former West Germany. See also Tilly (1992) for another example in distinguishing different categories of part-timers.

7   In fact, both the modal and mean weekly working hours for all part-timers is 20 hours in the SCELI survey. Hakim (1990) noted that the average working hours of part-timers have remained stable at 20 hours a week over the last ten years. Numerical significance, however, does not provide any theoretical ground to use 20-hour as the cut-off point for finer distinction among part-timers.

8   In fact, part-time workers represented about one-quarter of all the female respondents in our sample. Of all 3,041 female respondents in the main survey of SCELI, 4% were self-employed, 31% were in full-time paid work, 24% in part-time work and 41% were not working in the reference week of the survey. Our focus will be on wage work and hence the self-employed category will not be dealt with.

9   Our focus will be on industrial employment, hence employment in the primary sector which consists of extractive industries and farming will be excluded from the subsequent discussion.

10   The validity of the schema has been tested and was found to be closely associated with a range of relevant occupational characteristics. These include employment and payment conditions as well as future prospects. See Evans (1992) for a discussion of the schema's validity. It was also noted that this schema has particular advantages in mobility study; see the discussion of Ganzeboom and his associates (1992).

11   The distinction between market and work situations was made by Lockwood (1958) in his study of office workers.

12   For a detailed description of the class schema, see Erikson and Goldthorpe (1993:35-47).

13   In their study of the class structure of Britain, Marshall and his associates (1988) found that the work situation and the mobility

path of individuals in rank-and-file sales and service occupations were similar to semi-/unskilled manual occupations and were rather different from those who were in routine clerical occupations.

14   The lower unionization rate of the part-time workforce has also been noted by Elias and Main (1982). Using the data from the National Training Survey, they found that while four out of ten women in full-time employment were trade union members, only 20% of women who worked part-time belonged to a union.

15   Previous studies have attempted to explain membership rates in terms of structural factors which make it difficult for unions to recruit or retain members, or in terms of personal characteristics of workers which strengthen or undermine trade union allegiance. For a discussion of the trend of membership rate, see Metcalf (1994); for an assessment of the various factors which determine union membership, see Gallie (1989).

16   These latter two subjects are often associated with the term 'skill' but not distinguished from that used with reference to the job, as pointed out by Craig and her associates (1984).

17   Martin and Roberts (1984) recorded in the 1980 Women and Employment Survey a similar difference between women working full-time and those working on a part-time basis. However, since their sample consisted of women only, one cannot tell whether the difference is due to working-hour status per se or to gender.

18   In a study of promotion decisions of personnel managers, Bills (1988) found that over half of the appointing managers he interviewed used schooling as a promotion criterion.

19   This finding is in line with the analysis of actual promotion by Glover (1994) for working women in teaching and white-collar occupations. She found that the part-time status of a worker significantly reduced her chance of being promoted.

20   In the 1980 Women and Employment Survey, respondents were asked whether they received paid holidays, whether they were entitled to sick pay, and whether they belonged to a private occupational pension scheme if their employers provided one. For each of these items, women who worked part-time fared worse

than those who worked full-time. Ginn and Arber (1993) also found that part-time status significantly reduced the likelihood of entitlement to a private occupational pension scheme.

5 The work situation of part-time work

While job rewards form a major part of an individual's employment experience and the way in which the labour market is segmented, the work situation is another equally important facet. Not only do jobs carry different packages of rewards, they are also embedded in diverse technical settings and social relations which characterize their workplaces. The allocation of jobs thus entails both differences in pecuniary job returns and disparate authority relations for workers. Previous studies have shown that the type of authority relations which an individual experiences at work affects his or her personality and is a major agent of socialization (Kohn and Schooler, 1983; Mortimer et al. 1983; Blauner, 1964). It is, therefore, pertinent to examine the different aspects of social relations at the workplace, that is, features which Lockwood (1958) called the work situation.

In Chapter one, it was noted that the work situation is the primary theoretical concern of a version of segmentation theory which stresses managerial control over the labour process. This version argues that the development of different types of control regimes at the workplace has led to labour market segmentation. Different labour market segments are characterized by the way the labour process is controlled and regulated. In this chapter, we shall look at the extent to which the full-time/part-time distinction can be characterised by distinct patterns of discipline and control of the labour process.

The discussion in Chapter one also pointed out that the flexible firm thesis considers the use of part-time work as one of the major measures which firms adopt to attain numerical flexibility. Part-time workers are deployed to match changing business needs. They are recruited to cover non-standard working-hour arrangements, for example, twilight shifts, overlaid shifts or peak running. The analysis in Chapter three shows that an increase in the use of shift-work is related to a greater use rate of part-timers at the establishment level. This association between shift-work and part-time work is analysed at the organizational level and does not tell us the different incidence rates of shift-work among workers who work full-time and part-time. For the latter, we need an analysis of the association at the level of individual workers. In addition to shift-working, the extent to which part-time workers are involved in other kinds of non-standard working-hour arrangements, as compared to that of full-timers, will also be examined.

The rest of this Chapter will be divided into two sections. The first section will examine the authority relations in which part-time workers are embedded in at the workplace, and assess the extent to which one version of segmentation theory can be applied to the full-time/part-time distinction. The second section will discuss the different extents to which full-time and part-time employees are involved in various non-standard working-hour arrangements.

As in the last Chapter, the analysis in this Chapter will focus on two questions. The first is : are part-timers worse off than full-time workers in the ways which segmentation theory suggests? Secondly, is the part-time workforce further segmented on the basis of working-hour statuses?

Authority relations at the workplace

Among existing studies, the market situation of part-time work has been studied more often than its work situation. Except for a few (Rubery et al. 1994; Robinson and Wallace, 1984), little is known about the work situation of part-time workers; for example, what kind of authority relations they are involved in, how much say they have in their work, and how they differ from their full-time counterparts. An analysis of the work situation is particularly relevant as authority relations have been suggested by some segmentation theorists as being one way to differentiate the labour market into segments.

In Chapter one, we noted that one version of segmentation theory attributes the cause of segmentation to employers' desire to exercise greater control over the labour process. This version argues that different labour market segments are characterized by the way workers are disciplined. Each segment is associated with a particular type of workplace disciplinary pattern.

We shall focus on the version formulated by Edwards (1978, 1979) who distinctively associates labour market segments with three different ways through which the labour process is controlled and the type of supervision that prevails at the workplace. According to Edwards, there are three modes of control through which employers

126

govern the labour process : simple control, technical control, and bureaucratic control. Simple control involves the exercise of personal power by foremen and supervisors. Personal despotism rules the workplace and favourable treatments are given out to workers arbitrarily. Workers who work under the simple control system are treated as commodities and as a variable cost of production instead of as assets to the firm. The secondary labour market is characterized by this mode of control. Jobs which belong to the secondary market segment are those in small manufacturing establishments, retail sales, temporary jobs, and in manual office work. The labour process in these workplaces is subject to simple control. Workers are tightly supervised instead of being given discretionary power to perform their job tasks.

In the technical mode, the control mechanism is built into the physical technology used in production. The pace and intensity of work is monitored and directed by the machines used in the production process. The supervisory function of foremen is replaced by assembly-lines and mechanized production methods. Work which is organized around assembly-lines and in heavily mechanized industries is subject to the technical mode of control. So are machine-paced clerical jobs. These jobs form the subordinate primary market.

The third one, bureaucratic control, is also an impersonalized form of control. It involves the institutionalized power of capitalists and managers. There are rules and regulations which govern the exercise of managerial power at the workplace, the determination of wage rates and the allocation of job positions. The disciplining of employees is governed by bureaucratic and standardized rules and regulations. Jobs in large corporations which tend to be oligopolists or monopolists are in the independent primary segment where the bureaucratic mode of control prevails at the workplace.

Edwards argued that the labour market was segmented according to these three modes of control :

> Labour markets are segmented because they express a historical segmentation of the labour process; specifically, a distinct system of control inside the firm underlies each of the three market segments. The secondary labour market is the market expression of workplace organized according to simple control. The subordinate primary market contains those workplaces (workers and jobs) under the 'mixed' system of technical control and unions. And the independent primary market reflects bureaucratically controlled labour process.....
> (Edward, 1979, p.178).

In applying Edwards' notion of secondary labour market to authority relations at the workplace, the questions that we shall address are : are part-timers more likely to be subject to the simple mode of control and the personal discipline of their supervisors, and less likely to experience bureaucratically regulated discipline at work, as compared to full-time workers? Are they given less job autonomy and are more closely supervised at the workplace; while their full-time counterparts enjoy a greater degree of self-direction and discretion in their work?

In the following analysis, several indicators are used to examine the authority relations at the workplace : the supervisory responsibility, discretionary power, the closeness of supervision and the determinants of work intensity. In the last Chapter, we noted that part-time jobs were concentrated in the routine non-manual class and the semi-/unskilled manual working class. Previous studies have shown that the amount of discretionary power one can exercise over his or her job is closely related to the class position to which the job belongs (Lincoln and Kalleberg, 1990; Evans, 1992, Marshall et al. 1988, Birkelund et al., 1994). Hence, in comparing the different working-hour statuses, we shall also assess whether the working-hour differences still hold after class is taken into consideration. In addition to the data from the main survey, the information from an area-specific question is also used for comparing the degree of formality of management-employee relations in which full-timers and part-timers are respectively involved.

Supervisory responsibility

Central to the system of work discipline and control at the workplace are the supervisory relations in which workers are involved. Primary and secondary workers are allocated to job positions which are different in terms of their supervisory statuses. The commitment of primary workers to the firm is valued and is actively sought after by employers. Delegating workers a certain degree of discretionary power is one means through which management can foster in them an identification with the goals and interests of their employing organizations. They are given supervisory statuses. On the contrary, secondary workers are regarded as dispensable by employers. It is unlikely that they are allocated to jobs which carry supervisory duties. This section deals with the question as to whether part-timers are less likely to be delegated some supervisory responsibilities, as compared to full-timers.

In the survey, respondents were asked whether they were directly responsible for supervising other employees or not. Table 5.1 shows the percentages of workers in each working-hour status who said they were responsible for supervising others. It also shows the percentages broken down by three classes. These classes, as we noted in the last Chapter, had a relatively higher proportion of part-timers.

Table 5.1

Percentages of workers who said they had supervisory duties by class and by working-hour status

Working-hour status (%)	Class				
	All workers	Service	Routine non-manual	Semi-/unskilled manual	N
Short-hour part-timers	7	22	2	7	(295)
Long-hour part-timers	15	54	7	3	(364)
Female full-timers	32	59	22	10	(986)
Male full-timers	45	70	34	18	(2,140)

<Question : "Are you directly responsible for supervising other employees?">

Table 5.1 indicates that taken as a whole, part-timers differed significantly from full-timers in terms of their likelihood of being supervisors. Among part-timers, those who worked shorter hours were even less likely to have supervisory responsibilities. The gap remains when the working-hour statuses were disaggregated by the class position to which the job belonged. Table 5.1 shows that within each class, part-timers were less likely to be delegated supervisory responsibilities. Among employees in the service class, short-hour part-timers were particularly unlikely to have supervisory duties. Among routine non-manual workers, the distinction between the full-time and part-time workers is more marked than the difference among the part-

timers. Within the semi-/unskilled manual working class, the full-time/part-time gap is narrower. It is also noticeable that holding the working-hour status constant, full-time working women, whether taken as a whole or disaggregated according to the class positions to which their jobs belonged, were less likely than their male counterparts to be given supervisory duties.

While the presence or absence of supervisory responsibility generally indicates a formal position in the organization, it may not reflect the extent of discretionary power which the worker can exercise over the job in actual practice. To examine this aspect of the authority relations at the workplace, we turn to the second indicator, namely, the extent to which workers can make decisions related to their worktasks.

Discretion at work

It was suggested that the work situation of workers also differs in terms of the decision-making power delegated to them by the management. The differences in the skill requirements of the job are associated with the amount of discretionary power which the job-holder would enjoy. Work tasks of jobs which involve higher skill levels cannot be specified in great details by the management. Workers need to be given decision-making power so that they can cope with the complexity and the related uncertainties at work. Moreover, allowing workers a high level of discretionary power not only helps employers secure allegiance from them, it also encourages the employee to work conscientiously. Primary workers whose jobs are more skilled and whose allegiance is sought after by the management are given much discretion over the way they carry out their work tasks. On the contrary, workers whose jobs involve unskilled work are likely to have their worktasks well-specified, leaving them with little room to exercise their own discretion. The analysis of the various skill indicators in Chapter four shows that part-time work is less skilled than full-time work. In this section, we examine the extent to which part-timers are disadvantaged in terms of the amount of discretionary power they can exercise over their jobs, as

The level of discretionary power can be indicated by the extent to which the workers can decide different aspects of their work. In the survey, respondents were asked a general question about the amount of choice they had over the way they did their jobs as an indicator of discretion. The percentage distributions of workers by the extent of choice is shown in Table 5.2a.

Table 5.2a shows that, taken as a whole, part-timers, as compared to female and male full-timers, were less likely to say they had a great deal of choice over the way they did their work (The difference among working women is significant at a p-value of 0.03). Among part-timers, short-hour part-timers were less likely to report a great deal of choice, as compared to their long-hour counterparts.

Table 5.2a
Working-hour status by the extent of choice over the way the job was done

Working-hour status (%)	Extent of choice				
	A great deal	Some	hardly any	None	N
Short-hour part-timers	42	32	11	14	303
Long-hour part-timers	45	28	13	13	369
Female full-timers	48	33	9	10	1,001
Male full-timers	56	28	8	8	2,131

<Question : "How much choice do you have over the way in which you do your job : a great deal, some, hardly any, or none at all?">

While the question which SCELI used to indicate discretionary power at work is a general one, the 1984 Social Class in Modern Britain asked more questions to measure discretionary power. This survey asked respondents whether they could decide on several specific aspects of their jobs. These include : (1) the particular tasks or jobs carried out from day to day; (2) the time they arrived at and left work, whether officially or unofficially; (3) changing the pace of work for a day; (4) introducing a new task or work assignment that they would do on their job. An analysis of the survey found that less than half of the female part-timers could decide their workpace, as compared to more than half of female and male full-timers. Part-timers were also less likely to be able to design or introduce new tasks at their jobs.[1]

To ascertain the net effect of working-hour status on the level of discretionary power, we need to take into consideration the class position of the job. Previous studies have found that jobs in the service class give workers a higher level of decision-making power than jobs in the semi-/unskilled manual working class (Mann, 1986; Birkelund et al. 1994).

Table 5.2b
OLS regression on the extent of choice over job for working women

Variables	Unstandardized coefficient	S.E.	T-value
Class			
service	-0.402	0.08	-4.76**
routine non-manual	-0.07	0.06	-1.07
technicians & skilled manual	-0.125	-0.03	-0.47
semi-/unskilled manual	-	-	-
Formal qualification			
no qualification	0.223	0.08	2.78**
vocational	0.151	0.12	1.27
O-level	0.118	0.08	1.46
A-level	0.156	0.103	1.51
higher education	-	-	-
Age group			
20 - 29	0.148	0.08	1.90*
30 - 39	0.083	0.08	1.11
40 - 49	-0.017	0.08	-0.23
50 - 59	-	-	-
Working-hour status			
short-hour PT	0.045	0.07	0.045
long-hour PT	0.068	0.06	1.074
full-time	-	-	-
Constant	1.78	16.55	

R-square = 0.052; Adjusted R-square = 0.052; N=1,645; significant at 0.05 (**) and (*) 0.1 level

Besides the class position to which the job belonged, two individual attributes of the worker will also be taken into account, namely, formal educational level and age. Employers would regard more educated workers as more capable of independent judgement and decision-making, and hence be able to be given more choice in the way they do their work. Employers may also regard older workers as more experienced and mature, and thus can be delegated some discretionary power. A multiple regression was conducted to assess the effect of working-hour status independent of the class, education and age factor. The results are given in Table 5.2b. Because of the way the dependent variable was coded (1 equals a great deal of choice and 4 equals none at all), a positive coefficient means a lower level of choice.

Table 5.2b shows that when the other factors were taken into account, shorter weekly working hours had no significant effect on the extent of choice which a worker enjoyed on the job, although the results indicate that both groups of part-timers had a lower degree of choice, as compared to full-timers. In line with findings in other studies, workers who were in service class positions had a greater level of choice over the way they did their work, as compared to semi-/unskilled manual workers. Workers who lacked formal qualifications were allowed a lower degree of choice, as compared to workers who had a degree or non-degree higher education qualifications. Younger workers aged between 20 to 29 were given fewer choices than older workers. Hence, with respect to discretionary power on the job, our findings do not lend support to the argument that the full-time/part-time delineation forms a distinct segmentation boundary.

Closeness of supervision

To the extent that part-time work belongs to the secondary labour market, we would expect that part-time workers are subject to close supervision. In SCELI, respondents were asked a general question about the extent to which they were closely supervised. For those who did not have supervisory responsibilities, the percentages of workers who said they were closely supervised among each of the three working-hour statuses and a breakdown by three classes are shown in Table 5.3a.

The table shows that, instead of a negative relation between working hours and the likelihood of being subject to close supervision as hypothesized by Edwards' secondary labour market theory, our findings suggest the opposite. Both groups of part-timers were less likely to be subject to close supervision, as compared to male and female full-timers. Moreover, among the four groups of workers, short-hour part-timers were the least likely to be closely supervised rather than not. If we consider only the working women, the difference between the three working-hour status was significant at a p-value of 0.03.

Table 5.3a
Percentages of workers who said they were closely supervised by working-hour status and by class

Working-hour status (%)	Class				
	All workers	Service	Routine non-manual	Semi-/unskilled manual	N
Short-hour part-timers	31	*	43	25	283
Long-hour part-timers	38	33	38	41	313
Female full-timers	42	32	37	52	679
Male full-timers	41	34	49	43	1,185

*absolute N fewer than 30

Table 5.3a also shows that when the working-hour statuses are disaggregated by class, the relation between the likelihood of being closely supervised or not and the working-hour status varies according to the class position to which the job belonged. Within the service class, part-timers were as likely to be closely supervised as both male and female full-timers. Among working women who belonged to the routine non-manual class, short-hour part-timers were more likely to experience close supervision as compared to long-hour part-timers and female full-timers. However, the difference failed to reach the statistical significance level of 0.05 or 0.1. Within the semi-/unskilled manual class, short-hour part-timers were much **less** likely to be closely supervised, as compared to long-hour part-timers and to female full-timers. They were also considerably less likely than male full-timers to be closely supervised (The difference among these three groups of working women is significant at the 0.05 level).

Besides being asked about their current situation, respondents who had a job five years ago were also asked to compare the closeness of supervision which they were then subject to with that of their current situation. Table 5.3b shows the percentages of workers in each working-hour status who reported an increase, no change, or a decrease in the tightness of supervision which they experienced in their job.

From Table 5.3b, we can see that among working women, short-hour part-timers were least likely to report an increase in the closeness of supervision, as compared to the other three groups (The difference among the working women was significant at the 0.05 level).

Table 5.3b
Changes in the tightness of supervision by working-hour status

Working-hour status (%)	Nature of change			
	Decrease	No change	Increase	N
Short-hour part-timers	17	72	10	175
Long-hour part-timers	17	61	22	284
Female full-timers	21	57	22	799
Male full-timers	28	51	21	1,942

<Question : "I would like you to compare your current job with what you were doing five years ago. For `the tightness of supervision over your job', would you say there had been a significant increase between then and now, a significant decrease or little or no change?">

These different relations between working hours and the closeness of supervision lend little support to the proposition which we can derive from Edwards' notion of secondary labour market when it is applied to the full-time/part-time distinction. The hypothesis that part-time work belongs to a secondary labour market and workers are more likely than full-timers to be subject to close supervision is not borne out by our

135

findings. Taken as a whole, part-timers were actually less likely to be closely supervised. When they were further classified according to their working hours, those who worked shorter hours were less likely to experience close supervision. When the working-hour status was disaggregated by the class position to which the job belonged, in only one out of the three classes were part-timers more likely than full-timers to be closely supervised, yet the difference was insignificant. Instead of a negative relation between the closeness of supervision and working hours, our analysis shows that systematic patterns cannot be detected for the relation between working-hour status and the level of supervision.

Determinants of work effort

The final indicator of authority relations at the workplace pertains to the determinants of work effort. In the survey, respondents were asked whether a particular reason was important in determining how hard they worked in their jobs. They were given a range of choices. Table 5.4 shows the percentages of workers in each working-hour status who said a certain factor was important in determining their work pace and effort.

Table 5.4
Percentage of workers who gave a particular reason for their work intensity

Reason	Working-hour status			
	Short-hour part-timers	Long-hour part-timers	Female full-timers	Men
Supervisors/boss	22	21	29	28
Machine/assembly line	3	4	6	9
Clients/customers	40	40	41	35
Fellow workers	25	26	41	35
Pay incentives	4	7	11	20
Reports/appraisals	5	7	17	17
Own discretion	57	62	60	62

*The column percentages do not add up to 100 as respondents can give more than one reason.

The simple control mode which Edwards suggested to be a characteristic of the secondary labour market would lead us to expect that part-time workers would be disciplined primarily by their supervisors or employers. Our findings show that less than one-third of the workers in all three working-hour statuses said it was their supervisors or employers who determined their work effort. Moreover, part-timers were actually **less** likely than full-timers to give this as an important determinant of their work effort.

For each of the four categories of employees, less than 10% gave a machine or an assembly line as an important determinant of their work intensity. Since part-time work, as we have noted in Chapters three and four, is concentrated in the service sector, we would expect that the work pace is more likely to be affected by the amount and demands of customers than by a machine or an assembly line. The latter is more pertinent to work in manufacturing industries. Table 5.4 shows that for each of the two part-time categories, 40% of the workers gave customers as the main reason for their work pace. This reason was rated as important by 41% of female full-time workers. Thus, if there is any resemblance between the labour process of part-timers and that of Edwards' secondary labour market segment, the work intensity of part-timers is more likely to be paced by the customers they serve rather than by machines or the personal rule of the management.

Few part-timers rated pay incentives or reports as important determinants of their work effort. The proportions of part-timers who considered these two as important determinants were lower than that of full-timers.

In fact, contrary to the implication which we can draw from Edwards' argument about the labour process of the secondary labour market, part-timers and full-timers were similarly likely to say that it was their own discretion which determined their work effort. Over half of the workers in each of the four categories said it was their own discretion which determined the amount of work effort they put into their jobs. Moreover, this reason was the one most frequently cited among all the reasons shown in Table 5.4. Thus, with respect to influences on work effort as indicative of the way in which the labour process is regulated at the workplace, our data show little differences between part-timers and full-timers, or among part-timers themselves.

Formalization of management-employee relations

A major distinction between employment in the primary and the secondary segment suggested by segmentation theory is the degree to which rules and regulations at the workplace are formalized. Primary

137

employment is characterised by bureaucratically administered rules and regulations at the workplace. Capricious and arbitrary supervision, on the contrary, prevails at the workplaces of the secondary segment. Edwards suggested that personal favouritism was another feature of workplaces in which the labour process is subject to the mode of simple control. In one of the six localities of SCELI, namely, Swindon, respondents were asked 'do managers have any favourites who get away with poor quality work or bad time-keeping?'. While 23% of short-hour part-timers reported that their management practised personal favouritism at the workplace, this is the case for 27% of long-hour part-timers, 37% of female full-timers and 39% of male full-timers. These figures suggest that contrary to the implication derivable from Edwards' argument about the secondary labour market, part-timers were actually less likely to work in workplaces where management gave personal favours to workers, as compared to full-timers.

According to segmentation theorists, secondary employment is characterized by a higher degree informality of the management-employee relations, as compared to that of the primary labour market. An indicator of the extent to which management-employee relations is formalized is the means which management use to communicate with employees. In one of the six localities of SCELI, Swindon, respondents were asked whether their employers used certain means to explain policies or communicate with employees. We would expect that the shorter the hours an employee works, the more informal the management-employee relations which he or she would be involved in, and, therefore, the less likely that he or she would be involved in a formal means of communication. Table 5.5 gives the percentages of respondents who said their employers used specific means to communicate with them.

It can be seen that management was less likely to use formal means to communicate with part-timers. Among part-timers, those who worked shorter weekly hours were much less likely than those who worked longer hours to participate in formal workplace meetings.[2] While only one-third of the part-timers received workplace newsletters, this is the case for more than half of the female and male full-timers. The uses of videos or films and of personal letters were also less common among part-timers than among full-timers. Finally, while none of the part-timers were members of quality circles, this is the case for 8% and 16% of the full-timers. These figures suggest that the management is less concerned with involving part-time employees in formal channels of communication as a way to regulate the management-employee relations.

Table 5.5
Availability of means of communication by working-hour status
(Swindon)

Means of communication	Working-hour status (% of workers who responded yes)			
	Short-hour part-timers	Long-hour part-timers	Female full-timers	Men
Formal workplace meetings	23	41	48	57
Workplace newsletters	33	37	55	64
Videos or films	12	19	37	40
Personal letters to staff	-	-	8	16
Number of respondents	53	47	170	350

*The column percentages do not add up to 100 as the percentages shown here are for each individual means

To sum up, the different indicators of authority relations examined in this section lend little empirical support to the proposition that part-time work can be characterised as belonging to a secondary labour market. With respect to managerial control as indicated by the level of discretionary power, the closeness of supervision, and the determinants of work efforts, our findings show that part-timers were not significantly worse off than full-timers. The only indicator which marks off part-timers from full-timers is supervisory duties. They were less likely than full-timers to be given supervisory duties. Previous findings suggest that employees in low-status, non-supervisory jobs were still expected to work without close supervision (Craig et al. 1982, 1985). It is also likely that worktasks were allocated in such a way that those which part-timers performed were less pivotal to the operation of their employing organization. Hence, although their worktasks were well-specified and they were left with little room to exercise choice, their scanty job content and the low skill level of their work meant that there was little need for the management to supervise closely their day-to-day job performance. This is also likely to be the reason underlying the informal management-employee relations in which part-time employees were involved.[3]

A flexible workgroup? Non-standard working-hour arrangements

Besides authority relations at work, the other aspect of the work situation which is held to distinguish core workers from those in the peripheral workforce is the degree of flexibility to which they are subject. We noted in Chapter one that the flexible firm thesis argues that the peripheral workforce into which part-time workers are classified is an important lever which enables employers to attain flexible manning levels. The thesis claims that core/primary workers enjoy more stable work arrangements while secondary/peripheral workers are assigned to non-standard working-hour schedules to meet various contingencies of the organization's work, to extend operating hours, or to cover unsocial working hours. This section will examine whether, in terms of working-hour arrangements, part-timers are more likely than full-timers to be assigned to various non-standard working-hour schedules. Few studies have examined in detail the working hours of *both* men and women. The findings will be compared to a more recent survey which did examine in detail an array of working-hour patterns in which working men and women were involved, namely, the 1989 Hours of Work Survey (HWS), to assess the extent to which the differences between full-timers and part-timers can be generalized.[4]

In SCELI, employees were asked whether their jobs involved the following working-hour schedules : shift work, frequent night work, flexi-time, being on call out of normal hours, and frequent overtime. Table 5.6 shows the incident rates of these different working-hour schedules among workers in the three working-hour statuses.

The general picture indicated by Table 5.6 is that except for flexi-time, men were more likely to work irregular working hours, as compared to both full-time and part-time working women. The difference is most marked in terms of frequent overtime work and being on call out of normal hours. Over half of the male employees in our sample often worked overtime; this is the case for less than one-third of each category of the female workers. While one-third of the male employees were involved in work outside the normal hours, this type of working hours was less prevalent among either the full-time or the part-time working women. The HWS also noted that the incident rates of overtime work and of working extra hours at short notice were higher among men than among either full-time or part-time working women.[5]

Table 5.6
Percentages of employees in each status who said their work involved irregular working-hour arrangements

Working-hour schedule	Working hour status*			
	Short-hour part-timers	Long-hour part-timers	Female full-timers	Men
Shift-work**	11	20	15	23
Frequent night work**	14	16	17	17
Flexi-time				
On-call out of normal hour	11	13	14	35
Frequent overtime**	10	22	27	53
Number of respondents	302	367	1,004	2,131

*the column percentages do not add up to 100 as what is shown here is the percentage of workers who responded yes to each item
**significant difference at 0.05 level and refers to the difference among working women

If we consider only working women, the differences between part-timers and full-timers vary according to the specific type of working-hour schedule. Long-hour part-timers were more likely to be involved in shiftwork, as compared to female full-timers and short-hour part-timers. This is due to the fact that a sizeable proportion of the long-hour part-timers were in the lower-grade service class, as it was noted in Chapter four. In our sample, occupations like teaching, nursing and social work professionals made up about 60% of occupations which were classified into this class category by the schema we adopt. Shiftwork is common in nursing which requires 24-hour care provision. Within the lower service class into which the nursing and the teaching occupations

141

were classified, while 21% of the long-hour part-timers said their jobs involved shift-work, this is the case for 16% of the female full-timers and 17% of the short-hour part-timers. Other studies have also noted the prevalence of shiftworking among part-timers in the nursing profession. For example, Beechey and Perkins (1987) found that, in the public sector, establishments which provided health and medical care recruited part-time nurses to do shiftwork. In the HWS, it was also noted that women who did shift work were concentrated in medical and healthcare professions.

Frequent night work was also more prevalent among the two types of part-timers than among female full-timers. Beechey and Perkins (1987) noted that part-timers were used to staff night shifts in the hospital and in the manufacturing establishments they studied. In our sample, among workers in either the semi-/unskilled manual class or the service class, part-timers were more likely to cover night work. Among semi-/unskilled manual workers, 15% of the short-hour part-timers and 13% of the long-hour part-timers were involved in frequent night work, this is the case for only 3% of the female full-timers. Within the service class, 27% of the long-hour part-timers did frequent night work, as compared to 17% of the short-hour part-timers and 14% of women who worked full-time.

For involvement in flexi-time, the incident rates for all three groups of female workers were very similar to each other. Less than one-fifth of the workers in each category said their work involved flexi-time.[6] The three groups also had similarly low incident rates of involvement in work outside the normal hours.

Finally, women working full-time were more likely than their part-time counterparts to work frequent overtime. Among part-timers, frequent overtime work was more prevalent for those who worked longer hours. In the HWS, it was also noted that among working women, part-timers were less likely to put in overtime work than full-timers.[7]

The findings here show that female part-timers were more likely to be deployed by the management to cover night work and shift work, as compared to their female full-time counterparts. However, they were less likely to put in extra hours of work, whether in the form of frequent overtime work or work which was outside their normal working hours. Our results suggest that the core/peripheral distinction which the flexible firm thesis uses to characterise full-time and part-time work does not enable us to distinguish the variations in the extent to which part-timers were involved in the different types of non-standard working-hour arrangements. Working hours which were less than that of a full-time job and which fell outside the standard nine-to-five schedules mark off the female full-time and part-time workers.

142

However, further flexibilization in the form of extra working hours, for example, over-time work, working at short notice, was an exception rather than a norm for part-time workers. Moreover, for the various types of non-standard working-hours which we examined here, the most noticeable differences are those between men and women, rather than in terms of working-hour status.

With its focus on the situation at the workplace, the flexible firm thesis overlooks the ways through which working hours may well be subject to supply-side influences that hamper further flexible uses of part-timers by employers. Factors which affect the supply side of part-time employment will be dealt with in Chapters seven and eight. For the present purpose of examining the extent to which the standard/non-standard working hours contrast is applicable to the full-time/part-time distinction, our findings show that instead of working-hour status, it is gender which divides the workforce.

Conclusion

In this Chapter, the usefulness of a version of segmentation theory in understanding part-time work has been evaluated. The aim is to assess the extent to which the work situation of part-time work resembles the features suggested by Edwards' version of secondary labour market. The findings about discretionary power, the closeness of supervision, the determinants of work intensity and the practice of favouritism at the workplace indicate that there is little empirical support for the proposition that part-time work belongs to the secondary labour market.

The other part of this Chapter then examined the flexibility level of part-timers in terms of their involvement in various non-standard working-hour schedules. The findings lend little support to the core/peripheral distinction drawn by the flexible firm thesis for full-time and part-time employees. Shift-work and night-work are the only two non-standard working-hour arrangements which are more prevalent among female part-timers than among their full-time counterparts. Part-timers are less likely to work extra hours to meet the contingencies of their employing organizations. The workforce which is most likely to experience extra working hours is male full-time workers.

While the focus was on the full-time/part-time distinction, attention was also given to possible variations among part-timers who had different working hours. Those who worked shorter weekly hours were less likely to have any supervisory responsibilities. However, the gap is a relatively minor one when compared to the full-time/part-time distinction. The differences with respect to other indicators also show that jobs with shorter working hours were not associated with the types of work situation which Edwards suggested to be characteristics of secondary employment.

This and the last Chapter examined in detail the market and work situations of full-time and part-time jobs. With respect to the full-time/part-time distinction, we noted in the last Chapter that the latter was worse than the former in terms of skill levels, training opportunities, the use of new technology, promotion prospects, wage rates and entitlements to an array of fringe benefits. In this chapter, we noted that part-timers were worse off than full-timers in terms of their likelihood of being allocated to supervisory positions at the workplace. However, the proposition about the discretion at work and the level of job security of part-timers vis-à-vis full-timers were not borne out by our data. Our findings show that there is little distinct differences between full-time and part-time work in terms of the regulation and disciplining of their work at the workplace. As the earlier discussion points out, that part-timers are not subject to close supervision can be explained by the low skill level of their work. This makes it unnecessary for the management to supervise the worker closely. Thus, in the survey, while they reported a lower degree of choice over the way they did their work, they did not experience close supervision.

The paucity of training and the low-skilled work of part-time jobs are unlikely to enhance the wage-earning capacity of the worker. These unfavourable employment conditions would, in the long-run, affect the labour market returns of an individual. In the next Chapter, we shall assess the long-term effect of part-time work experience on two major types of labour market returns - earnings and occupational mobility.

Notes

1   Details of these findings can be found in the doctoral work of my colleague, Makiko Nishikawa. I am grateful to Makiko for providing me with this information which is not reported in the book Social Class in Modern Britain, Marshall et al. (1989).

2   O'Reilly (1994) noted in her case study of French retail banking that part-timers were not involved in training/briefing meetings held at their workplaces.

3   However, a word of caution should be added to the above analyses. A formal supervisory position is likely to give its incumbent the final veto say. Therefore, it may be unwarranted to

give the different indicators of authority relations which we examined here the same emphasis. However, this cannot be resolved simply by assigning different weights to these indicators so that some are given a greater emphasis than others. A formal supervisory position may still not reflect in actual practice the decision-making power which a worker can exercise on a day-to-day basis. Unfortunately, we are limited by the availability of data about discretion at work in the main survey of SCELI. Moreover, as Marshall et al. (1988) commented, one problem with survey-type data on job autonomy is that it is difficult to put the responses given by the interviewees into a situational context.

4   For a report of the findings of the survey, see Marsh (1991). The survey also covered the different types of shift-systems which full-timers and part-timers were involved in. While in SCELI, the definition of shiftwork was left to the respondent, in the Hours of Work Survey, shiftwork was defined as 'a pattern of hours which changes over regularly after a fixed period of time'.

5   The survey recorded that while 31% of men worked extra hours at short notice, this is the case for 26% of female full-timers and 20% for female part-timers; and while 24% of men worked overtime, this is the case for 21% of women who worked full-time and 15% of female part-timers.

6   Flexi-time was found to be less prevalent among women than among men in the Hours of Work Survey (HWS). In the survey, respondents were asked 'Are your starting time and finishing times ever different from the week you have just told me about?' While 56% of men and 51% of women working full-time said their starting and finishing times did vary occasionally, only 39% of women working part-time ever varied their starting and finishing times.

7   In the HWS, while 24% of men worked overtime, this is the case for 21% of women who worked full-time and 15% of female part-timers.

6 Market rewards to part-time work experience

The last two Chapters dealt with the current unequal job rewards and workplace positions of part-time workers as compared to full-time workers. Considerable disparities were noted between the two. Part-timers were worse off in a number of job rewards and in certain aspects of their work situations. In addition to explaining cross-sectional differences, labour market theories are also concerned with the way long term employment attainment differs between individuals. Both human capital theory and segmentation theory recognize the role which previous work and non-work experiences play in shaping the current employment conditions. They differ from each other in terms of whether work experience is further differentiated or not, and whether some experiences are more favourable than others.

In this Chapter, the long-term effect of part-time work experience on women's labour market returns will be examined. Two major kinds of returns, namely, current earnings and occupational mobility, will be dealt with.[1] Throughout this chapter, the analysis is confined to women who were in paid work at the time of the interview.[2] This Chapter is divided into two sections. In the first section, the wage rate will be examined, and in the second part, the effect of part-time work experience on occupational mobility will be assessed.

Working experience and current earnings

As the discussion in Chapter one pointed out, human capital theory regards current earnings as determined largely by the investment in human capital which a worker has made previously. Workers are paid according to their productive capacity which, in turn, depends on the

147

amount of human capital they have. The greater the amount of human capital accumulated, the higher the level of earnings. A major part of a person's human capital is acquired through formal schooling. In Chapter four, we noted that the level of formal qualification is positively related to the wage level. Working experience is another source of human capital. More working experience enhances work skills and raises the productivity of the worker. It can, therefore, be hypothesized that the more working experience, the greater the amount of human capital and, thus, the higher the current wage level.

While we can generally expect male workers to have continuous participation in wage work over their worklife and hence a continuous accumulation of job skills and human capital, the same does not apply to women. Married women often interrupt their worklife to take up domestic responsibility. Human capital theorists, Mincer and Polachek (1974), used longitudinal panel data to study the wage growth of American married women who re-entered the labour market after a period of non-participation. They found that the wage level at the re-entry point was lower than that at the point of their withdrawal from the labour market. Time spent outside the labour market would lead to a lower wage level for two reasons. During periods of non-participation, skills previously acquired would depreciate due to non-use. Moreover, there is no new investment as no work skills are accumulated.

The same reasoning can also apply to the effect of time spent being unemployed. While previous skills become obsolete due to non-use, new skills are not acquired because the individual is not working on a job. The result is a lower current wage level. The longer the duration of non-participation in wage work, the more serious the obsolence of work skills and the lower the wage level will be. Thus, in addition to the level of formal qualification, we can draw two more hypotheses from human capital theory regarding previous work experience : (1) the more time spent in unpaid housework, the lower the wage level when the woman resumes wage employment; (2) the more time in unemployment, the lower the wage level when the woman takes up waged work again.

It was pointed out in Chapter one that human capital theory seldom makes a distinction between the different *kinds* of human capital which different jobs enable their incumbents to accumulate.[3] While most jobs provide general basic work skills, some are more likely to provide specific, and/or better work skills than others. Segmentation theory argues that the amount and the kind of job skills which a worker can accumulate is the result of employers' labour use strategy, instead of the choice of individuals. This implies that working experiences on different jobs do not have the same effect on the current wage level. In our case, there is a clear difference between full-time and part-time jobs in terms of whether they enhance the work skills of their incumbents. Findings in Chapter four show that part-time work is low-skilled and is unlikely to involve the use of advanced technology. It is also unlikely that part-time workers would receive job training as they work fewer hours, and there are more hours of non-use of any training that is provided for them. A rational employer would not incur such a waste to his or her training cost.[4] Thus, we can expect that part-time work experience is neither conducive to the acquisition of new work skills nor to the enhancement of the skills already acquired. It is, therefore, unlikely that working experience gained through part-time employment would lead to the formation of productive human capital. If it has any beneficial effect at all, it is likely to be limited to the upkeep of basic work skills.[5] It can be hypothesized that other things being equal, the more time spent in part-time work as a proportion of the individual's worklife, the lower the current wage level.

In the wage equation, to take into account the age difference of the respondents at the time of the interview, part-time work experience is expressed as a percentage of worklife. The percentage is calculated by first amassing the number of months spent in part-time work (according to the self-definition of the respondent) since the respondent entered the labour market after finishing full-time education, and then dividing it by the number of months elapsed between the entry point and the time of the survey. The other two non-working experience factors were derived in a similar way.

Besides non-working experiences and the formal qualification factor, three characteristics of the job also need to be controlled for to assess the net effect of part-time work experience on the current wage rate. These control variables were found to be significant in the wage analysis in Chapter four. They are : union representation at the workplace, the size of the workplace, and the class position to which the occupation of the job belonged. Whether the job is in a unionized workplace or not will be included as a dummy variable in our wage equation. Workplace size will be included as a dummy variable with workplaces which have 25 or more workers as the reference category. We shall continue to use the Goldthorpe class schema for our occupational classification. The category 'small proprietors' will be excluded as our focus is on paid employment.

The results of the regression analysis are shown in Table 6.1. The dependent variable takes the form of the natural logarithm of the gross hourly wage.

Table 6.1
OLS regression on log of gross hourly wage for working women

Variable	Model I		Model II		Model III	
	Unstandardis-ed Coefficient	T-value	Unstandardis-ed Coefficient	T-value	Unstandardis-ed Coefficient	T-value
Level of formal qualification						
no qualification	-0.676	-16.61*	-0.609	-14.88*	-0.440	-10.33*
vocational	-0.817	-10.47*	-0.591	-10.32*	-0.398	-6.98*
O-level	-0.587	-13.67*	-0.572	-13.61*	-0.414	-9.69*
A-level	-0.47	-0.30*	-0.468	-0.93*	-0.310	-6.41*
non-degree higher education	-0.241	-4.87*	-0.243	-5.03*	-0.215	-4.73*
degree	-	-	-	-	-	-
Work and non-work experience						
% of worklife in part-time	-	-	-0.003	-4.59*	-0.001	-2.27*
% of worklife being unemployed	-	-	-0.005	-4.81*	-0.004	-4.14*
% of worklife in housework	-	-	-0.004	-6.77*	-0.002	-4.39*

(continued)

Table 6.1 (continued)

Variable	Model I		Model II		Model III	
	Unstandardised Coefficient	T-value	Unstandardised Coefficient	T-value	Unstandardised Coefficient	T-value
Class						
high grade service	-	-	-	-	-	-
lower-grade service	-	-	-	-	0.171	-3.29*
routine non-manual	-	-	-	-	-0.33	-6.07*
retails and sales	-	-	-	-	-0.369	-6.78*
technicians and skilled manual	-	-	-	-	-0.286	-4.44*
semi-/unskilled manual	-	-	-	-	-0.425	-7.54*
Union representation						
present	-	-	-	-	0.109	4.91*
absent	-	-	-	-	-	-
Workplace size						
fewer than 25 workers	-	-	-	-	-0.135	-6.07*
Constant	1.521	41.16	1.613	42.91	1.72	29.23
R-square	0.22		0.268		0.362	
Adjusted R-square	0.22		0.264		0.354	

N = 1,286; *denotes significant at p ≤ 0.05 level.

151

In Model I, only the effect of formal qualification was considered. The result is in line with the hypothesis drawn from human capital theory. Women with degree qualifications earned more than those who had lower levels of formal qualification. The gap is biggest for those without any formal qualifications and smallest for those with non-degree higher education qualifications.

In Model II, the part-time work experience, unemployment and non-participation factors were introduced. The estimates of these three factors are negative. This is in line with the hypotheses discussed earlier. The more time spent in part-time work, the lower the current wage level. Non-participation due to involvement in unpaid housework and unemployment also reduced the current wage level.

It is interesting to note the difference in the magnitude of the negative effects of these three types of experiences. The negative effect of part-time work experience is smaller than that of non-participation and of unemployment. This may be because part-time work experience allows women to maintain a minimal level of general work skills, while non-participation and unemployment lower the current wage level through the depreciation of basic work skills and the job skills previously accumulated, *and* the absence of formation of new skills, however basic this is. Thus, the negative effect of non-participation and unemployment on the wage rate is more severe than that of part-time work.

In Model III, three sets of control variables were introduced to see whether part-time work experience was still significant. The results of the fifth and sixth column in Table 6.1 show that while class, workplace size and union representation are all significant in affecting the wage level, part-time work experience is still significant.[6]

Thus, women who interrupt their working life for household responsibility not only suffer from wage loss due to non-participation; their earnings are further penalized by the inferior nature of part-time work. In the next section, we shall examine whether part-time work experience also has a negative effect on occupational mobility in terms of the class position to which their first and current job belonged.

Worklife occupational mobility and part-time work experience

We have repeatedly seen that the class position to which an occupation belongs is closely related to a number of major employment conditions, such as wage level, promotion prospects, supervisory duties, etc. A change in the class position of the occupation would, therefore, entail critical changes in major types of job rewards and employment conditions. For example, a move from being a lower-grade manager to a clerical position is likely to result in a worsening of various employment conditions. Hence, it is pertinent to examine the effect of part-time work experience on occupational mobility in class terms. In this section, the focus is on whether part-time work experience results in changes in the net association between the class of the first job and that of the current job, and, if so, the nature and the direction of the mobility. The issue will be dealt with in a way which is different from that in the literature. Existing studies of women's occupational mobility will be discussed first to clear the ground for the issue to be addressed as well as the approach and the method of analysis which will be adopted. This will facilitate the discussion of the findings.

Existing studies of women's occupational mobility in Britain

Several studies on British women's occupational mobility have noted occupational downgrading which women experience at some points in their working lives (Joshi, 1984; Greenhalgh and Stewart, 1985; Dex, 1986; Dale, 1987; Elias, 1988). The downgrading, in some studies, is attributed to the interruption in women's working life during the stage of family formation. In particular, Elias (1988) associated the downgrading to participation in part-time work. Dex (1986) and Dale (1987) also noted that, after childbirth, the resumption of wage employment through part-time work led to downward occupational mobility. However, these studies are rather unsatisfactory either in the way occupations are classified or the method used to analyse the movement.

Greenhalgh and Stewart (1985) used average hourly earnings to rank occupations in a continuous manner. In a similar way, Elias (1988) used average hourly earnings to classify occupations into two broad categories, one above and one below the average level of earnings. He then used this ranking to study the occupational movements of women in different birth cohorts. Dex (1986) also used earnings to rank occupations in a hierarchical manner. She then used this ranking to measure the vertical occupational mobility of women during their family formation stage.

The earnings level of an occupation covers only one of the many aspects of the market situation of employment. Other types of market situation, for example, chances of advancement, the form which wage growth takes, employment security, are as pertinent as the absolute level of earnings. Besides these types of market situation, occupational positions also differ in terms of their extent of authority and job autonomy which their incumbents enjoy at the workplace, as we have seen in Chapter five. Hence, using one indicator to represent occupational mobility is likely to neglect a number of other salient aspects of labour market and workplace experience.

Besides being a partial indicator, another disadvantage associated with average earnings as a criterion for occupational classification is that earnings are susceptible to influences of individual characteristics and working experience, and hence may not reflect accurately the occupation's structural location within the system of economic production. As we have seen in the last section, wage level is affected by factors other than the class position of the job. Thus, instead of using earnings, we shall continue to use the Goldthorpe class schema to classify occupations.

The Goldthorpe schema was originally designed for a study of the mobility pattern among men only. This has rendered it unsuitable for analysing the mobility pattern among women. To make it more appropriate for the investigation of women's mobility through their own employment, the original routine non-manual class (class III) was later split into two groups : class IIIa which is made up of clerical occupations, and class IIIb which comprises shop assistants, shop cashiers, receptionists and lower-level attendants. In the ensuing analysis, these two classes will be distinguished from each other. The latter will form a separate category instead of being combined with the semi-/unskilled manual working class. There are two reasons for not classifying class IIIb and the semi-/unskilled manual workers together in the way which Goldthorpe and his associates did in their analysis of the mobility pattern of women (Goldthorpe et al. 1980:277-301). Firstly, information about finer occupational movements would be lost if the two categories are combined. Secondly, we have seen in Chapters three and four that part-time jobs were concentrated in personal services and retail industries. Since the purpose here is to examine the effect of part-time work on occupational mobility, it is necessary to separate these two occupational groups.

The Goldthorpe schema belongs to what is called the categorical approach to the stratification of occupations, in contrast to the continuous approach.[7] Opting for a categorical approach has significant methodological and substantive implications on the method of analysis for mobility. These implications are also related to other inadequacies in some of the existing studies. These weaknesses can be overcome by the categorical approach.

Greenhalgh and Stewart (1984, 1985) adopted ordinary least square regression to analyse occupational status change of men and women using the data of the 1976 National Training Survey. This method, however, does not allow for the change in the overall occupational structure. The expansion of various service industries and the decline of manufacturing industries have led to an overall increase in occupations like sales, personal services, clerical jobs, administrative and service professions. Under this circumstance, the observable changes in individuals' occupations may be induced by changes in the overall occupational structure, instead of by their differential employment experiences.

Our focus is on relative rather than absolute mobility. The issue which will be addressed is the way the relative fate of women who started their working lives in different classes is affected by the different extent of involvement in part-time work. In other words, the question which will be dealt with is the way an 'in-market' experience affects movements of different individuals, rather than movements which are induced by the overall change of the occupational structure. Linear regression does not deal adequately with the change in the relative size of each occupational grouping (or, technically, the marginal distribution of a mobility table). Hence, it may confound mobility which is due to the distributional difference and relative mobility which is related to the different labour market experiences. The categorical approach to analysing mobility enables us to control for the variation in the sizes of the different occupations, and thereby avoids confusing the effect of distributional difference and the associational effect. This, in fact, is more in line with one of the major concerns of the present study which is an application of segmentation theory to part-time work. The occupation of the first job and the 'pre-market' experiences which lead an individual to land in a particular class upon entry into employment need to be controlled for to assess how 'in-market' experience (and, in our case, part-time work experience) affects the final occupational outcome.

Another weakness about the existing studies is the rather limited reference time-frame against which women's occupational movement is analysed. Dex (1986), Dale (1987), McRae (1991), Brannen (1989) focused on the occupational movement across breaks for childbirths. The rationale behind this is to assess the effect of discontinuities (normally due to family formation or childbearing) of women's working lives on their occupational achievement. However, other works by Dex (1987), by Martin and Roberts (1984) and by Shaw (1983) have also found that women experienced a large amount of occupational mobility at other times in their worklife. If this is the case, then there are no good reasons for confining the analysis to the family formation stage.

Moreover, part-time work experience is not solely associated with childbirth. In our sample, about 23% of married women had not had any children. Yet, 24% of these women had had at least one part-time work spell. Since our purpose is to examine the effect of part-time work experience on worklife mobility, it is not pertinent to exclude these women and only focus on those who had had at least one childbirth. Instead of examining occupational movements with reference to one particular segment of women's working life, the entire working life will be taken as the basis for the analysis.

The other issue which is often addressed in the existing studies is the direction of the mobility. The focus is usually on whether women experience downward mobility across breaks of their worklife. Dex and Shaw (1986) noted a significant effect of part-time work on downward occupational mobility, even after a number of relevant variables have already been taken into account. In their analysis, downward mobility was defined as a move down an occupational scale defined by earnings (Dex and Shaw, 1986:103). We have pointed out earlier the deficiency of using earnings to rank occupations. Moreover, in their classification, it is not clear why intermediate non-manual occupations were ranked above clerical occupations, or why sales occupations were below semi-/unskilled factory work when other studies have shown that the latter two share similar market and work situations (Marshall, 1988; Evans, 1992). Moreover, the restriction of the analysis to a dichotomy of downward mobility or not, as in Dex's analysis (1986), does not allow other possible kinds of mobility to be detected. Besides being domestic carers, women should also be treated as workers whose occupational mobility experiences are susceptible to the different types of 'in-market' experiences which they have undergone. If this is so, the analysis of occupational movements should not be restricted to a dichotomy of downgrading or not. Other possible kinds of mobility should also be entertained. Furthermore, the use of linear regression as in the case of Greenhalgh and Stewart (1984, 1985) deals with immobility merely as another variety of mobility, with zero difference between the original and the destination state. The categorical approach, on the contrary, treats mobility as multi-dimensional and is more sensitive to immobility. Hence it is a more appropriate method to analyse movements, or the absence of movements.

Having clarified the substantive and the methodological ground for the analysis of worklife (im)mobility, the following discussion is divided into two stages. In the first part, the outflow pattern between the class position of the first job (defined as the job which a woman first took up when she entered the labour market after leaving full-time education) and that of the current job will be examined.[8,9] The extent of part-time work experience will then be introduced to see the way it alters the association between the class of the first job and that of the current job (hereafter these will be referred to as entry class and destination class respectively). This second stage of the analysis will be divided into two parts. In the first part, part-time work experience will be measured in terms of number of spells. In our sample, married women on the whole had had 1.2 spells of part-time work. Hence it is reasonable to combine two or more spells into one category. The mobility pattern and the extent of part-time work experience measured as three levels (no part-time work spell, one spell, two or more spells) will be examined. In the second part, the extent of part-time work experience is measured as a percentage of worklife spent in part-time work. This variable is derived in the same way as in the earlier earnings analysis. For both parts, the formal statistical test will be conducted through multinomial logistic regression.

The outflow pattern

In Table 6.2, the outflow pattern between the entry class and destination class is shown using Goldthorpe's seven-category class schema. Class IVa (small proprietors), IVb (small farmers) and VIIb (farm workers) were omitted, as the focus is on wage employment and industrial employment. The final classification consists of : class I = higher grade professionals, administrative and managerial occupations; class II = lower grade professionals, administrative and managerial occupations; class IIIa = intermediate non-manual occupations like clerical work and higher grade personal service occupations; class IIIb = lower grade personal service occupations and shop assistants; class V = technicians and supervisors of manual employees; class VI = skilled manual workers; class VIIa = semi-skilled and unskilled manual workers.

From Table 6.2, we can see that the commonest entry class is class IIIa, followed by class VIIa. Very few women were in higher grade service class (class I) or lower-grade technicians (class V) when they first entered the labour market. As for the destination class, the commonest one is also class IIIa, and the second commonest is also class VIIa. Similar to entry class, very few women's destination classes were I or V. When we compare the two margins, we can see that the size of class II has expanded while that of class VI has shrunk substantially. Other classes have also shown quite considerable changes in their share in the overall occupational structure. This indicates the importance of controlling the marginal distribution in examining occupational movements.

Next we can consider the outflow of women in each entry class. Looking down the cells on the diagonal line of Table 6.2, it can be seen that among all seven entry classes, the most immobile group are women who started their working life in class II. Over two-thirds of them stayed in this class in 1986. For the movers from this class, the commonest destination is clerical occupations. Few moved into manual occupations or sales and services occupations.

The second most immobile group are class VIIa entrants. Over half of them remained in this entry class by 1986. For the movers, the commonest destination is clerical occupations, followed by class II.

Table 6.2
The outflow pattern between entry class and destination class

Entry Class	Destination class (%)							Row N	Marginal %
	I	II	IIIa	IIIb	V	VI	VIIa		
I	45	17	31	-	-	-	-	15	1
II	5	74	10	4	1	-	6	114	9
IIIa	3	18	46	11	3	2	16	478	40
IIIb	1	13	19	22	4	5	36	190	16
V	-	20	21	12	8	-	39	13	1
VI	-	6	16	11	7	19	42	144	12
VIIa	1	12	14	7	3	5	57	226	19
Column N	33	239	334	134	46	60	350	1,197	
Marginal %	3	20	28	11	4	5	29		

Compared to class II and class VIIa entrants, those who started in classes IIIa, IIIb and VI were more mobile. For class IIIa entrants, less than half of them remained in the same class. The commonest destination of the movers is class II, followed by destination classes VIIa and IIIb. Very few movers reached the higher service class, and an equally small proportion became technicians or skilled manual workers.

Women who started working in class IIIb were also highly mobile. About one-fifth of them had remained in their entry class by 1986. About one-third had moved into class VIIb. The second commonest destination class for these women was that of clerical occupations. Similar to class IIIa entrants, few women in this entry class reached class I occupations.

For women who were skilled manual workers when they started their work life, only one-fifth were stayers. Nearly half of them moved into semi-/unskilled manual occupations, 16% moved into clerical jobs, and 11% moved into sales and service occupations.[10]

Table 6.2 shows that without introducing any other factors, we can see that the pattern of worklife mobility varies substantially by the entry class which a woman landed in when she entered the labour market. If we consider reaching classes I and II as upward mobility, and moving into class VIIa as downward mobility[11], the outflow pattern indicates that the propensity to move and the likelihood of moving into which specific destination class differ according to the entry class. While it is highly unlikely that classes I and II entrants have experienced downward mobility and moved into classes VI or VIIa, it is also unlikely for class VIIa entrants to make long-range upward mobility and move into classes I or II.[12]

Most of the movements occur with class IIIa, IIIb and VIIa entrants. More class IIIa entrants have moved upward than class IIIb and class VIIa entrants, and fewer IIIa entrants moved down to class VIIa than class IIIb entrants. These patterns of (im)mobility ask for a method which can deal with these differential mobility likelihoods, rather than a method which captures only one dimension of mobility.

The effect of part-time work experience I : number of spells

In this section, the extent of part-time work participation expressed as numbers of spells will be introduced into the outflow mobility Table 6.2. In order to avoid too few numbers in each cell when we introduce the part-time work experience variable and for the subsequent formal test, class I will be combined with class II, classes V and VI will also be collapsed into one category.[13] The outflow patterns for women in each entry class who had had no, one, and two or more part-time work spells are given in Table 6.3.

Table 6.3
Outflow patterns by extent of part-time work participation

Entry class	Destination class*						
	I+II	IIIa	IIIb	V+VI	VIIa	Total (%)	Row N**
I+II (%)	86	10	2	-	2	100	45
	70	18	5	-	7	100	42
	78	**9**	**4**	**2**	**7**	**100**	**42**
IIIa (%)	26	62	6	4	3	100	120
	19	38	13	4	25	100	138
	20	**42**	**13**	**8**	**17**	**100**	**216**
IIIb (%)	23	25	14	6	32	100	33
	11	15	25	8	41	100	51
	12	**19**	**23**	**11**	**35**	**100**	**105**
V+VI (%)	13	29	-	36	22	100	24
	1	9	17	26	47	100	51
	6	**10**	**13**	**31**	**39**	**100**	**81**
VIIa (%)	15	28	-	8	48	100	39
	9	12	7	14	58	100	69
	15	**9**	**9**	**5**	**62**	**100**	**114**

*The first row shows the outflow percentages for those who have not had any part-time work spell, the second row is for women who have had one part-time work spell, and the third row is for those with two or more part-time work spells.
**the row Ns do not add up to the same figures as those shown in Table 6.2 as for some women, the value for their part-time work participation is missing. These cases were excluded from the cross-tabular analysis.

From Table 6.3, we can see that the percentages of class I and II entrants who were stayers drop as we go up from none to one part-time work spell and then rise again with 2 or more spells. The destination of the movers, that is, those who were downwardly mobile, differed between the two levels of part-time work participation. For these movers, the commonest destination was class IIIa, very few moved into manual occupations, classes V, VI or VIIa alike.

Next we can consider class IIIa entrants. For those who had never had any part-time spell, over half were stayers. For the movers, some were upwardly mobile and had moved into classes I and II. Very few moved down to manual working class or retail and sales class. The picture changes when we consider those who had had some part-time work experience. Less than half were stayers. For the movers, the destination class varies between those who had had only one part-time work spell and those who had had two or more. If we only consider upward mobility into classes I and II and downward mobility into class VIIa, the effect of an increase in the number of part-time work spells does not seem to be a greater downward flow or a lesser upward flow (19% vs 20% for the upward flow; 25% vs 17% for the downward flow).

Class IIIb entrants were highly mobile. Less than one-third were stayers for all three levels of part-time work participation. For the movers, their movements were diverse. For those who had not had any part-time work experience, one-third moved into class VIIb and 23% into classes I and II. The experience of part-time work reduced the proportion of those who were upwardly mobile in classes I and II, and increased the proportion who moved into class VIIa. However, the extent of rise and drop does not differ much between those with one part-time work spell and those with two or more part-time work spells.

Class V and VI entrants were also highly mobile. Less than half were stayers for all three levels of part-time work participation. As for the movers, the percentage of the upwardly mobile drops as we go from none to one part-time work spell, but rises again for those with two or more part-time work spells. Nearly half of these entrants moved into class VIIa when they had had one part-time work spell. But the proportion dropped for two or more part-time work spells.

Finally, considering those who started their worklife in semi-/unskilled manual class, a sizeable proportion were stayers for all three levels of part-time work participation. As for those who were upwardly mobile into classes I and II, while fewer had made such a move when they had had one part-time work spells, more had made this move when they had had two or more part-time work spell. The percentage of those who moved into class IIIa drops with a rise in the level of part-time work participation.

What then can we say about the effect of part-time work experience on women's occupational mobility between their entry and destination class position in 1986? Putting this more technically : does the probability of those who started their worklife in a one class rather than another ending up in one class rather than another class vary with the level of part-time work participation?

To test precisely whether the net association between the entry class and the destination class is affected by the extent of part-time work experience, a formal statistical test was conducted for the three-way table. In the test, we examine the relative odds of being in one destination class rather than another for a woman who started her worklife in one entry class rather than another, and the way these odds vary between the three levels of part-time work participation. Substantively, the hypothesis that is being tested is whether the extent of part-time work participation (expressed as number of part-time work spells) has a significant effect on the net association between the class position of the first and the current job. In the standard form of log-linear notations, the null hypothesis that is being tested looks like this :

$$\log F_{ijk} = \mu + t_i^o + t_j^d + t_k^P + t_{ij}^{od} + t_{ik}^{op} + t_{jk}^{dp}$$

where F_{ijk} is the expected frequency in cell ijk of our three-way table comprising entry class (O), destination class (D), and the number of part-time work spells (P). On the right-hand side of the equation, μ is a scale factor, t_i^o, t_j^d and t_k^P represent the 'main' effects of the distribution of individuals over entry class, destination class, and number of part-time work spells, and the remaining terms represent the effects for the three possible two-way associations. The term t_{ij}^{od} means that there is an association between entry class and destination class. The terms t_{ik}^{op} and t_{jk}^{dp} mean that there is an association between the extent of part-time work participation and the entry class for the former, and the destination class for the latter. The equation hypothesizes that the net association between entry and destination class is not affected by the level of part-time work participation, since the three-way interaction term t_{ijk}^{odp} is not included.

The result of the test is given in Table 6.4. Model I is only presented as a reference to the second model which is our prime concern. The substantive proposition which Model I is testing : the extent of part-time work participation is associated with the entry class, and with the destination class, but there is no association between the entry and the destination class. This hypothesis is rejected as we can see from the index of dissimilarity that this model misclassifies about 25.2% of our cases. The p-value shows that we can reject the null hypothesis represented by this model. This means the two-way term, O-D, is significant and should be included.

Table 6.4
Testing the association between entry and destination class

Model	G^2	df	rG^2	rdf	p	ID
I. OP DP	473.5	48	-	-	0.00	25.2
II. OP DP OD	40	32	433	16	0.16	5.4

Keys : G^2 = scaled deviance; df= degrees of freedom; rG^2 = reduction in scaled deviance; rdf = reduction in the degrees of freedom; p = p-value; ID = index of dissimilarity

The proposition which the second model is testing is that part-time work participation does not affect significantly the net association between O and D, as the three-way term, O.D.P, is not included. The overall p-value shows that we cannot reject this null hypothesis. This model misclassifies only 5.4% of all our cases. In other words, the result of this test means that the relative odds of reaching one destination class rather than another for a woman who started her worklife in one entry class rather than another does not vary significantly between the different levels of their part-time work participation. Put differently, the result indicates that the chance of reaching or staying in one class rather than another for a woman who started her worklife in one class rather than another is not made better or worse by the amount of part-time work experience she has had. The hypothesis that more part-time work experience would lead to a weakening of the association between the entry and the destination class is not borne out by our findings.

The effect of part-time work experience II : duration

The spell measure used in the last section does not take into account the duration dimension of part-time work experience. The effect of a part-time spell which lasted only for several months is likely to differ from one which lasted for several years. In this section, the extent of part-time work participation will be expressed as percentage of worklife spent in part-time work. This way of measuring part-time work experience also takes into consideration the age difference of the respondents at the time of the interview. To represent the outflow pattern by the different percentages of worklife spent in part-time work would be highly cumbersome. Instead, we shall proceed directly to the test. There are three variables in this equation, the destination class (D) and the origin (O) class both of which have five levels as in the previous section, and PCT3 which represents the percentage of worklife spent in part-time work. The result of the test is given in Table 6.5.

Table 6.5
Testing the association between entry and destination class

	G^2	d.f.	rG^2	rd.f.
Base Model	4017	4988	-	-
+D.O	3317	4972	700	20
+PCT3.D	3285	4968	32	4
+PCT3.D.O	3269	4952	15	16

Keys : G^2 = scaled deviance; d.f. = degrees of freedom; rG^2 = reduction in scaled deviance; rd.f.= reduction in degree of freedom; O = entry occupational class; D = current occupational class; PCT3 = percentage of worklife spent in part-time work.

The base model simply means that reaching/remaining in a specific destination class does not depend on either one of the two factors. The reduction in the scaled deviance and the corresponding drop in the degrees of freedom as the two terms, D.O, D*PCT3, were introduced into the base model show that the entry class has a significant impact on reaching/remaining in a specific destination class, so is the time spent in part-time work participation. However, the term which is our main concern is the three-way interaction term, PCT3.O.D. This term hypothesizes that the net association between the entry and destination class is affected by the proportion of worklife spent in part-time work. The drop in degree of freedom and the corresponding decrease in the scaled deviance indicate that this term is insignificant.Substantively, the test shows that the net association between O and D is not affected by the amount of time spent in part-time work. In other words, the test gives us the same picture which we obtained in the last section : the relative odds of reaching one class rather than another for a woman who started her worklife in one class rather than another does not vary significantly with an increase in the time spent in part-time work. By using a measure which is more sensitive than the count variable, we arrive at the same result. The evidence which is available to us shows that greater part-time work experience does not affect the net association between the entry and the destination class.

Discussion

While previous studies which examined the occupational mobility of women stressed that part-time work led to downward occupational mobility of women, our analysis shows a more complicated picture. The chance of downward mobility from service class to routine non-manual class or to semi-/unskilled manual working class was not raised significantly by a greater extent of part-time work participation. Nor did it lower significantly the chance of upward mobility from semi-/unskilled manual working class or from routine non-manual class into the service class. The effect of a greater extent of part-time work participation was insignificant in both ways.

The question which our analysis addresses is substantively different from previous studies, especially that of Dex and Shaw (1986) who demonstrated, through a rigorous analysis of the data from the 1980 Women and Employment Survey, the negative effect of part-time work on British women's occupational mobility. Our earlier discussion has noted two weaknesses of the dependent variable in their analysis. One is related to the inadequacy of its dichotomous form, and the other is about using earnings as a criterion of measuring mobility. Moreover, we do not know the specific occupational destination to which women moved in their analysis, that is, we do not know whether the downward mobility is of a long-range or a short-range kind. Thirdly, part-time work as the independent variable in their analysis was dealt with as a single instance, that is, whether the woman took up a part-time job or not when she resumed wage employment after a break for childbirth. Without taking into account the duration aspect (whether in terms of the number of spells or the cumulative duration as the case in our analysis), Dex and Shaw could not ascertain the permanency of the negative effect of part-time work which they recorded.

There are several points which we can note to account for the insignificance of the part-time work effect recorded here. One is related to the classification schema which we adopted for the analysis. The five-level classification may allow us to detect only broad and drastic occupational movements, for example, from service class to semi-/unskilled manual working class or to routine non-manual workers. This classification may be too crude to capture any finer movement within each of these five categories. For example, the classification would not be able to capture a move from a ward sister to a rank-and-file nurse in the nursing profession as both occupations would be classified as service class occupations. This movement would be recorded as immobility by our classification. To capture more detailed occupational movements, one solution would be to use a classification which has more categories. However, a large enough sample would then be needed to avoid data sparsity in each individual cell of a mobility table formed by a more refined occupational classification schema and cross-classified by the number of part-time work spells.

Another possible explanation for the insignificance of the effect of part-time work is related to an assumption underlying the previous analyses which may not be tenable. In both the spell and duration analyses, the effect of each part-time job on the entry-destination association is assumed to be uniform. This may not be valid. The other aspect of part-time work experience not adequately captured by either the spell count or the duration measure is the remoteness dimension. In other words, the question here involves how far back a woman's part-time job(s) before her current employment was. The women whose part-time work experience we examine here were of different ages when they were interviewed. For older current workers who had taken up some part-time work previously, the experience could be in the remote past. And the involvement could be of a short or a long duration. It could also be a recent experience. The most extreme cases are those who were first time part-timers at the time of the survey. Remote part-time work experience may have a different effect on mobility compared to a more recent one, not just because of remoteness per se, but also because of other in-market experiences which the woman subsequently has. These experiences may offset whatever effects previous part-time work has had. For example, for the current full-timers who had had some part-time work experience before they resumed their current full-time employment status, the 'in-market' experience which they had after they left their last part-time job may have an impact on their destination class. This impact may cancel out (or exacerbate) whatever negative effect their previous part-time work experience had. Hence, the possible effect of a greater extent of part-time work participation is not borne out by our findings.

Those studies which recorded a negative effect of part-time work were based on a limited time frame. Hence, they could not detect whether the negative effect persisted beyond the time points against which the mobility experience was considered. By taking on a broader time frame, the results of the present analysis suggest that the adverse effect could have been cancelled out by other effects. To entertain the effect of remoteness of part-time work participation and the different possible combinations of this with the duration and count measure, and to introduce them into the categorical approach would make the analysis more complicated. This calls for further study with more sophisticated techniques that can consider simultaneously these three aspects and is beyond the scope of this Chapter.

Conclusion

In this chapter, two major aspects of labour market experience, namely, earnings and worklife mobility were examined. The main concern is whether part-time work experience has negative effects on both these two aspects, as analyses in the previous Chapters lead us to expect. The findings in the first section show that part-time work experience has an adverse effect on the current earnings. The greater the extent of part-time work participation, the lower the level of current earnings.

In the second part of this Chapter, the focus was on mobility and the issue addressed was whether part-time work experience leads to significant changes in the class position of the woman's occupation. The relative likelihood of ending in one destination class rather than another for women who started their worklife in different entry classes was first analysed in the standard mobility table. The way the likelihood varied with the extent of part-time work participation was then analysed. The overall picture suggested by the two formal tests shows that our evidence indicates that part-time work experience does not affect the net association between entry and current class. The findings highlight the need to pay more attention to the permanency of the negative effect of part-time work in causing downward occupational mobility.

Notes

1   Here, we are not dealing with occupational attainment as a general issue. Our focus is to examine the effect of part-time work experience, as a specific kind of in-market experience, on women's labour market attainment, rather than taking on the broader issue of occupational attainment. This latter issue theoretically also entails the analysis of effects of pre-market experience.

2   This means that women who were not working (non-employed and

unemployed alike) are excluded. Since the analyses of occupational mobility and current earnings require the woman to be in paid work, little can be done about this exclusion. Some studies, for example, Portocarero (1983), use the last job of those who were housewives at the time of the study to analyse occupational mobility. However, the duration of the time interval between the last job and the current housewife status is likely to vary greatly. These would have to be taken into account if the last job was used. To keep the focus of this study sharp, the practice of using the last job for a current housewife will not be adopted in the present study, and current unpaid houseworkers are not included in the analysis.

3   For a rare attempt by human capital theorists to make such a distinction, see Polachek (1981).

4   Studies in America also show that the amount of on-the-job training which employers provided for their employees was positively related to the working hours. For example, Duncan and Hoffman (1979) found that workers who worked fewer than 20 hours per week were only given half as long a training period as workers who worked 40 to 50 hours per week.

5   In the light of the differences between part-time and full-time working experience, the 'restoration of human capital' and 'wage rebound' phenomena suggested by Mincer and Ofek (1982) are dubious. In this more recent study, they noted that there was a rapid growth in wage when a woman returned to work after a period of non-participation. They attributed the wage growth to the restoration of previously eroded human capital. However, as will be indicated in Chapter eight, after a period of non-participation (which is normally spent in unpaid housework), a married woman is more likely to take up part-time rather than full-time work. Thus, in assessing the long-term impact of work experience, it is important to examine the type of job experience which a married woman takes up when she re-enters the labour market after a period of non-participation.

6   We do not introduce the factor percentage of working life spent in full-time work into the wage equation because of the problem of collinearity with the other three working experience factors. In other studies of women's earnings level (e.g. Jones and Long, 1979; Cocoran et al., 1983; Joshi, 1984; Dex et al., 1993; Ermisch and Wright, 1993), part-time work experience as absolute numbers of

years (or months) was also found to have a negative effect on the current wage level of working women.

7   See Ganzeboom et al. (1992) for a comparison of the categorical approach and continuous approach to the study of occupational stratification.

8   Admittedly, representing mobility by the first job and current occupation neglects movements in between these two time-points, and also any orderliness of women's career paths. But our concern here is more modest. Instead of a detailed mapping out of all the possible occupational changes with each employment status change, the focus is sharper and narrower for testing segmentation theory with regard to part-time work experience. For examples of the way segmentation theory can be applied to each work event in the case of men, see Carroll and Mayer (1986, 1987). See also Chan (1994) for an empirical study of the sequential order of worklife class mobility by using Hong Kong as an example.

9   It is possible that the first job is the same as the current job, especially for young respondents. However, since we are here dealing with married women or women living in single-parent households, it is unlikely that their current job is also their first job. The married women sample in the main survey of SCELI had had an average of five work events, and two spells of interruptions. Hence, it is unlikely that their current job is also their first job.

10   A similar pattern of mobility was noted by Marshall and his associates in their study. See Marshall et al. (1988:123-126).

11   Whether a move from class IIIb into class VIIa can be considered as downward mobility is doubtful as the employment conditions of class IIIb has been found to be akin to that of class VIIa. Thus, taking a more conservative position, we shall only use downward mobility to refer to those moves which are from class I, II and IIIa to class VIIa.

12   Similar patterns of occupational movement have been noted for British men. See Goldthorpe (1987).

13   However, unlike worklife mobility studies (for example, Goldthorpe, 1987; Marshall et al., 1988) which also adopt the Goldthorpe class schema, classes V, VI and VIIa were not collapsed

into one category as this would entail further loss of information from the seven-by-seven table.

7 Part-time work participation I : self-selection ?

So far, our discussion has been focusing on the limitations of part-time work at the organizational and job level. In the previous Chapters, the job structure and rewards of part-time employment were examined. The wage rate and promotion prospects of part-time jobs were found to be worse than that of full-time jobs, although they were not associated with a higher level of job insecurity or a greater risk of job loss. With regard to workplace authority relations, part-time workers were more likely to be subordinates rather than supervisors and generally enjoyed a lower level of discretionary power over their jobs, as compared to their full-time counterparts. To a considerable extent, their unfavourable legal status was exacerbated by their jobs' disadvantageous market situation.

The findings in Chapters four and five also indicate that it is unwarranted to treat the part-time workforce as a homogeneous group. When disaggregated, it was found that there were disparities between part-timers with different legal statuses. In terms of promotion chances and entitlement to fringe benefits, part-timers who worked fewer hours were worse off than those who worked more hours per week. The former were also less likely to be in supervisory positions.

The cumulative effect of part-time work experience was assessed in Chapter six. With respect to earnings, the findings indicate that part-time work experience had a negative effect on the current wage level. As for its impact on occupational mobility, the analysis shows that it has no significant effect on the net association between the entry and the destination class.

In this and the next Chapter, the analysis will focus on the supply side of part-time employment. Specifically, we shall examine women's participation in part-time work. This Chapter will assess the argument

171

that this is closely related to a set of work attitudes which accords a lower priority to wage work vis-à-vis other life domains.

One of the contentious issues about women's participation in part-time work is - is it voluntary despite its unfavourable employment conditions? Hakim (1991) argues that taking up part-time work is related to women's personal desires. Their acceptance of the inferior conditions and the limited opportunity offered by part-time work is closely related to their level of employment commitment. Women are not 'pushed' into part-time work by the labour market structure, nor by childcare responsibility. They choose to reduce their number of working hours out of their personal preferences. Hakim further argues that these preferences are, in turn, related to the different rankings women accord to various life domains. Since part-time workers, in our case, are mainly working mothers, the self-selection argument further suggests that they internalize the traditional idea of motherhood and home-maker, and give greater importance to family life and domestic activity and a lower priority to wage work. Taking up a part-time job is an outcome of the preference they give to their gender role.

The argument put forward by Hakim is very similar to the one which underlies one of the explanations of the secondary labour market discussed in the introductory Chapter. Certain attitudinal traits and dispositions of workers are emphasized in explaining why some socio-economic groups (in our case, married women) are recruited to secondary employment. Individuals in these social groups develop their work attitudes through their involvement in other life domains. Specifically, these work attitudes are about their lower level of subjective attachment to wage work. Workers bring these work attitudes into the workplace. Their level of attachment to employment is then reflected in behaviours like absenteeism, frequent turnover and withdrawals from the labour market.

Devotion to wage work involves at least two analytically distinct concepts which need to be distinguished from each other before the voluntary or constrained nature of participation in part-time employment can be discussed. Thus, to clear the conceptual ground and for the subsequent analysis, these two different meanings of subjective attachment to work will be discussed first. We shall also draw from one of these two concepts the specific propositions which we shall examine.

Subjective work attachment and labour market participation

The two labour market theories reviewed in Chapter one have different views on the nature and the level of subjective work attachment. Neo-

172

classical theories posit that an instrumental orientation is a general feature shared by workers in their labour supply. Individuals decide to enter into and withdraw from the labour market by balancing the costs and benefits they can derive from wage work. Similarly, remaining with an employing organization or switching employers also involves a process of balancing the financial incentives offered by different employers. Workers are committed to wage work primarily for its financial rewards.

Segmentation theory, however, considers workers as different in terms of their subjective levels of attachment to employment. This is considered as pivotal to the segmentation of the labour market. There are, however, two different concepts of attachment to work which need to be distinguished from each other. The first concept is subjective devotion to work as a general attitude. This means commitment to employment *per se*. The second concept refers to dedication to a particular employing organisation, that is, organizational commitment. The meaning of commitment to employment *per se* will be discussed first. This, as we shall then note briefly, is different from organizational commitment which is posited as an outcome of the different employment conditions in the primary and the secondary labour market.

The concept of employment commitment

Commitment to employment *per se* refers to a *generalized* (as some argue, a normative[1]) attitude towards wage work. A commonly adopted definition of employment commitment stresses the relative importance of wage work to an individual's identity.[2] A person who is strongly committed to wage work would regard his or her work role as central to his or her sense of self and a primary source of personal identity. Such a kind of person would consider having a job, rather than living as an economic dependant, as a norm, or even a moral virtue. (S)he will be an active job-seeker if (s)he becomes unemployed.[3]

As Bielby and Bielby (1988) suggested, commitment would involve a distributional dimension. Individuals allocate or trade off their time and effort between different types of activities to which they are more or less committed and to which they give different rates of importance and priorities. A person who is dedicated to employment would consider it a major source of personal identity. Wage work would be regarded as a more important life domain than other domains like family life or leisure. He or she would allocate more time and effort to the former. When competing demands arose from other spheres of life, paid work would take priority as they rate their work roles as more salient than their roles in other social institutions.

173

The difference in employment commitment is put forward by segmentation theory to explain why workers are recruited to or remain in different labour market segments. Workers who have a higher level of employment commitment are likely to be favoured by employers, being regarded as more trainable; employers will find it worthwhile to give them advancement prospects, more training opportunities, a preferential wage rate and more fringe benefits. Workers who have a lower level of employment commitment are regarded by employers as having a strong turnover intention and liable to frequent exits from the labour market. These dispositions make it not worthwhile for employers to invest these employees with job training and advanced work skills. They are given secondary rather than favourable conditions of employment.

In their discussion of the contrast between the primary and the secondary workforce, Berger and Piore contended that workers who made up the secondary workforce belonged to distinct groups whose work orientations and values were formed through their socialization outside the workplace :

> The labour force in these jobs is composed of distinct groups who derive their principal identity from social roles outside the workplace: women, adolescents, peasant workers, or temporary migrants. Such workers are typically unstable, with a high rate of voluntary turnover, and frequent movement in and out of the labour force (Berger and Piore, 1980, p.18).

In other words, the identities associated with non-work roles underlie these workers' weaker attachment to wage work. The identities which they derive from non-work domains override the centrality of their work roles. This is then used to explain their movements in between different employing organizations as well as frequent entries into and withdrawals from the labour market.

This explanation stresses the primacy of non-work factors in shaping the level of employment commitment. It sees devotion to wage work as a function of the personal characteristics and the immediate social milieux of the worker.

In the case of women, we noted in Chapter one that segmentation theorists Doeringer and Piore (1971) argued that their employment commitment is strongly influenced by their gender role. Their principal identity is home-maker. Being a wage-earner for the household is a secondary status for them. Their gender identity is developed and formed prior to their entry into any specific work organization. A high voluntary turnover rate and frequent exits from the labour market are behavioural manifestations of their non-committal orientation to employment.

Besides the level of employment commitment, Doeringer and Piore also pointed to the differences about the motivation to work. They argued that working mothers (and other socio-demographic groups which are more likely to be in the secondary labour market) hold an instrumental and calculative attitude towards employment. They work for money rather than because the nature of the job is inherently interesting or because wage work itself is a prime source of personal fulfilment and identity. They stay with a specific employer or remain employed on a purely cost-and-benefit calculative orientation. What matters to working mothers are their personal economic interests and the welfare of their families, rather than the interest of the organization or any intrinsic meanings of wage work. Attachment to employment and to an employing company is, therefore, likely to be transient and volatile for workers with this kind of orientation. They stay with their employing company until a better alternative becomes available. They remain employed for the economic rewards which paid work offers. If they can have other sources of financial support (for example, welfare payments, earnings of other family members, especially from husbands in the case of married women), they would give up whatever current jobs they have and withdraw from the labour market into the domestic domain from which they derive their principal identity. The intrinsic nature of paid work is of minor importance, as compared to family life and domestic activities. In other words, the work attitudes of secondary workers (whether the motivation to remain in the labour market or to stay with their employing organization) resemble the type of attitudes which neo-classical labour market theory postulates for workers who are in a perfectly competitive labour market.

In contrast to workers in the secondary labour market, workers in the primary segment are more likely to be committed to employment *per se*. They value work in itself. Their principal source of personal identity lies with their employment. The nature of their work involves them psychologically and is intrinsically rewarding. Hence, they would remain in the labour market even if they had other sources of financial support.

A work perspective of employment commitment

The explanation of the employment commitment of secondary workers put forward by Doeringer and Piore is from a non-work perspective. The

175

emphasis is on influences from life spheres beyond the workplace. However, besides this perspective, there is another one which emphasizes aspects of work as the major factors in determining employment commitment. This perspective, which can be called the work perspective, is premised on the tenet that job features exert a great influence on personal attitudes and identity (Kohn et al. 1983; Kanter, 1977; Mortimer et al., 1983). It argues that the ways in which jobs are structured in specific organizational and occupational contexts give workers very diverse socialization experiences. These, in turn, affect the extent to which individuals are committed to employment. According to this perspective, it is features of the job that matters in shaping employment commitment. Previous studies have noted that the work conditions and the labour market opportunities of the job which an individual holds are strong determinants of his or her employment commitment. Workers who are in jobs which give them a higher degree of job autonomy, better promotion prospects and higher status are more committed to employment *per se* (Warr, 1982; Kanungo, 1982; Lorence, 1987; Pittman and Orthner, 1989; Loscocco, 1989). A major cross-national comparative study of work values finds that workers who enjoy greater degree of discretion at work, more learning possibilities are more likely to value the intrinsic value of work, while employees whose jobs are of low-quality are more likely to have an instrumental orientation towards wage work (Meaning of Work, 1987).

We thus have two different explanations of employment commitment. The work perspective leads us to expect that a higher or lower level of employment commitment is primarily determined by the favourable or unfavourable market and work situations of a job. The non-work perspective emphasizes the effect of disparate personal attributes. To the extent that part-timers are less committed to employment than full-timers, is this due to their personal characteristics or to the unequal rewards between full-time and part-time jobs? More specifically, with respect to work motivations, are part-timers primarily concerned with the financial rewards rather than the intrinsic value of wage work? These work attitudes form the first set of issues which this Chapter will address.

Organizational commitment

Employment commitment is different from an employee's subjective attachment to an organization. The latter refers to attachment to a *specific* employing company or an employer, while the former is a more generalized attitude.

Segmentation theory argues that employers are concerned with building a stable workforce which is committed to the organization. This aim can be realised by giving a certain fraction of employees more favourable job returns and work situations. Employees who receive a wage rate above that which they can obtain from a perfectly competitive labour market are likely to have a weak turnover intention. Their inclination to stay with their current employers would be reinforced if their jobs offer advancement prospects within the firm and if they are entrusted with a high degree of job discretion, work autonomy and supervisory authority.

A worker's organizational commitment would be strongest when it is built on a normative basis.[4] When a worker is normatively committed to his or her employing company, he or she identifies himself or herself with the organization. He or she would also take on the company's goals and values as his or her own. Work effort would be exerted conscientiously for the welfare of the company. Workers who have this kind of allegiance are unlikely to leave their employing company. They are also likely to have a stable employment history which is embedded in the company and tied to a job hierarchy within the organization. Employers who aim at minimizing the cost and the loss of specific human capital due to frequent turnover are willing to offer these employees better job returns and accord them an asset-like status in the company. The favourable job rewards and work situation further strengthen the worker's allegiance and loyalty to the employing company. A strong sense of commitment to the work organization, favourable job returns and work situation are thus mutually reinforcing.

We shall not deal with the issue of organizational commitment as we are concerned with the self-selection argument which pertains more to commitment to employment *per se*. Admittedly, organizational commitment of workers can also have a reciprocal effect on employers' labour use strategies which then further sharpen the distinction between different labour market segments. To keep the analysis in sharp focus, this will not be addressed here. Moreover, we are also restricted by the availability of data to examine the difference in the organizational commitment between full-time and part-time workers in the main survey of SCELI.

Employment commitment and job satisfaction

Related to employment commitment is the issue of job satisfaction. Kalleberg (1977) suggested that job satisfaction is associated with the expectation and the degree of importance attached to wage work. Workers who are less devoted to employment and more committed to other life domains would have a lower expectation from their job, as

177

their prime concern and main interest would not be with their attainment in wage work, but with involvement in other life activities. A low level of expectation from their job means that they can be easily satisfied with whatever jobs they have. On the contrary, workers who are more committed to employment seek for personal fulfilment in their jobs. Their involvement in wage work is their central life interest. They will, thus, have a higher level of expectation from their job and a higher threshold of job satisfaction. Compared to workers who are less committed to employment, these employees may have a lower level of job satisfaction as they expect a great deal from their jobs to fulfil their aspiration. If the choice of a reduced number of working hours is underlined by the difference in the workers' commitment to employment and their expectation from wage work, are part-timers more satisfied with their jobs than full-timers?

Furthermore, to the extent that part-timers accommodate their participation in wage work to their preference with other life domains, this would be evident in their satisfaction with non-work life domains as they are matching their job choice with their preference for non-work life activities. In the Household and Community Survey, a sub-sample of the original respondents of the main survey were re-interviewed. They were asked how satisfied they were with a number of life activities. With this information, albeit from a sub-sample, we can then explore the extent to which part-time working women are contented with their involvement in other life domains, as compared to full-timers.

The ensuing analysis is divided into four sections. In the first section, the focus is on employment commitment. Full-timers will be compared to part-timers in terms of their employment commitment and the relative importance they accord to wage work vis-à-vis other life domains. This will be followed by a discussion of other salient factors which would also affect employment commitment. An assessment of the effects of unequal job rewards and of personal characteristics on employment commitment will then be conducted through a logistic regression.

The second aspect of work attitudes which is held to be a characteristic of the secondary workforce is their instrumental motive towards wage work. In the second section, we shall examine the difference between full-timers and part-timers in terms of their reason for working.

The third section deals with attitudes towards the sexual division of labour which has been suggested to be a crucial factor in affecting women's work decision and employment commitment. The central question this section addresses is : are part-timers more traditional in terms of their attitudes towards the sexual division of labour, as

178

compared to full-timers? Several indicators will be used to measure attitudes towards female labour market participation and the division of labour within the household.

The last section will examine job and life satisfaction. The main part of the analysis will be on job satisfaction. Information concerning the life satisfaction of a sub-sample of the respondents in the main survey will also be drawn on to compare women working full-time with those working part-time.[5]

Employment commitment of working women

In the main survey of SCELI, as a general indicator of devotion to employment, those respondents who were employees and self-employed at the time of the survey were asked : "If you were to get enough money to live as comfortably as you would like for the rest of your life, would you continue to work, not necessarily in your present job, or would you stop working?".[6] While 68% of the male employees said they would continue, this is the case for 63% of all working women.[7] If we consider only female employees, 65% of the full-timers said they would carry on working, and 59% of all part-timers said they would.

Besides commitment to employment in an absolute sense, the earlier discussion suggested that primary and secondary workers would differ in terms of the relative importance they give to wage work vis-à-vis other life activities. However, in only two out of the six local areas of SCELI were there questions asked to tap this difference between workers. These two areas are Swindon and Kirkcaldy. Compared to Kirkcaldy, Swindon had experienced a relatively lower level of unemployment in the mid-1980s. While we do not know the extent to which the findings can be generalized, this additional information would, nevertheless, indicate whether part-timers differ from full-time workers in terms of their commitment to wage work relative to other life domains.

In both Swindon and Kirkcaldy, those respondents who were employed at the time of the interview were asked to rate how important they thought their wage work was as compared to (1) spending time at home with the family; (2) working on projects to improve the house; (3) going out and enjoying oneself. The percentages of female full-timers and part-timers who said their wage work was more important, equally important or less important than family life, leisure activity and domestic work are shown in Table 7.1.

If part-time workers are less committed to wage work and accord a higher priority to other life domains as compared to full-timers, we would expect that they would be more likely than full-timers to rank

179

wage work as less important than family life and leisure activity. We would also expect that they would be more likely than full-timers to rank family life and leisure activity as more important than wage work.

Table 7.1
Relative importance of wage work for working women
in Kirkcaldy and Swindon

	Kirkcaldy		Swindon	
	% of full-timers	% of part-timers	% of full-timers	% of part-timers
Compared to family life, my wage work is				
more important	13	5	26	28
equally important	32	18	26	17
less important	53	76	45	53
not applicable/don't know	2	1	2	3
Compared to projects at home, my wage work is.......				
more important	51	38	41	29
equally important	19	25	22	34
less important	23	33	31	34
not applicable/don't know	7	5	6	3
Compared to leisure activity, my wage work is				
more important	43	50	37	32
equally important	21	20	24	21
less important	35	48	38	46
not applicable/don't know	2	0.5	1	2
N	139	111	152	121

<Question : 'Thinking about how much work matters to you in comparison to other aspects of life, I'd like you to tell me how important work is, in relation to each of the following'.>

From Table 7.1, it can be seen that in both Swindon and Kirkcaldy, female part-timers were indeed more likely than their full-time counterparts to rate wage work as less important than family life, working on projects at home and leisure activity. For instance, in Kirkcaldy, while 76% of the part-timers rated their wage work as less important than their family life, this is the case for 53% of the full-timers. Conversely, full-timers were generally more likely than part-timers to rank wage work as more important than family life, working on projects at home and leisure activity. For example, in Swindon, while 41% of those women working full-time ranked wage work as more important than working on projects at home, this is the case for 29% of the part-timers.

In Swindon, respondents were also asked whether they agreed with the statement 'unpaid work in the home is just as worthwhile as paid work'. While 64% of full-timers agreed with the statement, this is the case for 74% of part-timers. Thus, in both an absolute and a relative sense, part-timers were less committed to employment as compared to full-timers.

In order to assess whether it is unequal job rewards and labour market positions or personal characteristics which contribute to the level of employment commitment, we shall take into account four factors which have been found in previous studies to be significant in affecting employment commitment. Age is negatively associated with employment commitment (Warr, 1982; Hanlon, 1986; Vecchio, 1980; Gallie, 1994). A preference for leisure or declining health are some of the reasons why older workers are less committed to employment when compared with younger workers. Compared to single women, married women would also be less committed to employment as their socially prescribed gender role would mean that they would regard wage work as less important than family life (Gallie et al. 1994; Loscocco,1989).

Attitudes towards the sex roles of men and women would also have an impact on employment commitment. Women who hold a more traditional attitude towards the gender division of labour would give greater emphasis to their domestic role and would, therefore, be less committed to employment, as compared to women who hold an egalitarian attitude. Two indicators were used to tap attitudes towards gender role in the main survey. Respondents were asked the extent to which they agreed with two statements : (1) In times of high unemployment married women should stay at home; (2) I am not against women working but men should still be the main breadwinner in the family. We would expect women who agreed with these two statements to rank their family role as more salient than their work role and hence would be less likely to be committed to employment, as compared to those who disagreed with the two statements.

The fourth possible source of variation in employment commitment is educational level. More educated people are likely to seek for intrinsic rewards from wage work, instead of regarding it merely as a means of living. Hence, they would be committed to wage work even without the financial needs. Higher educational level would, therefore, be positively related to employment commitment. Gallie (1994) found that for both men and women, the higher the level of formal qualification, the more likely that the worker is committed to employment.

According to the work perspective of employment commitment, we would expect that jobs which are more prospective and which offer better wages, greater job autonomy and supervisory status would have a positive effect on employment commitment, and vice versa. The class position to which the job belongs is used to differentiate favourable and unfavourable jobs. We would expect that workers whose jobs are in the service class would be more committed to employment, as compared to semi-/unskilled manual workers whose labour market prospects and work situation are worse than those in the service class.

Following the reasoning of the work perspective, the poorer job rewards and promotion prospects, as well as the non-supervisory status of part-time work vis-à-vis full-time work noted in Chapters four and five, would lead us to expect that working-hour status would also contribute to employment commitment. The poorer market and work situations of part-time jobs mean that holding other factors constant, women working part-time would be less committed to employment, as compared to women working full-time.

Table 7.2a shows the percentages of workers in these subgroups who said they would continue to work even in the absence of financial needs. It can be seen from Table 7.2a that older workers were less likely to say that they would continue to work if financially it was not necessary, as compared to younger workers. While over 70% of those aged 20 to 29 were committed to employment, this is the case for less than half of those aged between 50 and 59. Educational level is positively associated with the likelihood of being committed to employment or not. Women who had a higher education (degree or non-degree) qualification level were more likely to say they would continue working, as compared to women who did not have any formal qualification. Married women were less likely to be committed, as compared to single women. Women who held a traditional attitude towards the sexual division of labour were less likely to be committed than women who favoured female labour force participation. Women working full-time were more committed than women working part-time.

182

Table 7.2a
Percentages of workers in each subgroup who said they would continue to work even without financial need

	Percentage	(N)
All working women	62	(1,653)
Age group		
20-29	74	(473)
30-39	62	(497)
40-49	58	(410)
50-59	48	(273)
Marital status		
single	73	(349)
married	59	(1,384)
Attitudes towards sexual division of labour		
Men should be the breadwinner		
agree	54	(805)
no strong opinion	60	(139)
disagree	71	(704)
In times of high unemployment, married women should stay at home		
agree	54	(365)
no strong opinion	56	(120)
disagree	65	(1,160)
Education qualification		
none	53	(658)
vocational	57	(102)
O-level	64	(405)
A-level	65	(145)
higher education	78	(343)
Working-hour status		
full-time	64	(918)
part-time	59	(735)
Class position of the job		
service	70	(395)
routine non-manual	64	(671)
technicians or skilled manual workers	57	(143)
semi-/unskilled manual workers	54	(444)

Finally, workers who were in service class jobs were more likely to be committed, as compared to semi-/unskilled manual workers. To assess the net effects of job features and the personal characteristics on employment commitment, a logistic regression was conducted in which the dependent variable takes the dichotomous form of whether or not he or she would carry on working even without the financial need. A composite variable is created for the sex role attitude. Those who agreed with both statements were classified into one group and compared to those who had no strong opinion and to those who disagreed with the two statements. The results are shown in Table 7.2b and Table 7.2c.

Table 7.2b
Logistic regression on the employment commitment of working women

Variables	G^2	D.F.	rG^2	rD.F.
Null model	661	413	-	-
+age	607	410	54	3
+marital status	596	409	11	1
+education level	545	405	51	4
+attitudes towards gender role	530	403	16	2
+class position of the job	528	400	2	3
+working-hour status	527	402*	3	1

*this is included into the model in which the four personal characteristics were included and after the class variable was removed. G^2 = scale deviance, D.F. = degree of freedom, rG^2 = change in scale deviance, rD.F. = change in degree of freedom

Table 7.2b shows that when the class variable is added to the model in which variables related to the personal characteristics were already included, it does not give a significantly better-fitted model. When the working-hour status variable was added, the improvement in the fit also failed to reach the 0.05 significance level. This suggests that our findings do not lend support to the explanation of employment commitment in terms of the workplace constraints and opportunities. In our case, the significant factors are the personal characteristics of the worker and the attitudes towards gender roles.

Table 7.2c
Estimates for employment commitment of working women

Variables	Estimates (log-odds)	S.E.	Multiplicative estimates
Constant	1.316	0.186	3.72
Age			
20 - 29	-	-	1
30 - 39	-0.416	0.150	0.659**
40 - 49	-0.467	0.160	0.627**
50 - 59	-0.857	0.175	0.424**
Marital status			
single	-	-	1
married	-0.418	0.139	0.659**
Formal qualification			
none	-	-	1
vocational	-0.228	0.223	0.769
O-level	0.218	0.136	1.24
A-level	-0.017	0.202	0.983
higher education	0.854	0.157	2.35**
Attitude towards gender role			
egalitarian	-	-	1
no strong opinion	-0.394	0.194	0.674**
traditional	-0.467	0.120	0.627**

$G^2 = 530.2$, d.f. = 403, N = 1,676, **denotes significant at <0.05 level, S.E. stands for standard error.

In Table 7.2c, the exponentiated log-odds of the individual estimates are given together with the standard errors and the additive estimates (the log-odds). We can see from the odds ratio that age has a negative effect on employment commitment. Being aged between 50 and 59 reduced the odds of being committed to employment rather than not by a factor of 0.424, as compared to workers who were in the age group 20 to 29. Women who were married were also less likely to be committed to employment, as compared to single women. Compared to workers without any formal qualification, those who had a higher education qualification level were more likely to be committed to employment. Women who held an unfavourable attitude towards female employment were less likely to be committed to employment, as compared to women who favoured female labour market participation.

This section shows that the difference in the level of employment commitment among working women is associated with the personal rather than the job characteristics of working women. The findings lend support to the non-work perspective rather than the work perspective of employment commitment. To the extent that part-timers are self-selecting themselves into part-time jobs, our analysis shows that this can be traced back to influences which are beyond the workplace. However, from the results, we cannot distinguish the different specific motives underlying labour market participation. This will be the focus of the next section.

The motive to work

We have noted in the earlier discussion that the second attitudinal trait which is held to characterize secondary workers is their instrumental orientation towards wage work. They are concerned primarily with the economic rewards which employment offers, rather than with any intrinsically rewarding nature of the job or of working. The issue that we shall address in this section is whether part-timers can be characterized as instrumentally oriented towards wage work. To tap the specific motives of work, respondents were asked to give their first and second main reasons for wanting a job. The differences between female full-time and part-time workers are given in Table 7.3a.

It can be seen that a sizeable proportion of *both* full-timers and part-timers said they wanted a job primarily for its monetary reward. While 60% of full-timers said they worked for the monetary rewards, this is the case for 64% of part-timers. Full-timers were no less instrumental than part-timers in wanting a job. The difference is whether the income is for basic essentials or to buy extras. Full-timers were more likely to say that their income was for basics, while part-timers were more likely to say that their income was of a supplementary nature. This may be explicable in terms of their marital status. As we shall see in the next Chapter, a great majority of the part-timers were married (whether in a *de facto* or legal sense) and their male partners were more likely to be employed rather than unemployed. It is likely that female part-timers had a main wage-earner for their households and hence a greater proportion of them said they wanted a job to cover supplementary expenditure rather than for basic essentials.

Table 7.3a
First and second main reason for wanting a job for working women

Reason	Nominated as first reason		Nominated as second reason	
	% full-time	% part-time	% full-time	% part-time
Working is the normal thing to do	4	2	4	2
Need money for basic essentials	44	30	9	5
To earn money to buy extras	16	34	18	18
For the company of other people	1	3	6	10
Enjoy working	10	8	16	14
To use my abilities to the full	6	3	10	4
To feel that I'm doing something worthwhile	6	5	9	7
To give me a sense of independence	10	11	21	24
To get out of the house	1	5	4	14
Don't know	2	-	-	-
Total	100	100	100	100

<Question : 'Here are some reasons for wanting a paid job. At the moment, which one would come closest to your own main reason for wanting a job? And which would be your second most important reason?'>

As for the other reasons, Table 7.3a shows that similarly small proportions of full-timers and part-timers gave 'working is normal' as their main reason for wanting a job. Likewise, similar proportions of women in the two working-hour statuses said they worked because they enjoyed working, or because working gave them a sense of independence. Thus, part-timers do not differ much from full-timers in terms of wanting a job primarily for its economic benefits or for the intrinsic or expressive values of wage work.

From the distribution of the second main reason, it can be seen that contrary to the implication which we can draw from the secondary labour market theory or the neo-classical theory, part-timers were actually as likely as full-timers to value some intrinsic and expressive values of wage work. Similar proportions of full-timers and part-timers gave intrinsic reasons for wanting a job. For example, while 24% of part-timers said they worked because working gave them a sense of independence, this is the case for 21% of full-timers. While 14% of part-timers said they worked because they enjoyed working, this is the case for 16% of full-timers.

On the whole, our findings suggest that part-timers were similar to full-timers in wanting a job because of the extrinsic or the intrinsic and expressive values of employment.

We have noted that segmentation theorists Doeringer and Piore (1971) posited that women who are in the family formation stage would be more likely to work for economic rewards as their income is needed to finance the household expenditure, especially when their children are still financial dependants. For working women who are in their family formation stage, are part-timers more likely than full-timers to work for the monetary rewards of wage work? For the purpose of comparing those who work primarily for monetary rewards with those who work for the intrinsic or expressive values of wage work, the first main reasons for wanting a job shown in Table 7.3a are classified into two categories : extrinsic reasons which comprise the two monetary reasons, and intrinsic reasons which include the other reasons. Table 7.3b shows the percentages of part-timers and full-timers in these two categories for four life-cycle stages.

It can be seen from Table 7.3b that among working women who were in the family formation stage and with economically dependent children (either pre-school or school age), part-timers were as likely as full-timers to work primarily for economic benefits. For women whose youngest child was 15 years old or above, those working part-time were **less** likely to work primarily for financial rewards, as compared to their full-time counterparts who were in the same life-cycle stage. Finally, for married women who had not had any children, full-timers and part-timers were similarly likely to work for the intrinsic or financial values of wage work.[8]

188

Table 7.3b

Percentages of working women who worked for extrinsic and intrinsic reason by their life-cycle stage and by their working-hour status

Life-cycle stage	Reason for wanting a job	
	Intrinsic	Extrinsic
Youngest child under 5		
% full-time (N = 50)	29	71
% part-time (N = 152)	29	71
Youngest child between 5-15		
% full-time (N = 195)	36	36
% part-time (N = 310)	64	64
Youngest child above 15		
% full-time (N = 165)	31	69
% part-time (N = 162)	41	59
Married no children		
% full-time (N = 294)	42	58
% part-time (N = 103)	46	53

The motive to work can also vary according to the individual's occupation. Workers whose jobs which do not involve them psychologically would be more likely to work for financial incentives than for the intrinsic nature of the work itself. We have noted in Chapter four that part-time jobs were mostly occupations which fell into the semi-/unskilled manual working class and few belonged to the service class. Table 7.3c shows that within each of the three class categories in which there were relatively more part-timers, the differences between full-timers and part-timers in terms of their work motives were insignificant. Part-timers and full-timers in the service class were similarly likely to work for extrinsic and intrinsic reasons. Likewise, within the semi-/unskilled manual working class, women working full-time and part-time were similarly likely to work for the monetary rewards which their jobs offered them.

Table 7.3c

Percentages of working women who worked for extrinsic and intrinsic reasons by occupational class and by working-hour status

Class	Reasons for wanting a job			
	Extrinsic	Intrinsic	Total	N
Service*				
% full-time	50	50	100	(310)
% part-time	45	55	100	(93)
Routine non-manual*				
% full-time	61	39	100	(387)
% part-time	58	42	100	(292)
Semi-/unskilled manual*				
% full-time	75	25	100	(146)
% part-time	73	27	100	(307)

*insignificant difference between full-timers and part-timers

The general picture indicated by the previous analysis is one in which the work motivation of part-timers cannot be characterized by a distinctively instrumental orientation to work. Taken as a whole, they are as likely as full-timers to work because of the economic rewards or intrinsic value of wage work. When their positions in the life cycle and the class position to which their job belonged were controlled for, female part-timers did not differ significantly from their full-time counterparts in wanting to work for expressive values of wage work.

Attitudes towards the sexual division of labour

The third part of the self-selection argument is about part-timers' attitudes towards the sexual division of labour. The argument advanced by Hakim (1991) suggests that women who internalize the traditional gender role for women, and hence regard gainful employment as relatively less important than their home-making and childcare role in the family, would have a lower extent of wage work participation :

Women's own 'traditional' sex-role attitudes, and a desire to defer to husbands with even more extreme views on women's role in the home, contribute to low levels of work commitment among women, but also contribute to high satisfaction with jobs that can remain relatively invisible to their husbands because women stay at home most of their time. (Hakim, 1991, p. 109)

We have seen that a traditional attitude towards sex roles contributed to a lower likelihood of being committed to employment. Is full-time/part-time wage work participation then related to attitudes towards gender roles? Table 7.4a shows the percentages of working women who agreed, disagreed or had no strong opinion about the statements (1) in times of high unemployment, married women should stay at home and (2) I'm not against women working but men should still be the main breadwinner in the family.

Table 7.4a
Percentages of working women who agreed or disagreed with two statements about gender roles

Gender attitude	Full-timers (%)		Part-timers (%)	
	Agree	Disagree	Agree	Disagree
Women should stay at home during times of unemployment*	19	75	26	65
men should be the main breadwinner in the family*	39	61	61	30

*the row percentages do not add up to 100. Those who did not have a strong opinion towards the two statements took up no more than 10% of either the full-timers or part-timers and are not shown in the Table.

It can be seen that part-timers were more likely than full-timers to have a traditional attitude towards the sexual division of labour. A

191

greater proportion of part-timers agreed that men should be the main breadwinner, as compared to full-timers. They were also more likely than full-timers to agree with the statement that women should leave the labour market when there were generally fewer job opportunities.

To further tap attitudes towards the sexual division of labour, respondents in Swindon were asked to give their opinions to two hypothetical situations. One was about the right thing for the wife to do if the husband gets a better job and accepting it means the couples have to move to another place.[9] More part-timers than full-timers said the wife should encourage the husband to take the job in the new place and began looking there for any job she could do; fewer part-timers than full-timers said the wife should ask the husband not to accept the offer before she could be sure of finding as good a job there as the one she had now. A similar question was asked in which the situation was reversed, that is, respondents were asked what the husband should do if the wife was offered a better job . More part-timers than full-timers said the husband should ask the wife not to accept the job before he could be sure of finding as good a job as he had now; fewer part-timers than full-timers said the husband should encourage his wife to take the job in the new place. This pattern of responses indicates that part-timers tended to hold a traditional attitude and accorded a higher priority to the employment of the husband than to that of the wife.

While the main survey of SCELI covered attitudes towards female labour market participation, the Household and Community Survey had questions which tapped normative attitudes towards division of labour between the two sexes within the household. Although only a sub-sample of the main survey's respondents were re-interviewed for the Household and Community Survey, this information will further indicate the attitudinal differences between women working full-time and part-time. Respondents were asked whether the male partner, the female partner or both *should* have the *ultimate* responsibility for the following three items : (1) ensuring that the housework is done properly; (2) ensuring that the family gets an adequate income and (3) looking after the children. The results are shown in Table 7.4b. It can be seen that part-timers were more likely to hold a traditional attitude about the ways in which domestic work should be divided between the two sexes. Three-quarters of them considered that the female partner should have the ultimate responsibility for housework, as compared to 45% of their full-time counterparts. While about two-third of the part-timers said the male partner should have the ultimate responsibility for income-earning, this was the case for only 30% of the full-timers. Part-timers were also more likely to say that the female partner should be responsible for childcare.

192

Table 7.4b
Normative attitudes towards domestic division of labour
by working-hour status

Domestic labour division	Full-timers (%)	Part-timers (%)
*Who should be responsible for housework ?**		
male partner	2	-
female partner	45	75
both	51	25
total	98	100
*Who should be responsible for ensuring adequate income for the family ?**		
male partner	30	61
female partner	-	-
both	64	39
total	94	100
*Who should be responsible for childcare?**		
male partner	-	-
female partner	13	28
both	45	55
total	58**	83
N	298	217

*the difference between full-timers and part-timers is significant at $p \leq 0.05$.
**the percentages do not add up to 100 as, for some respondents, the question was inapplicable.

Table 7.4b also shows that part-timers were less inclined to think that both male and female partner should share the responsibility towards division of labour within the household. While only one-quarter of the part-timers said both should be responsible for housework, this was the case for half of the full-timers. Likewise, while only 39% of the part-timers said both male and female partner should be responsible for bringing money into the family, this was the case for 64% of full-timers.

Besides emphasising women's own attitudes towards the sexual division of labour, the self-selection argument advanced by Hakim also stresses the affinity between the wife's and the husband's attitudes towards their respective sex roles. A woman's weaker attachment to wage work is likely to be a reflection of her husband's views. Hakim argues that a woman's desire to defer to her husband would influence her work decision.

> In effect, work orientations that give a secondary place to paid work, and accord low priority to pay, prospects and job security against convenience factors, may be imposed on wives by their husbands. High satisfaction with such jobs may in turn be a reflection of husbands' views as much as the wife's own feelings. Women who accept another person's views as regards whether to work, and if so where, will also accept and internalize their husband's assessment of the endeavour." (Hakim, 1991, p. 109)

Two propositions can be drawn from Hakim's argument about the effects of attitudes of the husband on the work decision and job choice of the wife. One is that the husband's attitudes would have a direct impact on the wife's labour market behaviours, irrespective of the wife's own attitudes. We shall discuss this in the next Chapter. The other proposition is that the wife's attitudes towards paid employment and her family role are shaped by her husband's sex-role attitudes.[10] Hakim's argument implies that women who work convenient part-time hours would be more likely to share their husbands' attitudes towards their respective sex roles, as compared to full-timers. In the Household and Community Survey, male partners of the female respondents were also asked to give their opinions as to who should have the ultimate responsibility towards housework, ensuring adequate income for the family and childcare. The percentages of female full-timers and part-timers who had the same attitudes towards sex roles as those of their husbands are given in Table 7.4c.

The first section of Table 7.4c indicates that part-timers were more likely to agree with the traditional attitude of their husbands, as compared to full-timers. Among those part-timers whose husbands said women should have the ultimate responsibility for housework, 79% of them held the same attitude; while this is the case for 61% of the full-timers. Among full-time working wives whose husbands were egalitarian about the responsibility of housework, 74% of them had the same attitude. However, this is only the case for 34% of the part-timers.

Table 7.4c
Attitudes of working wives by their male partner's normative attitudes towards sex roles

Male partner's attitudes towards domestic labour division	% of full-timer female partners who had the same attitude	% of part-time female partners who had the same attitude
Who should be responsible for housework ?		
female partner	61	79
both male and female	74	34
Who should be responsible for ensuring adequate income for the family ?		
male partner	45	68
both male and female	75	52
Who should be responsible for childcare ?		
female partner	*	33
both male and female	69	63

*absolute N fewer than 30.

With regard to the breadwinner role of the husband, the discrepancy between full-time working wives and their husbands is greater than that between part-time working wives and their husbands. Among full-time working wives who were married to traditional-oriented husbands, only 45% of them said men should have the ultimate responsibility for wage-earning. Among part-time working wives whose husbands had a traditional attitude, 68% of them also held a traditional attitude towards men's role as the family's breadwinner. On the other hand, among full-time working wives whose husbands held an egalitarian attitude, 75% had the same attitude; while this is the case for 52% of part-time working wives. With respect to childcare responsibility, among full-time working wives whose husbands were egalitarian, 69% held the same attitude as that of their husbands. This is the case for 63% of the part-time working wives. These results indicate that if women working part-time were more deferential towards their husbands than women working full-time, the deference is towards the traditional rather than the egalitarian orientation of their husbands.

The overall picture which the findings indicate is one in which female part-timers held a more traditional attitude towards female labour force participation and domestic division of labour, as compared to full-timers. However, it has also been argued that participation in part-time work may still be constrained by the unequal division of labour within the household regardless of attitudes. Joshi (1992), Ruggie (1983), Lane (1993), Dex and her associates (1993) argued, in similar manner, that the inadequacy of public provision of childcare predisposed the inequality in the division of domestic labour between husbands and wives and contributed to the greater concentration of women with pre-school children in part-time work in Britain as compared to other European countries. We shall discuss this in the next Chapter. In the next and last section of this chapter, the self-selection argument will be further assessed by examining the full-time/part-time difference in terms of job satisfaction and the levels of contentment with several life domains.

Frustrated or contented workers?

It was suggested earlier that if the self-selection argument holds and that part-timers match their personal preferences with their labour market behaviours, they would then have a lower level of expectation from their jobs as their main interest and concern lie with their involvement in other life domains rather than with success in employment. They would be satisfied with their jobs, even though the employment conditions were inferior. On the other hand, to the extent that full-timers are more concerned with employment, they would have a higher level of job aspiration and expectation and hence would be less satisfied with their jobs, as compared to part-timers.

In the survey, respondents were asked to rate their levels of satisfaction with various specific aspects of their jobs and with the job taken as a whole on an ten-point scale. As our concern is with the argument that part-timers are self-selecting themselves into inferior jobs, we shall focus on the overall job satisfaction, hours of work,

196

promotion prospects, pay and the actual work itself. In terms of the last three aspects, it was noted in Chapters four and five that part-time jobs was worse than full-time work. Table 7.5a gives the mean levels of satisfaction of full-timers and part-timers with these four aspects and with the job as a whole.

Table 7.5a
Mean level of job satisfaction for working women[a]

Aspect of job	Full-timers	Part-timers
Promotion prospects*	5.66	5.80
Total pay**	5.91	6.65
Actual work	7.92	7.97
Hours of work	7.77	8.55
Overall job satisfaction*	7.84	8.28
N	936	744

[a]the higher the figure, the more satisfied the worker.
difference of mean significant at 0.1(*) level or 0.05 (**) level.

We can see from Table 7.5a that part-timers were indeed more satisfied with their jobs, as compared to full-timers, whether with the specific aspect or with the job as a whole.[11] The gap is the biggest for hours of work and smallest for the actual work itself. If we focus on part-timers, it is worth noting that the average satisfaction levels for promotion prospects and for pay are lower than that for hours of work. In particular, among the four specific job aspects, they were least satisfied with the promotion prospects their jobs offered. This suggests that, even if part-timers chose jobs with the hours of work to accommodate their gender role in the household, this does not mean that they also accept indifferently the inferior employment conditions which are associated with a reduced number of working hours.

There are several sources of variation for job satisfaction which are worth considering to further assess the self-selection argument about part-time work participation. Previous studies have found that older workers, in general, have a higher level of job satisfaction (Kalleberg and Loscocco, 1983; Wright and Hamilton, 1978; Gallie and White, 1994). There are several reasons to account for the negative relation between age and the level of job satisfaction. It could be that older workers have found their ideal job for which they have been searching; or their central life interest no longer lies with wage employment; or they have scaled down their aspirations and expectations as they gradually come to terms with reality and what they can realistically attain. It could also be that workers who are dissatisfied have opted for early retirement.

Job satisfaction is also related to the range of possible job choices which workers have. An unrestricted job choice would mean a worker is more likely to match successfully her desire or preference with the type of job she can get, thereby resulting in a higher level of job satisfaction. Conversely, a worker facing a limited range of choice is likely to have to take up a job which is not the one she would most prefer. In the survey, to tap job mismatch, respondents were asked the range of choice they had when they were looking for their current job. The difference between full-timers and part-timers is given in Table 7.5b. It can readily be seen that part-timers were more limited in the amount of choice they had, as compared to full-timers. They were less likely to say they had some choice, as compared to full-timers.

Table 7.5b
Amount of choice when looking for a job by working-hour status for working women

Extent of job choice	Working-hour status	
	Full-timers (%)	Part-timers (%)
a great deal	17	10
some choice	38	28
hardly any choice	32	44
none at all	12	18
N	895	682

<Question : 'When you were looking for your current job, how much choice would you say you had over the type of job you could get : a great deal, some, hardly any or none at all?'>

Job mismatch also occurs when a worker has to take a job for which he or she is over-qualified. Over-qualification can be indicated by the discrepancy between the formal qualification requirement of the job and the worker's own level of formal qualification. Table 7.5c shows separately for full-timers and part-timers the distribution of their own qualification levels by the qualification requirements of their job.

It can readily be seen that part-timers were more likely than full-timers to work at a job with a qualification requirement which was lower than their own level of qualification. For instance, 64% of those part-timers with an O-level qualification had jobs which had no qualification requirements, as compared to 32% of their full-time counterparts. While 22% of those part-timers who had a non-degree higher education qualification were working at a job which did not require any qualification, this is the case for only 9% of their full-time counterparts. In other words, these part-timers were over-qualified for their jobs. A worker who is over-qualified for his or her job is likely to be under-utilizing his or her skills or formal training. Moreover, the job rewards which he or she receives is unlikely to be commensurate with the market value of his or her qualification. Such a mismatch may well lead to a lower level of job satisfaction.

Table 7.5c
Percentages distribution of own qualification by job qualification for working women

Own qualification	Job qualification							
	None	Vocational	O-level	A-level	Non-degree	Degree	Total	N
None								
% PT	88	5	6	1	0.3	2	100	359
% FT	70	10	14	4	-	2	100	291
Vocational								
% PT	69	14	12	-	5	-	100	44
% FT	38	23	29	6	4	-	100	62
O-level								
% PT	64	10	21	3	2	1	100	160
% FT	32	9	47	5	4	2	100	252
A-level								
% PT	59	8	25	6	-	2	100	36
% FT	19	6	29	36	7	2	100	110
Non-degree								
% PT	22	4	12	4	51	6	100	68
% FT	9	4	12	8	59	9	100	123
Degree								
% PT	14	4	9	8	6	58	100	37
% FT	9	1	7	7	9	68	100	133

The average levels of job satisfaction for part-timers sub-divided according to their age, whether they were over-qualified for their job or not and whether they had any choice or not when they were looking for their job, are shown in Table 7.5d.

Table 7.5d
Mean level of job satisfaction for women working part-time
divided into sub-groups

	Aspect of job					
	Promotion prospects	Total pay	Actual work	Hour of work	Job as a whole	N
Extent of job choice[a]						
some	6.22	7.07	8.42	8.85	8.74	257
no	5.50	6.35	7.64	8.35	7.91	424
difference	0.72[b]	0.72[b]	0.78[b]	0.50[b]	0.83[b]	
Own and job qualification[c]						
same	5.90	6.80	8.10	8.70	8.40	315
overqualified	5.20	6.60	7.30	7.90	7.60	174
difference	0.70[b]	0.20	0.80[b]	0.80[b]	0.80[b]	
Age						
20-29	4.77	6.29	7.33	8.04	7.63	115
30-39	5.66	6.50	7.81	8.40	8.27	276
40-49	6.05	6.84	8.23	8.74	8.39	210
50-59	6.54	6.98	8.44	8.96	8.69	143

[a]'a great deal of' and 'some choice' were grouped together as first group; 'hardly any' and 'no choice' were grouped as the second group.
[b]difference significant at $p \leq 0.05$ level.
[c]those who were under-qualified for their jobs were not considered here as our focus is on the possible negative effect of the discrepancy between the qualification a worker has and the type of job she gets.

Table 7.5d shows that part-time workers who had a restricted range of choice were less satisfied with their jobs, as compared to those who had some choice, whether in terms of each of the specific aspects or with the job taken as a whole. It can be noted that the gap between those who had no choice and those who had some choice was widest in terms of the job as a whole. Likewise, part-time workers who were over-qualified for their jobs were also less satisfied with each of the specific aspects or with the job as a whole. The difference is greatest for the actual work itself and the hours of work. Age and the level of job satisfaction were negatively related to each other. The younger the worker, the less satisfied she was either with any one of the four aspects of her job, or with the job as a whole. It is worth noting that female part-timers who were in their 20s were particularly dissatisfied with the promotion prospects which their jobs offered, as compared to the other age groups.

In terms of job satisfaction, the findings indicate that part-timers were generally more satisfied with their jobs, as compared to women who worked full-time. However, a more detailed investigation reveals that there were variations among the part-time workforce, which suggests that the self-selection argument overlooks the heterogeneity of the part-time workforce. The evidence we have indicates that part-timers who were in their 20s, those who said they had a limited range of choice, and those who were over-qualified for their jobs were less satisfied with the specific employment conditions or with the job as a whole.

Another notable point that arises from the analysis is the different levels of satisfaction with individual aspects of the job. Part-timers may well have a preference for a reduced number of hours of work so that more time can be allocated to other life domains. This preference is evident in the high level of satisfaction with the hours they worked across all age groups and whether they said they had any choices over the type of jobs which they could get. However, the lower levels of satisfaction with pay, promotion prospects, and the actual work itself indicate that a preference for a reduced number of working hours does not then follow that they were indifferent to the adverse employment conditions which their jobs offered. Choosing a job with the working hours which they desired does not imply that part-timers also preferred the employment conditions which employers ascribe to jobs with shorter weekly working hours. The lower satisfaction level of those part-timers who were in their 20s and those who were over-qualified for their jobs suggests that in taking up jobs which had the hours of work they preferred, these part-timers were at the same time limited by employers' labour use policies which differentiate the employment conditions of part-time and full-time work as a cost-saving measure.

These workers may well be trading off better employment conditions for the hours of work which they preferred.[12]

In the earlier discussion, it was pointed out that to the extent that part-timers matched the level of their wage work participation with the preferences and priorities which they gave to other spheres of life activities, they would have a higher level of satisfaction with these life spheres. To examine this proposition, we can turn to the Household and Community Survey which asked respondents their levels of satisfaction with various life domains.

In the Household and Community Survey, a sub-sample of the original respondents in the main survey were asked to rate their level of satisfaction with : (1) their social life; (2) the amount of leisure time they had; (3) their family life; (4) their present arrangements for dividing up or sharing the work around the house on a ten-point scale. The average levels of satisfaction of full-timers and part-timers with each of these four items are shown in Table 7.6.

Table 7.6
Mean levels of satisfaction with four spheres of life activities for working women

Working-hour status	Spheres of life activities[a]				
	Social life	Amount of leisure time	Family life	Housework division	N
Full-timers	7.04	5.60	8.24	7.15	296
Part-timers	6.41	6.57	8.38	6.90	217
difference	0.63**	0.83**	0.06	0.25*	

Difference significant at 0.1(*) level and 0.05(**) level; [a]a higher figure means a higher level of satisfaction

The findings shown in Table 7.6 do not fit well with the proposition that female part-timers were more contented than their full-time counterparts with their involvement in life domains outside the workplace. While part-timers were indeed more satisfied with the amount of leisure time they had and with their family life as compared to their full-time counterparts, they were, however, less satisfied with

203

their social life and with the way housework was divided within their household. To identify the source of dissatisfaction with their social life is outside the scope of this Chapter. For our present concern, the evidence available to us does not lend consistent support to the self-selection argument about part-timers matching their wage work participation with their preference for domestic life.

Conclusion

In this Chapter, various types of work attitudes of part-timers were examined. The central focus was on the extent to which women's participation in part-time work can be explained as an outcome of self-selection. In the first section, the analyses show that personal factors had a significant effect on employment commitment, while the labour market constraints or opportunities associated with the job did not play a significant role. The findings about the motive to work suggest that to characterize part-timers as driven primarily by the financial incentives of wage employment is too simplistic a description and overlooks some of the intrinsic and expressive values which they attached to employment. In terms of attitudes towards gender role, part-timers were more traditional than full-timers.

The last section of this Chapter turned to the issue of job satisfaction and life satisfaction. While part-timers were generally more satisfied with their jobs than were full-timers, there were variations in terms of specific aspects of the job. Part-timers were most satisfied with their hours of work but less contented with the promotion prospects and the total pay. Moreover, the dissatisfaction among over-qualified and young part-timers suggest that it is unwarranted to claim that part-time work participation can be fully explained by a set of work attitudes which accord low priority to wage work and hence a lower level of expectation. To assess the attitudinal effect and the opportunities or constraints which the labour market engenders for women, an analysis which takes into consideration both sets of factors is needed. The next Chapter will deal with labour market participation in a more comprehensive manner.

Notes

1   This meaning of employment commitment is, as pointed out by Rose (1988), subsumed under the general rubric of work ethic. It is not my intention here to give a full discussion and empirical study of work

ethic. My focus is narrower. My concern is to distinguish organizational commitment which is dependent on the actual work conditions in a specific employing organization from employment commitment which is relatively a more general attitude and less contingent on the organizational context.

2   See Bielby (1992) for a review of the recent works which adopt this line of conception.

3   In a more recent survey, Gallie and his associates found that employment commitment was positively related to the amount of effort which unemployed people spent in job-search. See Gallie et al.(1994).

4   See Lincoln and Kalleberg (1990) for a discussion of the concept organizational commitment and an empirical study of Japanese and American workers.

5   It needs to be stated here the analysis that follows is not to trace a causal relation between employment commitment, self-selection in part-time work, and job and family life satisfaction. The attempt undertaken here is to examine whether full-timers and part-timers differ from each other in the way suggested by the self-selection argument. To establish a definitive test for the self-selection argument, the best research strategy is a panel study of the way employment commitment earlier in life affects subsequent labour market participation and employment opportunities by following individuals over a considerable period of time, say, from the time they are in the last stage of their schooling up to the time when they are in their mature adult life. For an example of such a study, see Shaw (1983).

6   This question, in slightly different wording, is widely used in similar studies both in Britain and in America. For a review of results of studies in Britain and America, see Hakim (1991). For examples of ways to operationalize employment commitment, see Kanungo (1982), Lodahl and Kejner (1965), Yankelovitch et al. (1983).

7   Other studies also recorded that women were less likely to be committed than men. See Warr (1982), Andrisani (1978), Hakim (1991) and Gallie et al. (1994).

8   In their intensive interview with groups of part-timers, Watson

and Fothergil (1993) also found that part-timers were motivated by the expressive and the intrinsic values of wage work.

9   The exact wordings of the question are : 'I'd like you to imagine a married couple who are in two equally good jobs. The husband got offered a still better job, but it means leaving the district. From this card, what, in your opinion, is the right thing for the wife to do?'

10   With cross-sectional data, we cannot assess whether it is the husband's attitudes that shape the wife's work orientation, or vice versa. The third possibility is assortive mating, that is, men and women who have similar attitudes are more likely to get married and stay together, whereas couples whose viewpoints are irreconcilable are more likely to split up. The best we can do here is to examine the way the affinity between the two varies according to the wife's working-hour status as suggested by Hakim.

11   Similar results were found in a recent cross-national study of job satisfaction of male and female workers in a number of countries. See Curtice (1993).

12   In the Hours of Works of Women and Men in Britain Survey, it was found that compared to men and women working full-time, women working part-time were more likely to say that they would like to choose a job with longer hours and more pay if they were to look for another job at the same hourly rate of pay (Marsh, 1991:75-76).

8 Part-time work participation II : a full assessment

In the last Chapter, it was argued that an explanation for part-time work participation which is premised on attitudes towards wage work and gender roles is not adequate. The opportunities and constraints engendered by the labour market also need to be considered. In this Chapter, women's participation in part-time work will be analysed in a more comprehensive way. While the focus of this Chapter is still the full-time/part-time distinction, this has to be put into the wider context of women's labour market participation. Thus, in addition to these two employment statuses, the status of non-participation will also be considered.

This Chapter is divided into three parts. In the first part, existing studies of female labour market participation in Britain will be reviewed briefly as they have already been covered in greater detail in Chapter one. The different emphases of these studies will be noted and the way the present one attempts to deal with the issue in a more appropriate way will be discussed. We shall then examine the specific hypotheses which can be drawn from the different theories about women's wage work participation. Alongside with these hypotheses, some bivariate analyses will be presented. In the third part, these hypotheses will be tested through a multivariate analysis.

Existing studies of British female labour market participation

Generally speaking, existing studies of the labour market participation of British women can be classified into two types. The first type analyzes data at the aggregate level. These studies seek to explain the trend of female labour market participation over time. The aim is often to detect systematic changes over time and the way these changes are related to relevant aggregate trends. For example, the study of Joshi and her associates (1985) addressed the secular increase of female labour supply over time. They tried to associate the trend with changes in fertility, unemployment rates and real hourly earnings. Rubery and Tarling (1988) examined the cyclical nature of women's employment in relation to the general economic recession and the expansion of service industries. They analysed aggregate data at the sectoral and the industrial level. Likewise, Mallier and Rosser (1987) used census data to examine the industrial distribution of female employment between 1951 and 1981. They found that the change was a secular increase and not of a cyclical nature. It was pointed out in Chapter one that studies of this type can give a general picture of trends of female participation in wage work. However, they do not address the heterogeneity of the female population. Women differ from each other in terms of their levels of formal qualification, their life-cycle stages, their household conditions and their age, etc. Analyses using aggregate data mask the variation in the extent of labour force participation among women.

The question of population heterogeneity is the focus of the second type of female labour market participation studies. These studies analyze data at the individual level. They treat participation in the labour market as an individual decision which involves economic calculation. The analysis is focused on the way the decision is affected by costs and benefits of various kinds, for example, the tax structure, the real or potential wage rate the woman can get from wage work, the income of the husband, the age structure of children etc. The decision is examined as a process of calculation of the benefits from wage work balanced against its costs (e.g. income tax) and the gains derivable from other sources of income (e.g. welfare benefits). Much interest is placed on the labour supply decision of married women. In these studies, the dependent variable usually takes a dichotomous form : whether to participate or not; economically active versus inactive; or in an aggregated form of annual working hours. The effects of a range of dependent variables are mostly estimated by means of linear probability model (Layard et al. 1980; Greenhalgh, 1980, Dex, 1988). For working women, part-time status is generally not dealt with as a distinct form of labour market participation and not distinguished from full-time status except in more recent studies (Perry, 1990; Dale and Ward, 1992; McRae,1994).

In view of the expansion of the service sector, it is untenable to treat female labour force participation as a dichotomous choice. In Chapter three, we noted that retail and personal services establishments have a particularly heavy demand for part-time workers. Hence, women do not have only two choices : either to work full-time or not work at all. In a more realistic sense, participation on a part-time basis becomes a viable alternative to working full-time or not working.

As it was pointed out in Chapter one, aggregating working hours on an annual basis assumes that labour supply takes the form of a continuous curve. A unit increase in wage leads to a unit increase in the number of hours of work supplied by workers. Furthermore, the effect of a unit wage is regarded as uniform across every single unit hour of work, that is, every unit of wage increase will bring forth the same extent of increase in the labour supplied. This assumption implies that employers can vary their demand for labour freely. Likewise, workers can alter the amount of labour they want to supply at their own will. However, realistically, both employers and workers are generally unlikely to be able to choose freely the number of working hours they demand for and supply.

In Chapter three, it was pointed out that the recruitment, administration and training of staff involve a certain amount of fixed costs that vary on a per-person basis rather than a per-hour basis. Having many workers each working a few hours is likely to raise these fixed costs. Instead of designing and providing jobs hour by hour, employers are more likely to design and allocate jobs as discrete ranges of working hours. Likewise, the supply of working hours also involves fixed costs on the part of the worker, for example, transport cost. Thus, there are certain thresholds of wages below which workers would not supply any working hours at all. These fixed costs in labour demand and supply mean that wage work participation is more likely to be in the form of discrete hour ranges rather than unit hours.

It was mentioned in Chapter one that some recent empirical studies in economics have recognized that there are constraints which inhibit workers and employers to supply and demand for working hours freely. For example, the study of Arellano and Meghir (1988) used data from the British Family Expenditure Survey and found that there were constraints to the hours of work supplied by married women. These studies imply that labour power, in a realistic sense, cannot be supplied freely in terms of unit hours. To deal with women's labour market participation in a more satisfactory way, the dependent variable in the analysis of this Chapter will be treated as a categorical variable with three levels, namely, full-time, part-time and not working[1], rather than as a continuous one like the aggregated hours of work, or a binary dichotomous one like not working versus working.

The next three sections will discuss the different labour market theories about women's labour market participation. In each of these sections, the hypotheses that can be derived from these theories about current employment status will be discussed.

Labour market segmentation and part-time work participation

Gershuny and Marsh (1994) pointed out that the accumulated employment-rated characteristics of an individual would affect his or her future employment opportunities. Employers would use these accumulated experiences to judge the suitability of candidates for jobs. In the review of labour market theories in Chapter One, we have noted that while human capital theory does not distinguish different types of work experiences, segmentation theory recognizes the roles which cumulative (dis)advantages of previous work experiences play in shaping current employment prospects. These experiences, together with the barriers between labour market segments, have an inhibiting effect on workers' job choice. Jobs in the primary labour market involve firm-specific skills. The screening and training of workers to these jobs incur substantial costs for the employer. Despite the possible savings on wages which employers can make by opening these primary jobs to competition and frequent recruitment of outsiders, the costs associated with labour turnover and staff training discourage employers from doing so. Thus, incumbents of primary jobs are not subject to competition. They stand a better chance in holding onto their job rather than losing it to an outsider.[2] In other words, they enjoy an advantage over outsiders in the distribution of employment prospects in the primary labour market.

The disadvantages of outsiders in being recruited or allocated primary jobs would be made worse by working experience which does not enhance skills, or which only provides the most basic work skills. The analysis in Chapter three about employers' demand for part-time workers indicates that the prospects of part-timers in the labour market is limited by their employing organizations. Small firms in the private sector which had a particularly heavy demand for part-timers were much less likely to have upgraded their technology. In Chapter four, we noted that part-time jobs are low-skilled and are less likely to involve the use of modern technology. Workers who take up part-time jobs are unlikely to be able to acquire or accumulate productive work skills, or firm-specific skills. It can, therefore, be expected that greater experience in part-time work will not improve the worker's chance in securing good/primary jobs as there is no betterment of work skills. Instead, the greater the part-time work experience, the less likely that the worker would be able to secure jobs with favourable employment conditions. In other words, part-time work experience places women in a disadvantageous position in securing full-time jobs which have higher level of skills requirements and which involve the use of automated technology. Thus holding other factors constant, it can be hypothesized that the greater the previous part-time work experience, the lower the likelihood of getting a full-time rather than a part-time job.

Besides this constraining effect of previous part-time work experience on a worker's current labour market prospects, secondary labour market theory also argues that unemployment experience has a significant impact on employment prospects. The chance of getting a primary rather than a secondary job will be negatively affected by previous unemployment for two reasons. One is that the loss of a job denies a worker the opportunity of accumulating even the most basic and minimal job skills. The second reason is the attrition and obsolence of previous work skills during the period when they are unemployed. The longer the duration of unemployment, the more serious is the deterioration of previous work skills. This adverse effect together with the absence of formation of new skills means that those who are previously unemployed will be regarded by employers as unsuitable for primary job positions.[3] The chance of getting a job in the primary labour market segment diminishes as the duration of unemployment increases, and the greater is the likelihood of being recruited to a secondary job which is low-skilled. Thus, in applying the secondary labour market theory to part-time work, the second hypothesis that we want to test is : holding other factors constant, the longer the duration of previous unemployment, the more likely that a worker would be currently in part-time rather than full-time work.

Time spent being a housewife would also have a negative effect on the formation of work skills. While no new work skills are formed, those accumulated previously would become obsolete due to non-use. It is unlikely that employers would recruit workers with a prolonged period of non-participation to jobs which have a higher level of skills requirement, otherwise they would have to provide such recruits with training. Employers may consider such an investment not worth undertaking, especially if they regard housewives who return to the labour market after a long period of non-participation as less committed to wage work. Thus, in terms of getting a part-time rather than a full-time job, we can hypothesize that other things being equal, the greater the amount of time spent in domestic work, the more likely that a woman would get a part-time rather than a full-time job.

The main survey of SCELI collected the full work history of the respondent starting from the date he or she left full-time education. As described in Chapter two, the work history was collected on an event basis. Employment events were further classified into whether it was a self-employment, a full-time or a part-time employment spell. It is, therefore, possible to calculate the total amount of time which a woman has spent on part-time work ever since she entered the labour market. Likewise, the total amount of time during which a woman was unemployed, or when she was involved in unpaid domestic work, can also be enumerated. The way these previous work experience variables were derived has already been described in Chapter six.

As a preliminary analysis, the average amount of time spent in part-time work and unemployment was calculated for the whole female sample, and separately for current full-timers, part-timers and for those who were not working at the time of the interview. The female respondents of SCELI had had an average of 39 months of part-time work experience, 6 months of unemployment and 84 months of unpaid housework.[4,5] Those who were currently full-time workers had had an average of 23 months of part-time work and 44 months of unpaid domestic work. Those who were working part-time at the time of the interview had had 42 months of part-time work experience,[6] and 85 months of unpaid domestic work. Both current part-timers and full-timers had had four months of unemployment experience.

Since the respondents were at different ages when they were interviewed for the survey, a more appropriate way to measure time spent in different employment statuses is to convert the absolute number of months into percentages of their worklife in the same way as in Chapter six. Women who were working full-time at the time of the interview had spent an average of 8% of their worklife in part-time work, 3% being unemployed and 14% in unpaid domestic work. The similar figures for women who were working part-time are 14% for completed part-time work (30% if the current job tenure is included as well), 2% for unemployment and 29% for unpaid housework.

If we consider separately single and married women (whether in the *de facto* or the legal sense), the picture is very different for the two groups. Table 8.1 gives the average percentages of worklife spent in the three different employment statuses for current full-timers and part-timers by their marital status.

The involvement in part-time work and housework of single women is much lower than that of married women. In fact, 83% of the single women had not been a full-time housewife; 76% had not worked part-time before. Involvement in part-time work and unpaid housework was more prevalent among married women. Married women had had an average of five work events (full-time, part-time, self-employed and working on a government scheme alike). Of these five work events, 3.7 were full-time spells and 1.2 were part-time spells. On average, these women had interrupted their participation in paid work twice since they entered the labour market. Of these interruptions, 1.3 spells were unpaid housework and 0.43 spell was due to unemployment. Returning to full-time education was rarely a reason for interruption to wage work. Of all married women, 92% had never returned to full-time education after their entry into the labour market.[7] Unemployment was more common among single women than among married women. While 58% of the former had not experienced unemployment, this is the case for 74% of the latter. In the final multivariate analysis, we shall examine the whole female sample of SCELI, and then the married women sub-sample.

Table 8.1
Time spent in different employment statuses for current full-timers and part-timers

Work and non-work experience	Single women		Married women	
	FT	PT	FT	PT
part-time work as % of worklife	3	20*	10	14*
unemployment as % of worklife	4	6	3	2
unpaid housework as % of worklife	1.4	12	18	29
(N	234	11	785	668)

Keys : FT = full-time; PT = part-time
*the figure given here is calculated by subtracting the current job tenure from the total number of months spent in part-time work.

The preliminary analysis shown in Table 8.1 suggests that more time spent in part-time work and unpaid domestic housework is associated differently with the current full-time/part-time status. However, contrary to the proposition which we drew from segmentation theory, both full-timers and part-timers had only been unemployed for a fairly short duration.[8] Nevertheless, a formal test is needed to ascertain the effect of previous unemployment on the current employment status. We shall now turn to the relevant control variables which should be introduced into the test.

Formal qualification and labour market participation

The first crucial control variable which needs to be considered is formal qualification. The neo-classical approach regards job choice as a process of rational calculation. The worker balances the returns from wage work against the opportunity cost of non-participation and of engaging in other kinds of life activities. According to this approach, we can expect formal level of qualification to have a significant effect on woman's labour market participation.

In advanced industrial societies, the criteria for allocating rewards, in principle, is the achievement which an individual makes. A major kind of achievement is formal qualification. A higher level of formal qualification will be rewarded with a correspondingly high level of job rewards in the labour market. Women with a higher level of formal qualification will, therefore, bear a high opportunity cost by engaging in domestic work and not taking up wage work.

Furthermore, we can also expect that the formal qualification level will affect the choice between part-time and full-time job. According to the neo-classical approach, workers are assumed to have prior knowledge and perfect information about the amount and kinds of rewards which different jobs offer. They are also economistic, rational calculators. They will choose jobs which have a level of returns comparable to their own level of formal qualification. Chapters four and five show that part-time jobs were less well paid and less likely to offer promotion prospects, as compared to full-time ones. They were also more likely to be jobs which were subordinate job positions. Thus, it is unlikely that workers who had a higher level of formal qualification would choose part-time jobs. This is because the level of rewards and the organizational position of part-time jobs are not commensurate with the expected labour market values of their level of formal qualification. The economistic reasoning of job choice will, therefore, lead us to hypothesize that (1) the higher the level of formal qualification, the less likely that a worker will work part-time rather than full-time; (2) the higher the level of formal qualification, the more likely that a worker will be working rather than not working. Table 8.2 shows the distribution of employment status by the level of formal qualification.

It can be seen that more women who had higher education level (degree and non-degree alike) were working full-time rather than not working, as compared to women who did not have any formal qualifications, or women who had a vocational level of qualification. Similarly, fewer women who were degree-holders were in part-time work, as compared to women in all the other lower levels of qualification, except for those with an A-level qualification. It is also noticeable that there is a non-linear relation between the level of qualification and likelihood of being in the full-time, the part-time and the not working status. Women with non-degree higher education level are more likely than women with O-level or A-level qualification to be working part-time.

Table 8.2
Percentage distribution of employment status by level of formal qualification

Level of formal qualification	Employment status				
	Full-time	Part-time	Not working	Total	N
None	24	28	48	100	1,353
Vocational	33	22	45	100	205
O-level	38	23	39	100	726
A-Level	50	15	34	100	241
Non-degree higher education	50	28	22	100	255
Degree	55	16	29	100	251

Household conditions and woman's labour market participation

It was noted in Chapter four that in our sample, over 90% of part-timers were women. The distribution of the three employment statuses is also skewed in terms of the type of household in which they were living. For women who were in a partnership household, 31% were working full-time, 29% worked part-time and 40% were not working. For women who were not living with a male partner, the similar figures were 46%, 9% and 44%. In Chapter one, it was pointed out that the household is considered by new home economics as a crucial factor in shaping women's labour market participation. The basic ideas of new home economics with respect to female labour market participation have been outlined and will not be repeated in details here. The approach posits that the pattern of sexual division of labour in the household and the labour market participation of married women are decided through a process of cost-and-benefit calculation. It was pointed out that the approach neglects the part which norms prescribing the sex roles of men and women play in the explanation of the sexual division of labour.

In contrast to the new home economics approach, the functional approach considers the sexual division of labour as subject to normative constraints. The gender norms prescribe women's primary role in the family as childcarer and homemaker, and men as the wage earner. The wage earning activity of women is secondary to their domestic responsibilities. The approach further posits that the form of employment which women take up should not run into conflict with their gender role in the family, otherwise marital stability will be jeopardized and the proper functioning of the nuclear household would, in turn, be upset.[9]

Both the new home economics approach and the functional approach lead us to expect that a woman's work decision, especially that of a married woman, is shaped by her household's situation. Two crucial factors can be expected to affect the labour market participation of a married woman, namely, the presence of young children and the employment of the husband.

A significant determinant of women's labour market participation is childcare responsibility. The amount of time which a woman needs to devote to childcare varies according to the age of the child. Infants of pre-school age demand a great deal of care and hence the amount of time which a woman can devote to wage work is reduced. In the case of Britain, it is now well established that the age of a woman's youngest child is a major factor which influences her labour market participation (Joshi, 1984; Martin and Roberts, 1984). It has been argued that the constraining effect of childcare on female labour market participation is particularly strong in Britain as there is inadequate provision of public childcare service for pre-school child as compared to some of her European counterparts (Ruggie, 1983; Joshi and Davies, 1992; Briar, 1992; Dex, et al., 1993, Lane, 1993).[10] In Britain, schooling starts at the age of five. Women with children under five, therefore, have to shoulder more demanding childcare duties than women with older children or women not living with any children. A part-time job enables a woman to accommodate her wage work participation to her childcare duties. Thus, we will expect that women with pre-school children would be less likely to work, and if they work at all, they are more likely to work part-time rather than full-time, as compared to women with older children, or women without any children.

Besides their demand on women's time, children can also lead women to engage in wage work. Dependent children who are still below the school-leaving age are likely to be economically inactive and are financially dependent on their parents. Women with children under the age of 15 are, therefore, likely to take up employment to supplement the income of their husbands and to finance the household expenditure. We noted in Chapter four that part-time work is lower paid than full-time work. Hence, a woman who is released from heavy childcare duties and whose earnings are needed for household finance will choose to work full-time rather than part-time in order to maximize the use of their time.

Thus, with regard to the age of the youngest child in the household, we can hypothesize that : (1) the likelihood of engaging in housework rather than wage work diminishes with an increase in the age of the youngest child in the household; (2) the likelihood of working full-time rather than part-time rises with an increase in the age of the youngest child. Table 8.3 shows the distribution of employment status by the presence and the age of the youngest child in the household.

Table 8.3
Percentage distribution of employment status
by the presence and age of the youngest child

Presence and age of youngest child	Employment status				
	Full-time	Part-time	Not working	Total	N
Child below 5	11	22	67	100	675
Child 5 - 15	27	35	38	100	851
Child above 15	37	31	32	100	523
Living with partner no children	55	16	29	100	600
Single no children	76	4	20	100	383

It can be seen readily that women whose youngest child was under five were least likely to be working full-time and most likely to be not working. Compared to this group of women, mothers with school children were more likely to be working part-time rather than full-time, and less likely to be not working at all. The higher percentage of women in this category who worked part-time can be related to the short school-days in Britain and the shortage of after-school care. Hence, the wage work participation of women with school children was still constrained by their childcare duty, although it was less time-consuming and onerous than the kind which pre-school children need. For women who had minimal childcare duties or not living with any children, that is, the last two categories in Table 8.3, they were more likely to be in full-time work, less likely to be part-time workers or not working at all, as compared to women whose youngest child was of pre-school age.

Besides the childcare factor, the employment of husbands (or male partners) can be another crucial predictor of women's labour market participation. Women married to men who are in professional and managerial occupations are less likely to have to work for economic reasons. Wives of men who are in occupations which offer lower income and poorer employment security may need to take up paid work to supplement the earnings of their husbands. Thus, women whose husbands are semi-/unskilled manual workers would be more likely to work, as compared to women whose husbands are in professional and managerial occupations. And if wives of semi-/unskilled manual workers work at all, they are likely to work full-time rather than part-time due to economic necessity. Here, we shall continue to use the Goldthorpe class schema for classifying the occupation of the husband. Table 8.4a gives the distribution of married women's employment status by the class position to which their husbands' (or male partners) occupations belonged.

Table 8.4a indicates that over half of the wives married to men in each of the seven classes were working, either full-time or part-time, rather than not working. A greater proportion of the wives of class I and II men were not working, as compared to women married to men in other classes. Wives of semi-/unskilled manual workers were more likely to be working part-time rather than not working, as compared to women who were married to class I and II men. However, the percentage distribution between full-time and part-time work does not vary in such a way that wives of working-class husbands were more likely than the wives of service class husbands to work full-time rather than part-time. For instance, women who were married to technicians were more likely to be working part-time rather than full-time, as compared to women married to men in other classes. Wives of husbands who were in the routine non-manual class were more likely to be working full-time rather than part-time, as compared to wives of husbands in other classes.

Table 8.4a
Percentage distribution of employment status by
class of husband (or male partner)

Husband's class	Employment status				
	Full-time	Part-time	Not working	Total	N
Higher grade service class	34	26	40	100	343
Lower grade service class	35	29	36	100	387
Routine non-manual	39	29	32	100	114
Small proprietors	32	29	39	100	239
Technicians	34	38	27	100	130
Skilled manual	31	35	34	100	385
Semi-/unskilled manual	35	31	33	100	438

While the findings about husbands' occupations do not seem to lend support to the proposition which we can derive from the new home economics approach, we need also to take into account another factor, namely, the unemployment of the husband, to ascertain fully the effect of the husband's employment on the wife's labour market participation. An absence of earnings for the household due to husband's unemployment would prompt the wife to take up wage work because of financial necessity. In our sample, 6% of the female sample were living with an unemployed male partner at the time of the interview. Their participation rate in wage work, as compared to those women whose male partner was employed or self-employed, is shown in Table 8.4b.

The percentage distribution shown in Table 8.4b does not lend support to the hypothesis that the unemployment of the husband would lead to a greater likelihood of the labour market participation of the wife. Instead, women married to an unemployed husband were more likely to be not working rather than working full-time or part-time.

Table 8.4b

Percentage distribution of employment status by the employment status of male partner

Women's employment status	Employment status of male partner not unemployed	unemployed
Full-time	33	10
Part-time	30	15
Not working	37	75
Total	100%	100%
(N	2,177	196)

The bivariate analysis here is in line with a number of previous studies which have noted the negative effect of the husband's unemployment on the wife's labour market participation (Moylan et al. 1984; Layard et al. 1980). Previous studies have noted that there are disincentives which may well offset the 'added-worker' effect. In her case studies of households with unemployed husbands, Morris (1984) found that the ideology of men being the main bread-winner of the family discouraged the wives of these unemployed husbands from taking up wage work. Similarly, Barrere-Maurisson and her associates (1985), McKee and Bell (1985) found in their studies that the traditional idea of men being the wage-earner for the family discouraged wives of unemployed husbands to take up wage work. Kell and Wright (1990) used cross-sectional information from the 1983 Family Expenditure Survey and the Labour Force Survey and argued that the entitlement to social security benefits, and to supplementary benefits in particular, were severe disincentives in the labour supply of a wife whose husband was unemployed. Davies and his associates (1994) used the work history data of SCELI and noted that the longer the unemployment duration of the husband, the less likely that the wife would be in wage work. They concluded that the extent to which this was the result of the benefits system or of the influences associated with the gender roles of husbands and wives remained unresolved. However, in their analysis of the wife's labour market participation, part-time work was not distinguished from full-time work. The dependent variable in their analysis takes the form of a dichotomy of in paid employment or not in paid employment.[11] In our multivariate analysis of labour market participation, the wife's attitudes towards the sexual division of labour will be assessed together with the husband's employment status.

Gender norms and women's labour market participation

We saw in the last Chapter that attitudes towards the sexual division of labour had a significant effect on the employment commitment of working women. The analysis of the different indicators showed that part-timers were more likely than full-timers to hold a traditional attitude towards the sexual division of labour. In this section, the analysis will be extended to include non-working women. To the extent that norms are internalized and have a guiding effect on behaviours, a woman's labour market participation would be affected by her attitudes towards the sexual division of labour.[12]

A variable is derived from the two statements about attitudes towards the sexual division of labour which were examined in the last Chapter. To facilitate the following discussion, it is necessary to restate the two statements. They are (1) in times of high unemployment, married women should stay at home and (2) I'm not against women working but men should still be the main breadwinner in the family. According to whether they disagreed with, agreed with or did not hold strong opinion towards these two statements, respondents were classified into three groups. Those who agreed with the two statements were classified as traditional, those who did not have strong opinion were considered as neutral, and those who disagreed with the two statements were regarded as egalitarian. The distribution of employment status by these three types of sex role attitudes is given in Table 8.5a.

Table 8.5a
Percentage distribution of employment status by attitudes towards the sexual division of labour

Employment Status	Attitude towards the sexual division of labour		
	egalitarian (%)	neutral (%)	traditional (%)
Full-time	46	41	27
Part-time	19	25	27
Not working	35	32	45
Total	100	100	100
(N	1,011	234	1,786)

From Table 8.5a, it can be seen that a traditional attitude is associated with a greater likelihood of not working rather than working full-time or part-time. Compared to women who held a traditional attitude, those who held an egalitarian attitude were more likely to be working than not working, and if they worked, they were more likely to work full-time rather than part-time.

In the previous Chapter, we noted that both the woman's own attitudes and her husband's viewpoints about who should have the ultimate responsibility towards housework, income-earning and childcare were closely associated with the woman's working-hour status. Unfortunately, the questions regarding these three items were only asked in the Household and Community Survey. We are not able to include these attitudinal factors as an independent variable in the final multivariate analysis for the female sample of the main survey of SCELI. Nevertheless, it is still useful to extend the analysis to women who were not working at the time of the Household and Community Survey. This will enable us to examine in greater details the relation between sex role attitudes and labour market participation. We shall first deal with the relation between the woman's own attitude and her employment status.

Table 8.5b shows that women who held a traditional attitude towards the sexual division of labour were more likely to be not working, as compared to women who were held an egalitarian attitude. For instance, 49% of those respondents who thought women should be responsible for housework were not working, while 35% of those who held an egalitarian attitude were not working. And among those women who considered wage-earning as men's ultimate responsibility, 51% were not working, as compared to 27% of those women who thought both men and women were equally responsible for bringing money into the family.

In terms of the full-time/part-time distinction, women who held a traditional attitude were more likely to be working part-time rather than full-time. For instance, 31% of those respondents who considered that housework should be shouldered by women were in part-time work; amongst women who regarded that housework should be shared equally between men and women, 22% were working part-time. Similarly, women who were traditional about their childcare and wage-earning role in the household were more likely to be in part-time rather than full-time work, as compared to women who held an egalitarian attitude.

Table 8.5b
**Percentage distribution of women's employment status by their own
attitudes towards sex role**

Own attitudes	Women's employment status				
	FT	PT	Not working	Total	(N)
who should be responsible for housework					
man (%)	-	-	-	-	- *
woman (%)	20	31	49	100	(415)
both (%)	48	22	29	99	(194)
who should be responsible for family's income					
man (%)	17	32	51	100	(331)
woman (%)	-	-	-	-	- *
both (%)	46	27	27	100	(254)
who should be responsible for childcare					
man (%)	-	-	-	-	- *
woman (%)	15	29	56	100	(164)
both (%)	28	33	38	99	(290)

Keys : FT = full-time; PT = part-time
*absolute N fewer than 30.

With respect to the husband's attitudes towards the sex role of men
and women, cross-tabulations shows that this is also closely related to
the wife's extent of wage work participation. Table 8.5c gives the
percentage distribution of the three employment statuses at the time of
the Household and Community Survey by the husband's attitudes
towards the same three items examined in Table 8.5b.

It can be seen that wives of husbands who held an egalitarian
attitude towards the sharing of housework were more likely to be
working full-time rather than part-time or not working, as compared to
respondents whose husbands thought women should bear the ultimate
responsibility of housework. Similarly, those respondents whose
husbands considered that both men and women should be wage-earners
for the family were more likely to be working full-time rather than

part-time or not working, as compared to women whose male partners held a traditional attitude. A similar percentage distribution can be noted for the partner's attitude towards who should be responsible for childcare.[13] The findings shown in Table 8.5c indicates that generally speaking, the more traditional the attitude of the husband, the lower the extent of wage work participation of the wife.

Table 8.5c
Percentage distribution of women's employment status by their partner's attitudes towards sex role

Male partner's attitude	Women's employment status				
	FT	PT	Not working	Total	(N)
who should be responsible for housework					
man (%)	-	-	-	-	-*
woman (%)	25	29	45	99	(428)
both (%)	38	24	36	98	(100)
who should be responsible for family's income					
man (%)	19	30	51	100	(386)
woman (%)	-	-	-	-	-*
both (%)	47	25	26	98	(211)
who should be responsible for childcare					
man (%)	-	-	-	-	-*
woman (%)	16	34	50	100	(136)
both (%)	28	30	41	99	(325)

Keys : FT = full-time; PT = part-time
*absolute N less than 30.

Although we are not able to include these attitudinal factors about who should have ultimate responsibilities towards wage-earning, childcare and housework in the final multivariate analysis, cross-tabular analyses show that the wife's own attitudes towards these three items are related closely to whether she agreed or disagreed with the statement that men should be the main bread-winner for the family which was covered in the main survey. Women who thought men should bear the ultimate responsibility of wage-earning for the family were more likely to agree that men should be the main breadwinner in the family than not. Women who considered housework and childcare as the duties of wives were also more likely to agree with the statement than not. Conversely, women who thought that childcare and wage-earning responsibilities should be shared between husbands and wives were more likely to disagree with the statement that men should be the main breadwinner for the family than not. Thus, the variable derived from the two statements asked in the main survey would enable us to capture the effect of the attitudes towards the sexual division of labour tapped in the Household and Community Survey.

Testing the three sets of hypotheses

In this section, a multivariate analysis is conducted to test the hypotheses which were derived in the preceding sections by means of multinomial logit regression. In the analysis, there are three possible pairwise comparisons, namely, full-time versus part-time; full-time versus not working; part-time versus not working. The question whether, after taking into account the effect of formal qualification, the childcare responsibility and the attitude towards the sexual division of labour, previous part-time work and non-working experiences still have significant effects on the odds of currently being in part-time rather than full-time work. Two analyses were conducted, one for the whole female sample, and the other one for the subsample of married women. In the latter, the husband's employment was included.

The results of the regression for both the whole female sample and the married women sub-sample are shown in Table 8.6a, 8.6b and 8.6c.

The Null Model in Table 8.6a simply means that the odds of being in full-time work versus part-time work, full-time work versus not working, and part-time work versus not working do not depend on any factors. When the qualification factor and childcare factor are included into the model, the reduction in the scaled deviance and the corresponding decrease in the degrees of freedom show that both are significant in affecting the odds ratios in each of the three pairwise comparisons. In the married women subsample, the husband's employment is also included. This predictor is a composite variable which is derived from both the class position of the husband's occupation and his unemployed/employed status.

Table 8.6a
Multinomial logistic regression for employment status

Model	For all women				For married women			
	G^2	df	rG^2	rdf	G^2	df	rG^2	rdf
Null model	6916	6296	-	-	4855	4420	-	-
+qualification	6564	6284	353	12	4725	4408	131	12
+ childcare	5973	6276	590	8	4361	4402	363	6
+ partners' employment	-	-	-	-	4270	4392	91	10
+gender attitude	5919	6272	54	4	4214	4388	55	4
+part-time work experience	5825	6270	67	2	4167	4386	47	2
+unemployment	5849	6268	3	2	4167	4384	0.26	2
+housework experience*	5663	6268	188	2	3982	4384	185	2

Keys :

G^2 = scaled deviance

rG^2 = reduction in scaled deviance by the addition of one more predictor

df = degrees of freedom

rdf = reduction in the degrees of freedom by the addition of one more predictor

*this term is added after the unemployment factor is taken out of the model

Finally, after all these factors are included, part-time work experience, unemployment duration and housework expressed as continuous variables are added to this model one after the other. The decrease in the scaled deviance and the corresponding drop in the degrees of freedom suggest that while previous part-time work experience significantly affects the current employment status, the unemployment factor does not give a better fitted model.[14] This term is taken out of the model and the housework factor is included into the model. As indicated by the decrease in the scaled deviance and the corresponding drop in the degrees of freedom, this factor is also significant. The estimates of the parameters are shown in Table 8.6b and 8.6c.

Since the focus is on the full-time/part-time comparison, the additive estimates of the first column section in Table 8.6b and 8.6c are exponentiated to give the multiplicative estimates (that is, the odds ratios). The results are shown in Table 8.6d.

Part-time versus full-time comparison

For both the full female sample and the married women sub-sample, the results show that the level of formal qualification affects the probability of working part-time rather than full-time. When the estimates are exponentiated to give the multiplicative estimates, we can see that the higher the level of qualification, the lower the odds for working part-time rather than full-time. For the full female sample, a degree level of qualification reduces the odds of being in a part-time rather than a full-time job by a factor of 0.35, relative to the absence of any formal qualification. An A-level qualification also reduces the odds of working part-time rather than full-time by a factor of 0.40. In the married women model, the figures are 0.29 and 0.37 respectively.

It is also noticeable that the negative relation between educational level and the likelihood of working part-time rather than full-time is a non-linear one. In the full female sample, the negative effect of non-degree higher level of qualification is lower than that of the other four levels except for the vocational level.

227

Table 8.6b
Parameter estimates and standard errors of the model for all women

Parameter	Full-time vs part-time		Full-time vs not working		Part-time vs not working	
	S.E.	Estimate	S.E.	Estimate	S.E.	Estimate
Constant	0.07	-0.027	0.06	0.64	0.06	0.62
Formal qualification						
no qualification	-	-	-	-	-	-
vocational	0.23	-0.197	0.19	-0.581	0.21	-0.385
O-level	0.13	-0.424*	0.12	-0.744*	0.13	-0.320*
A-level	0.23	-0.921*	0.18	-0.988*	0.23	-0.066
non-degree	0.18	-0.276	0.18	-1.49*	0.20	-1.214*
higher education degree	0.22	-1.038*	0.17	-1.291*	0.23	-0.253
Presence and age of youngest child						
below 5	-	-	-	-	-	-
5 - 15 years old	0.18	-1.041*	0.16	-1.650*	0.14	-0.609*
above 15	0.19	-1.711*	0.17	-2.293*	0.16	-0.582*
married no child	0.19	-2.090*	0.16	-2.458*	0.16	-0.368*
single	0.32	-3.586*	0.17	-2.575*	0.30	1.010*

(continued)

228

Table 8.6b (continued)

Parameter	Full-time vs part-time		Full-time vs not working		Part-time vs not working	
	S.E.	Estimate	S.E.	Estimate	S.E.	Estimate
Attitudes towards gender role						
egalitarian	-	-	-	-	-	-
neutral	0.21	0.304	0.17	0.160	0.21	-0.144
traditional	0.12	0.664*	0.10	0.653*	0.12	-0.011*
Previous work experience						
% of worklife completed in part-time work	0.003	0.023	0.003	-0.0028	0.003	-0.026*
% of worklife being housewife	0.002	0.021*	0.002	-0.0121*	0.002	-0.033*

*denotes significant at <0.05 level, s.e. stands for standard error.

Table 8.6c

Parameter estimates and standard errors of the model for married women

Parameter	Full-time vs part-time		Full-time vs not working		Part-time vs not working	
	S.E.	Estimate	S.E.	Estimate	S.E.	Estimate
Constant	0.08	0.25	0.53	0.079	0.07	0.281
Formal qualification						
no qualification	-	-	-	-	-	-
vocational	0.26	-0.379	0.24	-0.534*	0.25	-0.155
O-level	0.15	-0.334	0.15	-0.453*	0.15	-0.119
A-level	0.26	-0.994*	0.24	-0.882*	0.27	0.112
non-degree higher education	0.21	-0.142	0.23	-1.119*	0.23	-0.977*
degree	0.25	-1.24*	0.23	-1.282*	0.27	-0.042
Presence and age of youngest child						
below 5	-	-	-	-	-	-
5 - 15 years old	0.19	-0.984*	0.19	-1.561	0.15	-0.576*
above 15	0.21	-1.664*	0.20	-2.291*	0.18	-0.626*
no child	0.21	-2.177*	0.18	-2.526*	0.18	-0.349*

(continued)

Table 8.6c (continued)

Parameter	Full-time vs part-time		Full-time vs not working		Part-time vs not working	
	S.E.	Estimate	S.E.	Estimate	S.E.	Estimate
Male partner's class						
service	-	-	-	-	-	-
routine non-manual	0.28	-0.122	0.28	-0.455	0.29	-0.332
small proprietors	0.21	-0.306	0.20	-0.149	0.21	0.157
technicians/skilled manual workers	0.16	0.041	0.16	-0.302	0.16	-0.344*
semi-/unskilled workers	0.17	-0.194	0.17	-0.424*	0.17	-0.23
unemployed	0.33	0.207	0.28	1.476*	0.25	1.269*
Attitudes towards gender role						
egalitarian	-	-	-	-	-	-
neutral	0.23	0.251	0.23	0.396	0.25	0.144
traditional	0.13	0.745*	0.13	0.892*	0.14	0.148
Previous work experience						
% of worklife completed in part-time work	0.004	0.017*	0.004	-0.011	0.004	-0.027*
% of worklife spent as housewife	0.003	0.02*	0.003	-0.018	0.003	-0.038*

*denotes significant at 0.05 level.

Table 8.6d

Multiplicative estimates for part-time versus full-time

Variables	For all women	For married women
Formal Qualification		
no qualification	1	1
vocational	0.82	0.68
O-level	0.65	0.72
A-level	0.40	0.37
non-degree higher education	0.76	0.87
University degree	0.35	0.29
Presence and age of the youngest child		
below 5	1	1
5 - 15 years old	0.35	0.37
above 15	0.18	0.19
married no child	0.12	0.11
single no child	0.03	-
Male partner's class		
service	-	1
routine non-manual	-	0.88
small proprietor	-	0.74
technicians & skilled manual	-	1.04
semi-/unskilled manual	-	0.82
partner was unemployed	-	1.23
Attitude towards gender role		
egalitarian	1	1
neutral	1.36	1.28
traditional	1.94	2.10
Previous work experience		
% of worklife in PT work	1.023	1.017
% of worklife spent as housewife	1.021	1.021

In the married women sample, the negative effect of a non-degree higher education level were also lower than the other levels. This may be because, in our case, the nursing qualification is classified as non-degree higher education qualification. In our sample, 67% of those women who had a non-degree higher education qualification held a nursing qualification. We have noted in Chapter four that a sizeable proportion of part-timers were in the lower grade professional and managerial class into which the nursing profession was classified. This may explain why there is a non-linear negative relation between formal qualification level and the likelihood of working part-time rather than full-time.

Table 8.6d shows that women without any children, whether living with their husbands (or male partners) or single, were much less likely to be working part-time rather than full-time, compared to women whose youngest child was of pre-school age. Being single reduced the odds of working part-time rather than full-time by a factor of 0.03, as compared to women with pre-school children in the full female sample. In the married women sample, the presence of a child who was beyond school age reduces the odds of working part-time rather than full-time by a factor of 0.19, relative to women whose youngest child was below five.

The attitude towards the sexual division of labour is also in line with the earlier discussion. A traditional attitude towards the sexual division of labour raises the odds of working part-time rather than full-time by a factor of 1.94 in the full female sample and a factor of 2.1 in the married women sample, as compared to an egalitarian attitude.

The results for the married women sample show that the class to which the husband's occupation belonged does not have a significant effect on the odds of working full-time or part-time. Nor does the presence of an unemployed husband raise the likelihood of full-time participation. The 'added-worker' hypothesis is not supported by our findings here. However, the same factor has a different effect in the other two pairwise comparisons. We shall come onto this in the next section.

Finally, after holding all these factors constant, the results for the proportion of worklife spent in part-time work and in housework are in line with the two hypotheses which we derived from the secondary labour market theory. Previous part-time work experience had a channelling effect on the current job of women. In both the model for the full female sample and for the married women sub-sample, a greater proportion of worklife spent previously in part-time work increased the odds of currently being in part-time rather than full-time work. In the full female sample, it raises the odds by a factor of 1.023, and in the married women sub-sample, it raised the odds by a factor of 1.017. This indicates that part-time work carries a cumulative depressing effect on the labour market position of women. More part-time work experience raised the chance of remaining in a part-time rather than getting a full-time job. A similar penalty also arises from a total withdrawal from the labour market as evident in the negative effect of time spent in unpaid domestic housework. A greater proportion of worklife spent being a home-maker raised the odds of being in part-time rather than full-time work by a factor of 1.021.

Full-time versus not working and part-time versus not working comparison

As our focus is on the full-time/part-time comparison, the discussion of the other two pairs of comparison will be brief. Our findings support the hypothesis about the effect of formal qualification on labour market participation. The more educated the woman, the less likely that she was not working rather than working full-time. A degree or non-degree qualification reduces the odds of not working rather than working full-time or part-time, as compared to the lack of any formal qualification.

The childcare factor has a significant effect on labour force participation. The absence of a pre-school child reduces the odds of not working rather than working, whether full-time or part-time, with the exception of single women in the part-time/not working comparison. Being single raises the odds of not working rather than working part-time, as compared to mothers with a pre-school child. This is related to the job-seeking preference of single women who self-identified themselves as unemployed and were classified as not working in our analysis. The information about the job-seeking behaviour of the unemployed suggests that part-time job is unlikely to be option which single unemployed women would prefer. In the main survey of SCELI, those who self-identified themselves as unemployed were asked whether they had been looking for a job in the previous four weeks, and if so, whether they had been looking for only full-time, part-time or either type of work. Over half of the unemployed women who had been looking for a job said they were looking for a full-time job, 27% said they were looking for part-time work, 18% said either. More detailed examination of the job-seeking behaviour of the unemployed is needed to unravel the reasons why part-time work was unpopular among the unemployed. The analysis of Gallie and Vogler (1994) provided some evidence about the job-search orientation of the unemployed which helps explain the unpopularity of part-time work. Among the factors which they found to be significant in affecting the extent to which unemployed people were prepared to be flexible regarding the pay which they could get, they noted that single unemployed women were less likely to accept jobs the pay of which was lower than the average for the currently employed in their occupational class, as compared to married women. We have noted in Chapter four that part-time jobs were less well-paid than full-time jobs. This may well make it an unpopular option for single unemployed women who were seeking for jobs.

Among married women, contrary to the 'added-worker' hypothesis, being married to an unemployed husband actually raises the odds of the wife not working rather than working, whether in full-time or part-time work, as compared to women whose husbands were in professional and managerial class. This is in line with other cross-sectional studies which recorded that wives of unemployed husbands were more likely to be not working rather than working.

Conclusion

This Chapter has attempted to examine part-time work participation of women. Our concern is, however, broader than the conventional study of female labour supply. Instead of focusing only on the ways the human capital factor, or the childcare responsibility, or the gender attitude shapes women's labour market participation, we have also attempted to deal with the cumulative effect of previous working and non-working experience on the current labour market position of women. Through a series of bivariate and multivariate analyses, the findings indicate (1) the labour market structure has a significant effect on women's relative chances in getting full-time rather than part-time work, after the individual's formal qualification, the childcare factor and the gender attitudes factors were controlled for; (2) the restrictive effect comes from previous part-time work and non-work experience and not from unemployment experience. The current labour market position is not only a result of the household condition or the attitudes towards gender role. It is also an outcome of previous work and non-work history of the woman. Our findings show that more part-time work experience has an inhibiting effect on the woman's chance of getting full-time rather than part-time work.[15]

Notes

1   The 'not-working' status for women includes women who self-defined themselves as unemployed. Of all the 386 single women in the sample, 18% self-defined themselves as unemployed. Over two-third of these unemployed women were looking for work in the previous four weeks, and 88% of them were claimants of unemployment benefits. Among married women, 5% out of 2,655

self-defined themselves as unemployed. Of these 5% 'unemployed' women, 59% of these women were looking for work and 62% were unemployment benefits recipients. To create separate employment status category for these women will give rise to complication and computational difficulty. Moreover, as our focus here is the differential likelihood of working full-time rather than part-time, we, therefore, treat those who self-defined themselves as unemployed together with those who engaged in unpaid domestic work as a single category.

2   For an exposition of this insider/outsider theory of employment, see Lindbeck and Snower (1988).

3   See Payne and Payne (1993) for a discussion of the chance of unemployed people in getting part-time work and the trend over the years by using the Labour Force Survey for 1979-89.

4   Morgenstern and Barrett (1974) used American data and noted that retrospective information on unemployment understated the true extent of female unemployment.

5   It was also suggested that the way in which previous unemployment spell was enumerated in the work history may have underestimated the extent of unemployment among women. In the main survey and the household/community survey of SCELI, for those who self-defined themselves as currently not working or unemployed, they were further asked whether they were looking for a job in the last four weeks and whether they were recipients of unemployment benefits or supplementary benefits on the ground of unemployment. However, respondents were not asked these two questions when they defined themselves as having experienced unemployment in the past in the collection of the work history data. It could be that there were periods when the respondent was looking for a job or claiming unemployment benefits, but not defining that event as unemployment. This calls for the development of more sensitive ways to measure unemployment in the collection of work history data in future researches. The inclusion of time spent in domestic work would be able to make up for any underestimation of unemployment experience in the work history.

6   For the current part-time workers, this average was calculated by subtracting the current job tenure from the total amount of time

spent in part-time work. If the current job tenure is included, the average amount of time a part-timer has spent in part-time work is 93 months.

7 Using the 1980 Women and Employment Survey (WES), Wright and Hinde (1991) recorded that the mean number of spells for full-time employment is 1.72, 0.93 for part-time employment, and 2.23 for non-employment. Using the data from the National Child Development Study, Kerckhoff (1990) also found that only 8% of men and 6% of women returned to full-time education once after they entered the labour market. Similarly, Wright and Hinde (1991) recorded from the WES that less than 2% of the total number of work history spells were spells of full-time education.

8 See footnote 1.

9 See Oppenheimer (1977) for a discussion of the functional approach to women's economic role in the family.

10 Martin and Roberts (1984) recorded that for women who worked part-time, over half of them relied on their husbands for childcare while they were at work, and one-third relied on relatives while less than 5% used institutional forms of childcare, like nursery, creche, or employed private childminders.

11 See Ultee et al. (1988) for a cross-national study of unemployment between husbands and wives.

12 It is also possible that the influence runs in the opposite direction, that is, attitude is a result of behaviour. A panel study is needed to ascertain which way the causation runs, or how behaviours have a reciprocal effect on women's own attitude. Here, we shall focus on the first part of the chain, that is, the way attitudes are related to labour market participation. Our purpose is to contrast the choice guided by attitudes towards gender roles with the choice shaped by economistic calculation discussed in the section about formal qualification, and to the choice as shaped by the labour market structure. For a discussion of the causal influence between attitudes and behaviours, see Dex (1988).

13 It has already been pointed out in the last chapter that the causal direction between attitudes and behaviours cannot be determined with data collected in a cross-sectional manner. It is also possible

that the husband's attitudes are affected by the labour market behaviours of the wife. A panel study is needed to ascertain the causal direction between attitudes and behaviours.

14   Payne and Payne (1993) used the Labour Force Survey and had a different finding. Their analysis shows that being unemployed 12 months ago increases the chance of being in a part-time job 12 months later, even after the qualification and age of the youngest child were controlled for. In an unpublished paper, they also noted that the chance of leaving unemployment for a full-time job fell as unemployment becomes more prolonged, while the chance of leaving for a part-time job increases. On the face of it, this seems to contradict our findings here. But, to take into account the possible underestimation of unemployment experience among women, time spent in unpaid domestic work was also included. The inclusion of the housework factor would allow us to capture periods when the respondent was seeking for work and yet did not identify that period as unemployed in her recall of her work history.

15   While this chapter analyzes the entrapment effect of part-time work experience on remaining in a part-time rather than a full-time job, another way to gauge the entrapment effect is by examining the effect of a prolonged period of part-time work on the chance of leaving a part-time spell for a full-time job. See Wright and Hinde (1991) for an attempt which used proportional hazard model to examine transitions between full-time and part-time work spell by using the 1980 Women and Employment Survey data. They remarked that there were very few transitions between full-time and part-time status without an intervening spell of non-participation. Blank (1989) examined the employment status transition of American women by using proportional hazard analysis. She found that part-time work is an alternative to, rather than a bridge between, non-participation and full-time employment.

9 Conclusion

This study is an attempt to evaluate the usefulness of two major labour market theories in helping us understand part-time work which is expanding in Britain as well as in a number of advanced industrial societies. Another purpose to is relate part-time work to women's participation and fortunes in the labour market.

In the existing literature of part-time work, one approach has been to study it in relation to the way household responsibilities circumscribe women's labour market participation. It is viewed as a compromise between wage work and demanding childcare duties. Women are seen as home-makers whose labour market attainment is largely influenced by their domestic role. It is now well established that in Britain, part-time work is taken up mostly by women who are married with young children. However, when the employment conditions of part-timers are discussed and compared to those of full-time work, the differences are more often asserted rather than empirically investigated. In studies in which comparisons are made, the limited number of cases covered does not tell us the extent to which the findings can be generalized. The descriptive accounts which these studies give about the full-time/part-time distinction do not allow us to ascertain the effect of part-time work *per se* by taking into account other structural factors related to the labour market and the individual's characteristics. The existing literature provides an incomplete picture of part-time jobs, let alone a rigorous test of the two major labour market theories.

Another approach has been to investigate the way employers use part-time workers to cope with product market fluctuations, workload variations and the manning requirements brought about by uncertain business cycles. These studies emphasize the ways through which the working hours of part-time jobs enhance the labour use flexibility of employers and enable them to make savings in both wage and non-wage labour costs. Case studies or surveys based on organizations unravel rich details about the use of part-timers within their employing organizations. However, few of them investigate thoroughly the attitudes and household conditions of workers who supply part-time working hours.

This study brings together both the demand and the supply side of part-time employment. The analysis draws on the data from the Social Change and Economic Life Initiative which contain information about employers and employees. For the data about employees, there is information about the market and work situation of their jobs as well as their household conditions. Thus, this dataset enables part-time employment to be examined at three levels : establishment, job and worker.

In Chapter three, we examined various product market changes which were argued to be one set of major reasons for employers to use part-time workers as one type of non-standard labour use policies. The findings show that the flexible firm thesis gives an one-sided emphasis to changes in the business environment within which a firm operates to account for its use rate of part-timers. Our findings show that due recognition should also be given to those enduring effects which are related to the structural features of the firm. For reasons related to the scale of operation and fluctuations in the product demand patterns, small firms and establishments in retail and personal services industries had a particularly heavy demand for part-time workers. With respect to the public sector, establishments which provided healthcare, teaching and social services had a higher use rate of part-time workers than those which provided routine services. A finding common to both the public and private sector is that the greater the proportion of lower-skilled operatives, the higher the use rate of part-timers. However, contrary to the private sector, changes in the public's demand did not affect significantly the level of part-timers employed by the public sector.

Part-time work was then analysed at the job-level in Chapters four and five. It was compared to full-time work in terms of several major aspects of market and work situation. The findings indicate that part-time jobs were worse than full-time jobs in a number of aspects. The skill levels, wage rate and the promotion prospects of part-time jobs were poorer than those of full-time jobs. The analysis of the work situation in Chapter five shows that generally, part-time workers' positions in their employing organization were less likely to be supervisors, as compared to their full-time counterparts. The findings from a sub-sample of part-timers further suggest that they were more likely to be involved in an informal management-employee relations within their employing organization. However, the argument that part-time jobs are secondary jobs is not borne out by our analysis of the extent of job security, the closeness of supervision and the irregularity of working-hour to which part-time workers are subject. Whether in terms of the time horizon of their employment contract, their perception of the degree of security of their jobs or the chance of job loss, part-timers are not worse off than full-timers, despite the lesser extent of legal employment protection to which the former are entitled. With respect to the closeness of supervision at the workplace, the findings lend little support to the argument that part-time jobs are secondary jobs whose holders are under close supervision from the management. The analysis in Chapter five shows that while their work tended to involve non-standard working-hour schedules as compared to full-timers, further flexibilization in the form of over-time work and other irregular working hours schedules was more an exception rather than a rule. These aspects of market and work situation suggest that it is unwarranted to characterize, in a sweeping manner, part-time work as secondary employment.

We also noted that the conventional measure of full-time/part-time distinction has masked variations among part-time employees who worked different ranges of part-time hours and enjoyed different extent of legal employment protection. When the part-time workforce was disaggregated according to different legal statuses, it was found that there were variations among the part-timers. Those who worked shorter hours and were least well protected by the existing employment right legislations were the most unlikely to enjoy promotion prospects. They were also less likely to be offered various types of fringe benefits, as compared to part-timers who worked longer hours. With respect to being deployed to work irregular, non-standard working hours, short-hour part-timers were less likely than those who worked longer hours to be involved in shift-work. These variations among the part-time workforce undermine the argument that part-time work can be treated as a homogeneous form of employment.

The disadvantages associated with part-time work could be expected to be reflected in long term negative effects on the worker's earnings and occupational mobility. The hypothesized negative effect of part-time work is, however, only partially borne out by the findings in Chapter six. The analysis shows that while part-time work experience reduced the current wage level of working women, it did not affect the net association between the entry and the destination class position of the job.

Having given a comparative account of full-time and part-time work and the effect of the latter on the long-term labour market fortunes of women, the second part of the thesis then turned to the supply-side of part-time employment. Three opposing views were examined in Chapters seven and eight. In Chapter seven, the participation in part-time work was discussed in relation to the argument of 'self-selection' on the part of the worker. Several aspects of the work attitudes of part-time workers were examined. The first and foremost one is the level of employment commitment. The findings show that the significant factors that contribute to a greater or lower likelihood of employment commitment were the age, the formal qualification and the marital status of the worker as well as her own attitudes towards the sex roles of men and women. With respect to the motive to work, contrary to the proposition which we can derive from the neo-classical theory or secondary labour market theory, part-timers were not particularly instrumentally oriented towards wage work. That they worked for the intrinsic rewards of wage work should not be overlooked. The various measures of attitudes towards gender roles show that part-timers were more traditional than full-timers. However, the levels of their job and life satisfaction suggest that selecting a job with the desirable working hours does not necessarily entail a perfect match for other job conditions as well. The lower satisfaction level with the promotion prospects and with the total pay among younger and overqualified part-timers indicate discrepancy, in some cases, between the desire of a woman and the job opportunity which the labour market has to offer her. Taken as a whole, the analysis in Chapter seven suggests that an explanation of part-time work participation which is premised wholly on 'self-selection' is unsatisfactory.

In Chapter eight, a full assessment of the different factors on women's labour market participation was conducted. Hypotheses derived from secondary labour market theory are evaluated against propositions drawn from human capital theory and theories of gender division of labour. The analyses show that previous part-time work and non-working experience had a significant channelling effect on the current labour market position. They both raised the likelihood of getting part-time rather than full-time work, after we have allowed for the effect of formal qualification, the childcare responsibility and the attitudes towards gender role. Part-time work carries with it cumulative disadvantages which have a depressing effect on employment prospects.

Using part-time work as a case to assess two major approaches to labour market studies, this study shows that with respect to the demand side, the postulate that there is perfect competition among employers for workers does not help us understand the variation in the demand for part-timers. Our analysis also shows that the contemporary variant of segmentation theory, the flexible firm thesis, overemphasizes the changes in the business environment and does not give due recognition to the importance of the structural features of firms. Employers differ from each other in terms of their structural characteristics and the impact which the general business environment make on them. These influence their concern with wage cost minimization and labour use flexibility which, in turn, affect their demands for part-time workers. That the public and the private sector differ from each other in their use of part-timers as a cost-saving measure to meet changes in the product demand indicates that the flexible firm thesis has not given sufficient attention to the sectoral variations.

The differences between full-time and part-time jobs indicate that the gap between the two forms of wage work cannot be accounted for solely by the amount of human capital the job-holder has. A reduced number of working hours has a considerable negative impact on various kinds of job returns. The emphasis of segmentation theory on the labour use policies of employers help explain the advantages which full-timers have over part-timers regardless of their levels of formal qualification. However, to characterize part-time work as secondary employment is not tenable. In our case, job insecurity is not associated with other unfavourable employment conditions. Whether in terms of the worker's subjective assessment or their actual experience, our findings do not lend support to the proposition that there is a close relation between part-time work and job insecurity. This suggests that instead of asserting a definitional association between the different employment conditions, a more fruitful attempt would be to investigate empirically the extent to which the various unfavourable employment conditions are associated with each other.

As for the worker-side, this study shows that the 'economic man' explanation offered by human capital theory is insufficient in accounting for women's work decision and job choice. Nor is the explanation premised on norms which prescribe the sex roles of men and women an adequate one. This study shows that the current labour market position of working women is also shaped by their previous employment history. Part-time work experience carries cumulative disadvantages and has a negative effect on employment prospects.

Moreover, because of the low-skill nature of part-time work, it has a channelling effect on women's lifetime employment prospects. This study shows that while part-time work is not associated with job insecurity and unemployment, it constitutes a trap which lower women's lifetime employment prospects and earnings.

Theoretical and policy implications

Through a detailed examination of a particular form of wage work, this study shows that to understand fully the behaviours of the two major actors of the labour market, employers and workers, we need to consider not only their current circumstances, but also the specific previous experiences which they have undergone. On the employer side, the demand of part-time workers has grown as a response to the changes in the product market that necessitate more cost-effective deployment of manpower. However, we should not lose sight of the structural determinants which have enduring effects on the demand for part-timers. On the supply side, the choice of labour market participation is not only shaped by the cost-and-benefit calculation or by attitudes towards gender role, but also by previous work and non-working experiences. Thus, while the labour demand and supply are subject to the influence of the current situations of employers and workers, they are also shaped by their respective past experiences.

This study also implies that an improvement of the legal position of part-time workers would not directly benefit the worker if it is not accompanied by a change in the workforce policies of employers. The amendment of employment legislations is likely to serve only as a safety network which part-time workers can rely on for better employment security. This study, however, shows that part-time workers fare worse than full-timers in terms of promotion prospects, earnings and entitlement to fringe benefits, but not in terms of job security. Thus, extending some of the employment rights which full-timers enjoy to part-timers would only have at best a marginal effect on the enhacement of the overall job returns and employment prospects of part-time worker.

The question that needs to be addressed is what are the ways that can enhance the job returns and employment prospects of part-time workers. This is a particularly salient issue for young part-timers and those who are overqualified for their job. We have seen that these two groups of part-timers had a lower level of job satisfaction, especially with their promotion prospects. They were the ones who were likely to benefit most from a re-design of part-time jobs as higher skilled work and a better provision of work skills and training. As small employers tend to have a higher level of demand for part-timers, a betterment in the provision of training is more likely to be feasible if there is some public support for to enable these employers to provide training to part-timers. Finally, an improvement of part-timers' labour market position is unlikely to be accomplished fully unless there is also a change in the general social norms regarding the gender role of men and women.

Bibliography

Althauser, R. P. and Kalleberg, A. L. (1981), 'Firms, occupations, and the structure of labour markets' in Berg, I. (ed.), *Sociological Perspectives on Labour Markets*, Academic Press: New York.

Althauser, R. P. and Kalleberg, A. L. (1990), 'Identifying career lines and internal labour markets within firms : a study in the interrelationships of theory and methods' in Breiger, R. L. (ed.), *Social Mobility and Social Structure*, CUP: Cambridge.

Altonji, J. G. and Paxson, C. H. (1992), 'Labour supply, hours constraints and job mobility', *The Journal of Human Resources*, Vol. 27, pp. 256-78.

Amemiya, T. (1984), 'Tobit models : a survey', *Journal of Econometrics*, Vol. 24, pp. 3-61.

Amsden, A. H. (ed.) (1980), *The Economics of Women and Work*, Penguin: Suffolk.

Andrisani, P.J. (1978), *Work Attitudes and Labour Market Experience : evidence from the national longitudinal surveys*, Praeger: New York and London.

Arellano, M. and Meghir, C. (1987), *Labour Supply and Hours Constraints*, discussion paper no. 26, Institute of Economics and Statistics, Applied Economics, University of Oxford: Oxford.

Atkinson, J. (1984), 'Manpower strategies for flexible organizations', *Personnel Management*, August, pp. 28-31.

Atkinson, J. and Meager, N. (1986), 'Is flexibility just a flash in the pan?', *Personnel Management*, September, pp. 26-9.

Bakker, I. (1988), 'Women's employment in a comparative perspective', in Jenson, J., et al., (eds.), *Feminization of the Labour Force*, Polity Press: Cambridge.

Barrere-Maurisson, M., Battagliola, F. and Daune-Richard, A. (1985), 'The course of women's careers and family life', in Roberts, B., Finnegan, R. and Gallie, D. (eds.), *New Approaches to Economic Life*,

Manchester University Press: Manchester.

Barrett, M. and McIntosh, M. (1980), 'The family wage' in Whitelegg, E. (ed.), *The Changing Experience of Women*, Martin Robertson: Oxford.

Becker, G. (1981), *A Treatise on the Family*, Harvard University Press: Cambridge.

Beechey, V. (1987), *Unequal Work*, Verso: London.

Beechey, V. and Perkins, T. (1987), *A Matter of Hours*, Polity Press: Cambridge.

Berger, S. and Piore, M. (eds.) (1980), *Dualism and Discontinuity in Industrial Societies*, CUP: Cambridge.

Berk, R. A. and Berk, F. S. (1983), 'Supply-side Sociology of the family : The challenge of new home economics', *Annual Review of Sociology*, Vol. 9, pp. 375-95.

Bielby, W. and Bielby, D. D. (1988), 'Women's and men's commitment to paid work and family' in Gutek, B., et al. (eds.), *Women and Work*, Vol. 3, pp. 49-63, Sage: Beverly Hills.

Bielby, D.D. (1992), 'Commitment to work and family', *Annual Review of Sociology*, Vol. 18, pp. 281-302.

Bills, D. B. (1988), 'Educational credentials and promotions : does schooling do more than get you in the door?', *Sociology of Education*, Vol. 61, pp. 52-60.

Birkelund, G. E., et al. (1994), 'Job characteristics of men and women', paper presented at the conference "Work, Employment and Society in the 1990s : changing boundaries, changing experience." at University of Kent, Canterbury, September 22-24, 1994.

Blanchflower, D. (1984), 'Union relative wage effects : a cross-section analysis using establishment data', *British Journal of Industrial Relations*, Vol. 21, pp. 311-32.

Blanchflower, D. and Corry, B. (1986), *Part-time Employment in Great Britain : an analysis using establishment data*. Department of Employment. Research Paper No. 57, HMSO: London.

Blanchflower, D. (1992), 'Part-time employment and industrial relations in Great Britain', in Warne, B. D., et al. (eds.), *Working Part-time : Risk or Opportunities* , Praeger: New York.

Blank, R. M. (1988), 'Simultaneously modelling the supply of weeks and hours of work among female household heads', *Journal of Labour Economics*, pp. 177-204.

Blank, R. M. (1989), 'The role of part-time work in women's labour market choices over time', *American Economic Review*, Vol. 79, pp. 295-99.

Blauner, R. (1964), *Alienation and Freedom*, University of Chicago Press: Chicago.

Blossfeld, Hans-Peter and Hakim, C. (eds.) (forthcoming), *Between*

Equalisation and Marginalisation, to be published by OUP: Oxford.

Bosworth, D. and Dawkins, P. (1982), 'Women and part-time work', *Industrial Relations Journal*, Vol. 13, pp. 32-39.

Brannen, J. (1989), 'Childbirth and occupational mobility: evidence from a longitudinal study', *Work, Employment and Society*, Vol. 3. pp. 179-201.

Briar, C. J. (1992), 'Part-time work and the state in Britain, 1941-1987', in Warne, B. D. et al. (eds.), *Working part-time : risks and opportunities*, Praeger: New York.

Brown, C. and Medoff, J. (1989), 'The employer size-wage effect', *Journal of Political Economy*, Vol. 97, pp. 1027-59.

Buchtemann, C. F (1989), 'The socio-economics of individual working time reduction : empirical evidence for the Federal Republic of Germany', in Agassi, J. B. and Heycock, S. (eds.), *The Redesign of Working Time : Promise or Threat*, Ed. Sigma: Berlin.

Buck, N. H., et al. (1994), *Changing Households : the British Household Panel Studies, 1990-1992*, ESRC Research Centre on Micro-social Change, Essex: Colchester.

Carroll, G. R. and Mayer, K. U. (1986), 'Job-shift patterns in the Federal Republic of Germany: the effects of social class, industrial sector, and organization size', *American Sociological Review*, Vol. 51, pp. 323-41.

Carroll, G. R. and Mayer, K. U. (1987), 'Jobs and classes: structural constraints on career mobility', *European Sociological Review*, Vol. 3, pp.14-38.

Casey, B. (1991), 'Survey evidence on trends in "non-standard" employment', in Pollert, A. (ed.), *Farewell to Flexibility?*, Blackwell: Oxford.

Collinson, D. L. (1987), '"Picking" women : the recruitment of temporary workers in the mail order industry', *Work, Employment and Society*, Vol. 1, pp. 371-87.

Chan, T.W. (1994), *Social Mobility in Hong Kong*, unpublished D.Phil. thesis, Oxford: University of Oxford.

Corcoran, M., Duncan, G. J. and Ponza, M. (1984), 'Work experience, job segregation, and wages', in Reskin, B. (ed.), *Sex Segregation in the Workplace*, National Academy Press: Washington, D.C.

Court, G. (1990), *Continuity and Change in the Part-time Labour Market*, unpublished Ph.D. thesis, The School for Advanced Urban Studies, University of Bristol: Bristol.

Cousins, C. (1994), 'A comparison of the labour market position of women in Spain and the UK with reference to the "flexible" labour debate', *Work, Employment and Society*, Vol.8, pp. 45-67.

Craig, C., et al. (1982), *Labour Market Structure, Industrial Organization and Low Pay*, CUP: Cambridge.

Craig, C., et al. (1984), *Payment Structures and Smaller Firms*, research paper no. 48. Department of Employment, HMSO: London.

Craig, C., et al. (1985), 'Economic, social and political factors in the operation of the labour market', in Roberts, B., et al. (eds.), *New Approaches to Economic Life*, Manchester University Press: Manchester.

Curtice, J. (1993), 'Satisfying work - if you can get it', in Jowell, R., et al. (eds.), *International Social Attitudes: the 10th BSA Report*, Dartmouth: Aldershot.

Dale, A. (1987), 'Labour market structure in the United Kingdom', *Work and Occupations*, Vol.14, pp. 558-90.

Dale, A. (1987), 'Occupational inequality, gender and life cycle', *Work, Employment and Society*, Vol.1, pp. 326-51.

Dale, A. and Bamford, C. (1988), 'Temporary workers : cause for concern or complacency?', *Work, Employment and Society*, Vol. 2, pp. 191-209.

Dale, A. and Glover, J. (1990), *An Analysis of Women's Employment Patterns in the UK, France and the USA*, Department of Employment research paper No. 75, HMSO: London.

Dale, A. and Ward, C. (1992), 'Geographical variation in female labour force participation : an application of multi-level modelling', *Regional Studies*, Vol. 26, pp. 243-56.

Dale, A. and Ward, C. (1992), 'The impact of early life-course transitions on equality at work and home', *The Sociological Review*, Vol. 40, pp. 509-32.

Dale, A. (1992), 'Part-time working among young people in Britain', in Warne, B.D. et al. (eds.), *Working Part-time : Risks and Opportunities*, Praeger: New York.

Davidson, J. O'Connell (1990), 'The road to functional flexibility: white collar work and employment relations in a privatized public utility', *Sociological Review*, Vol. 38, pp. 689-711.

Davies, R., Elias, P. and Penn, R. (1994), 'The relationship between a husband's unemployment and his wife's participation in the labour force', in Gallie, D., et al. (eds.), *Social Change and the Experience of Unemployment*, OUP: Oxford.

Dex, S. (1984), *Women's work histories : an analysis of the Women and Employment Survey*, research paper no. 46. Department of Employment, HMSO: London.

Dex, S. and Shaw, L.B. (1986), *British and American Women at Work*, Macmillan: Basingstoke.

Dex, S. (1987), *Women's Occupational Mobility*, Macmillan: Hong Kong

Dex, S. (1988), *Women's Attitudes Towards Work*, Macmillan: Hong Kong.

Dex, S. (1991), 'The reliability of recall data : a literature review', working papers of the ESRC Research Centre on micro-social change, paper 11, University of Essex: Colchester.

Dex, S., Walters, P. and Alden, D. (1993), *French and British Mothers at Work*, Macmillan: Basingstoke.

Dey, I. (1989), 'Flexible "parts" and rigid "fulls" : the limited revolution in work-time patterns', *Work, Employment and Society*, Vol. 3, pp. 465-90.

Disney, R. and Szyszczak, E.M. (1984), 'Protective legislation and part-time employment in Britain', *British Journal of Labour Economics*, Vol. 22, pp. 78-100.

Doeringer, P. B. and Piore, M. (1971), *Internal Labour Market and Manpower Analysis*, D.C. Heath and Company: New York.

Duffy, A. and Pupo, N. (1992), *Part-time Paradox : connecting gender, work and family*, McClelland and Stewart: Toronto.

Duncan, G.J. and Hoffman, S. (1979), 'On-the-job training and earnings differences by race and sex', *Review of Economics and Statistics*, Vol. 61, pp. 594-603.

DuRivage, V. L. (1992), 'Flexibility trap : the proliferation of marginal jobs', *American Prospect*, Vol. 9, pp. 84-93.

Edwards, R.C. (1978), 'The social relations of production at the point of production', *Insurgent Sociologist*, Vol. 8, pp. 109-25.

Edwards, R.C. (1979), *Contested Terrains : the transformation of the workplace in the 20th Century*, Basic Books: New York.

Ehrenberg, R.G., Rosenberg, P. and Li, J. (1988), 'Part-time employment in the United States', in Hart, R. A. (ed.), *Employment, Unemployment and Labour Utilization*, Unwin Hyman: Boston.

Elias, P. and Main, B. (1982), *Women's Working Lives : Evidence from the National Training Survey*, Institute for Employment Research, University of Warwick: Coventry.

Elias, P. (1988), 'Family formation, occupational mobility and part-time work', in Hunt, A. (ed.), *Women and Paid Work*, Macmillan: Hong Kong.

Ermisch, J. F. and Wright, R.E. (1993), 'Wage offers and full-time and part-time employment by British women', *The Journal of Human Resources*, Vol.28, pp. 111-33.

Evans, G. (1992), 'Testing the validity of Goldthorpe class schema', *European Sociological Review*, Vol. 8, pp. 211-31.

Fleming, A. (1989), 'Employment in the public and private sectors', *Economic Trends*, No. 434.

Folbre, N. (1986), 'Hearts and spades : paradigms of household economics', *World Development*, Vol. 14, pp. 245-55.

Friedman, A. (1977), 'Responsible autonomy versus direct control over the labour process', *Capital and Class*, Vol.1, pp. 44-57.

Frenken, H. and Maser, K. (1992), 'Employer-sponsored pension plans - who is covered?', *Perspectives on Labour and Income*, Vol. 4, pp. 27-34.

Gaertner, K.N. (1980), 'The structure of organizational careers', in *Sociology of Education*, Vol. 53, pp. 7-20.

Gallie, D. (1989), *Trade Union Allegiance and Decline in British Urban Labour Markets*, SCELI working paper no. 9, University of Oxford: Oxford.

Gallie, D. (1991), 'Patterns of skill change: upskilling, deskilling or the polarization of Skills?', *Work, Employment and Society*, Vol. 5, pp. 319-51.

Gallie, D. and White, M. (1993), *Employment Commitment and the Skills Revolution : findings from the Employment In Britain Survey*, PSI: London.

Gallie, D. (1994), 'Are the unemployed an "underclass"?', *Sociology*, Vol. 28, pp. 737-57.

Gallie, D. and White, M. (1994), 'Employer policies, employee contracts and labour market structure', in Rubery, J. and Wilkinson, F. (eds.), *Employer Strategy and the Labour Market* , Oxford University Press: Oxford.

Gallie, D., et al. (1994), 'Job search effort and motivation in unemployment', in White, M. (ed.), *Unemployment and Public Policy in a changing labour market*, PSI: London.

Gallie, D. and Volger, C. (1994), 'Unemployment and attitudes to work', in Gallie, D., Marsh, C. and Vogler, C. (eds.), *Social Change and the Experience of Unemployment*, OUP: Oxford.

Gans, H.J. (1993), 'Time for an employees' lobby', *Social Policy*, Vol. 24, pp. 35-38.

Ganzeboom, H.B.G., et al. (1992), 'A standard international socio-economic index of occupational status', *Social Science Research*, Vol. 21, pp.1-56.

Gershuny, J. and Marsh, C. (1994), 'Unemployment in work histories', in Gallie, D., Marsh, C. and Vogler, C. (eds.), *Social Change and the Experience of Unemployment* , OUP: Oxford.

Ginn, J. and Arber, S. (1993), 'Pension penalties : the gendered divison of occupational welfare', *Work, Employment and Society*, Vol. 7, pp. 47-70.

Glover, J. (1994), 'Women teachers and white-collar workers : domestic circumstances and paid work', *Work, Employment and Society*, Vol. 8, pp. 87-100.

Goldthorpe, J. H. (1980), *Social Mobility and Class Structure in Modern Britain*, Oxford University Press: Oxford.

Goldthorpe, J. H. (1987) (2nd ed), *Social Mobility and Class Structure in*

Modern Britain, Oxford University Press: Oxford.

Goldthorpe, J. H. and Erikson, R. (1993), *The Constant Flux*, Clarendon Press: Oxford.

Gordon, D.M., Edwards, R. and Reich, M. (1982), *Segmented Work, Divided Workers: the historical transformation of work in the United States*, CUP: Cambridge.

Gornick, J. C. and Jacobs, J.A. (1996), 'A cross-national analysis of the wages of part-time workers : evidence from the United States, the United Kingdom, Canada and Australia', *Work, Employment and Society*, Vol. 10, pp.1-27.

Granovetter, M. (1974), *Getting A Job*, Harvard University Press: Cambridge, Mass.

Granovetter, M. (1981), 'Towards a sociological theory of income differences', in Berg, I. (ed.), *Sociological Perspectives on Labour Market*, Academic Press: New York.

Greenhalgh, C. (1980), 'Participation and hours of work for married women in Great Britain', *Oxford Economics Papers*, Vol. 32, pp. 296-318.

Greenhalgh, C. A. and Stewart, M. B. (1984), 'Work history patterns and the occupational attainment of Women', *The Economic Journal*, Vol. 94, pp. 493-519.

Greenhalgh, C. A. and Stewart, M. B. (1985), 'The occupational status and mobility of British men and women', *Oxford Economics Paper*, Vol. 37, pp. 40-71.

Gregory, A. (1991), 'Patterns of working-hours in large-scale grocery retailing in Britain and France : convergence after 1992?', *Work, Employment and Society*, Vol. 5, pp. 497-514.

Hakim, C. (1987), 'Trends in the flexible workforce', *Employment Gazette*. HMSO: London.

Hakim, C. (1989), 'Employment rights : a comparison of part-time and full-time employees', *Industrial Law Journal*, Vol. 18, pp. 69- 83.

Hakim, C. (1990), 'Workforce restructuring, social insurance coverage and the black economy', *Journal of Social Policy*, Vol. 18, pp. 471-503.

Hakim, C. (1991), 'Grateful slaves and self-made women: fact and fantasy in women's work orientations', *European Sociological Review*, Vol. 7, pp. 101-21.

Hakim, C. (1996), 'The sexual division of labour and women's heterogeneity', *British Journal of Sociology*, Vol. 47, pp. 178-88.

Hanlon, M. (1986), 'Age and commitment to work', *Research on Aging*, Vol. 8, pp. 289-316.

Harrison, B. and Kelley, M. R. (1993), 'Outsourcing and the search for flexibility', *Work, Employment and Society*, Vol. 7, pp. 213-35.

Hayward, M. D., Hardy, M.A. and Liu, M. (1994), 'Work after

retirement : the experience of older men in the United States', *Social Science Research*, Vol. 23, pp. 82-107.

Hinrichs, K., Roche, W.R. and Siranni, C. (eds.) (1991), *Working Time in Transition*, Temple University Press: Philadelphia.

Horrell, S., et al. (1989), 'Unequal jobs and unequal pay', *Industrial Relations Journal*, Vol. 20, pp. 176-91.

Horrell, S. and Rubery, J. (1991), 'Gender and working time : an analysis of employers' working time policies', *Cambridge Journal of Economics*, Vol. 15, pp. 373-91.

Humphries, J. and Rubery, J. (1985), 'The reconstitution of the supply side of the labour market : the relative autonomy of social reproduction', *Cambridge Journal of Economics*, Vol. 8, pp. 331-46.

Hunter, L.C. and Macinnes, J. (1991), *Employers' Labour Use Strategies - case studies*, Department of Employment. Research paper no. 57, HMSO: London.

Hurstfield, J. (1978), *The Part-time Trap*, Low Pay pamplet no.9, The Low Pay Unit: London.

Hurstfield, J. (1987), *Part-timers under pressure*, Low Pay pamplet no.47, The Low Pay Unit: London.

Ilmakunnas, S. and Pudney, S. (1988), *A model of labour supply in the presence of hours restrictions*, discussion paper no. 305, Centre for Labour Economics, London School of Economics.

Income Data Services (1985), *Part-timers, Temps and Job-sharers*, Employment and Law Handbook no.31. Income Data Services: London.

Jones, E.B. and Long, J.E. (1979), 'Part-week work and human capital investment by married women', *Journal of Human Resources*, Vol. 14, pp. 563-78.

Joshi, H. (1984), *Women's Participation in Paid Work : Further Analysis of the Women and Employment Survey*, Department of Employment, Research Paper No.45, HMSO: London.

Joshi, H., et al. (1985), 'Why are more women working in Britain?' *Journal of Labour Economics*, Vol. 3, pp. S147-76.

Joshi, H. and Davies, H. (1992), *Childcare and Mothers' Lifetime Earnings : some European contrasts*, Centre for Economic Policy and Research, discussion paper no. 600. London.

Joshi, H. and Hinde, P.R.A. (1994), 'Employment after childbearing in post-war Britain : cohort-study evidence on contrasts within and across generations', *European Sociological Review*, Vol. 9, pp. 203-27.

Kahne, H. (1994), 'Part-time Work : A reassessment for a changing economy', *Social Service Review*, Vol. 68, pp. 417-36.

Kalleberg, A. L. (1977), 'Work values and job rewards : a theory of job satisfaction', *American Journal of Sociology*, Vol. 42, pp.124-43.

Kalleberg, A. L. and Loscocco, K.A. (1983), 'Aging, values and rewards :

explaining age differences in job satisfaction', *American Sociological Review*, Vol. 48, pp. 78-90.

Kalleberg, A. L. and van Buren, M. E. (1992), 'Organizations and economic stratification : a cross-national analysis of the size-earning relation', *Research in Social Stratification and Mobility*, Vol. 7, pp. 61-93.

Kanter, R. (1977), 'The impact of hierarchical structures on the work behaviour of women and men', *Social Problems*, Vol. 23, pp. 15-30.

Kanungo, R. (1982), *Work alienation : an integrative approach*, Praeger: New York.

Kell, M. and Wright, J. (1990), 'Benefits and the labour supply of women married to unemployed men', *Economic Journal*, 400, pp. 119-26.

Kerckhoff, A. C. (1990), *Getting Started : transition to adulthood in Great Britain*, Westview, Boulder Colo : Oxford.

Knoke, D. and Kalleberg, A. L. (1994), 'Job training in U.S. organizations', *American Sociological Review*, Vol. 59, pp. 537-46.

Kohn, M. and Schooler, K. (1983), *Work and Personality*, Ablex.: Norwood, N.J.

Krahn, H. (1991), 'Non-standard work arrangements', *Perspectives on Labour and Income*, Vol. 3, pp. 35-45.

Lane, C. (1988) 'Industrial change in Europe: the pursuit of flexible specialization in Britain and West Germany', *Work, Employment and Society*, Vol. 2, pp. 141-168.

Lane, C. (1993), 'Gender and labour market in Europe : Britain, Germany and France', *The Sociological Review*, Vol. 41, pp. 274-301.

Layard, R., Barton, M. and Zabalza, A. (1980), 'Married women's participation and hours', *Economica*, Vol. 47, pp. 51-72.

Leeds, M. A. (1990), 'Part-time status and hourly-earnings of black and white men', *Economic Inquiry*, Vol. 28, pp. 544-54.

Lincoln, J. R. and Kalleberg, A. L. (1990), *Culture, Control and Commitment*, Cambridge University Press: Cambridge.

Lindbeck, A. and Snower, D. (1988), *The insider/outsider theory of employment and unemployment*, MIT Press: London.

Lockwood, D. (1958), *The Blackcoated Worker*, Allen and Unwin: London.

Lodahl, T. and Kejner, M. (1965), 'The definition and measurement of job involvement', *Journal of Applied Psychology*, Vol. 49, pp. 24-33.

Lorence, J. (1987), 'Age differences in work involvement', *Work and Occupation*, Vol.14, pp. 533-57.

Loscocco, K. (1989), 'The interplay of personal and job characteristics in determining work commitment', *Social Science Research*, Vol. 18, pp. 70-94.

McGregor, A. and Sproull, A. (1991), *Employer Labour Use Strategies :*

Analysis of a National Survey, Department of Employment. Research Paper No.83, HMSO: London.

McKee, L. and Bell, C. (1985), 'Marital and family relations in times of male unemployment', in Roberts, B., et al. (eds.), *New Approaches to Economic Life*, Manchester University Press: Manchester.

Mann, M. (1986), 'Work and the work ethics', in Jowell, R. et al., (eds.), *British Social Attitudes : 6th report*, Dartmouth: Aldershot.

McRae, S. (1991), 'Occupational change over childbirth: evidence from a national survey', *Sociology*, Vol. 25, pp. 589-605.

McRae, S. (1994), 'Labour supply after childbirth: do employers' policies make a difference?', *Sociology*, Vol. 28, pp. 99-122.

Main, B. G.M. (1988), 'The life-time attachment of women to the labour market', in Hunt, A. (ed.), *Women and Paid Work*, Macmillan: Hong Kong.

Mallier, A.T. and Rosser, M.J. (1987), 'Change in the industrial distribution of female employment in Great Britain, 1951-1981', *Work, Employment and Society*, Vol. 1, pp. 463-486.

Marsh, C. (1991), *Hours of Work of Women and Men in Britain*, Equal Opportunities Commission, HMSO: London.

Marsh, C. and Volger, C. (1994), 'Economic convergence : a tale of six cities', in Gallie, D. et al. (eds.), *Social Change and the Experience of Unemployment*, Oxford University Press: Oxford.

Marshall, A. (1989), 'The sequel of unemployment : the changing role of part-time and temporary work in Western Europe', in Rodgers, G. and Rodgers, J. (eds.), *Precarious Jobs in the Labour Market Regulation*, ILO : Geneva.

Marshall, G., et al. (1988), *Social Class in Modern Britain*, Unwin and Hyman: London.

Martin, J. and Roberts, C. (1984), *Women and Employment : A Lifetime Perspective*, HMSO: London.

Mastekaasa, A. (1993), 'Union-non-union wage differentials : individual level and organizational level of effects', *European Sociological Review*, Vol. 9, pp. 109-24.

MOW International Research Team, (1987), *The Meaning of Working*, Academic Press: London.

Mellow, W. (1982), 'Employer size and wages', *Review of Economics and Statistics*, Vol. 64, pp. 495-501.

Metcalf, D. (1994), 'Transformation of British industrial relations? institutions, conduct and outcomes 1980-1990', in Barrell, R. (ed.), *The UK Labour Market*, CUP: Glasgow.

Mincer, J. and Polachek, S.W. (1974), 'Family investments in human capital : earnings of women', *Journal of Political Economy*, Vol. 82, pp. 76-108.

Mincer, J. and Ofek, H. (1982), 'Interrupted work careers : depreciation and restoration of human capital', *Journal of Human Resources*, Vol. 17, pp. 3-24.

Montgomery, M. (1988), 'On the determinants of employer demand for part-time workers', *Review of Economics and Statistics*, Vol. 70, pp. 112-17.

Morgenstern, R.D. and Barrett, N.S. (1974), 'The retrospective bias in unemployment reporting by sex, race and age', *Journal of the American Statistical Association*, Vol. 69, pp. 355-57.

Morris, L. (1984), 'Redundancy and patterns of household finance', *The Sociological Review*, Vol. 32, pp. 492-523.

Mortimer, J. T., Lorence, J. and Kumka, D.S. (1983), *Work, Family and Personality*, Academic Press: New York.

Moylan, S., Millar, J. and Davies, R. (1984), *For Richer, for poorer? DHSS Cohort Study of Unemployed Men*, HMSO: London.

de Neubourg, C. (1985), 'Part-time work: an international quantitative comparison', *International Labour Review*, No. 124, pp. 599-76.

OECD (1985), *Employment Outlook*, OECD: Paris.

OECD (1987), *Employment Outlook*, OECD: Paris.

OECD (1994), *Employment Outlook*, OECD: Paris.

Oi, W. Y. (1991), 'Low wages and small firms', *Research in Labour Economics*, Vol. 12, pp. 1-39.

Oi, W. Y. (1962), 'Quasi-fixed labour costs', *Journal of Political Economy*, Vol. 70, pp. 538-55.

Oppenheimer, V.K. (1977), 'The Sociology of women's economic role in the family', *American Sociological Review*, Vol. 42, pp. 387-406.

O'Doherty, D. (1993), *Banking on part-time labour : management stratgey and the growth of part-time labour*, Leicester Business School, De Montfort University, Occasional Paper no. 8.

O'Reilly, J. (1994), *Banking on Flexibility : a comparison of flexible management in retail banking in Britain and France*, Avebury: Aldershot.

Payne, J. and Payne, C. (1993), 'Unemployment and peripheral work', *Work, Employment and Society*, Vol. 7, pp. 513-34.

Payne, J. and Payne, C. (1994), 'Recession, restructuring and the fate of the unemployed : evidence in the underclass debate', *Sociology*, Vol. 28, pp.1-19.

Perry, S. (1990), 'Part-time work and returning to work after the birth of the first child', *Applied Economics*, Vol. 22, pp.1137-48.

Piore, M. (1980), 'Economic fluctuation, job security, and labour market duality in Italy, France and the United States', *Politics and Society*, Vol. 9, pp. 379-407.

Pittman, J. and Orthner, D. (1989), 'Gender differences in the prediction of job commitment', in Goldsmith, E. (ed.), *Work and Family: theory, research and applications*, Sage: Newbury Park, California.

Polachek, S.W. (1981), 'Occupational self-selection : a human capital approach to sex difference in occupational structure', *Review of Economics and Statistics*, Vol. 63, pp. 60-69.

Pollert, A. (ed.) (1991), *Farewell to Flexibility?*, Basil Blackwell: Oxford.

Portocarero, L. (1983), 'Social mobility in industrial nations : women in France and Sweden', *Sociological Review*, Vol. 31, pp. 56-82.

Pratten, C. (1991), *The Competitiveness of Small Firms*, Occasional Paper 57, Department of Applied Economics, University of Cambridge.

Procter, S.J., et al. (1994), 'Flexibility, politics and strategy : in defence of the model of the flexible firm', *Work, Employment and Society*, Vol. 8, pp. 221-42.

Puckett, T.C. and Frederico, M. (1987), 'Part-time workers in welfare : who wins, who loses and why?', *Australian Journal of Social Issues*, Vol. 22, pp.50-62.

Pulkingham, J. (1992), 'Employment restructuring in the health service : efficiency, inititatives, working patterns and workforce composition', *Work, Employment and Society*, Vol. 6, pp. 397-421.

Reich, M., Gordon, D.M. and Edwards, R.C. (1973), 'A theory of labour market segmentation', *American Economic Review*, Vol. 63, pp. 359-65.

Robinson, O. and Wallace, J. (1984), *Part-time Employment and Sex-discrimination in Great Britain*, Department of Employment, Research Paper No. 43, HMSO: London.

Rodgers, G. (1989), 'Precarious work in Western Europe: the state of the debate', in Rodgers, G. and Rodgers, J. (eds.), *Precarious Jobs in Labour Market Regulation*, ILO: Geneva.

Rose, M. (1988), 'Attachment to work and social values', in Gallie, D. (ed.), *Employment in Britain*, Blackwell: Oxford.

Rosenfeld, R. and Spenner, K. (1988), 'Women's work and women's careers', in Riley, M. (ed.), *Social Structure and Human Lives*, Vol. 1, pp. 285-305, Sage: Newbury Park, California.

Rosenfeld, R. A. and Birkelund, G.E. (1995), 'Women's part-time work : a cross-national comparison', *European Sociological Review*, Vol. 11, pp. 111-34.

Rubery, J. and Tarling, R. (1988), 'Women's employment in declining Britain', in Rubery, J. (ed.), *Women and Recession*, RKP: London.

Rubery, J. (1989), 'Precarious forms of work in the UK', in Rodgers, G. and Rodgers, J. (eds.), *Precarious Jobs in the Labour Market Regulation* , ILO: Geneva.

Rubery, J., et al. (1994), 'Part-time work and gender inequality in the labour market', in Scott, A.M. (ed.), *Gender Segregation and Social Change*, OUP: Oxford.

Ruggie, M. (1983), *The State and Working Women : A Comparative Study of Britain and Sweden*, Princeton University Press: Princeton.

Ryan, P. (1981), 'Segmentation, duality and the internal labour market', in Wilkinson, F. (ed.), *The Dynamics of Labour Market Segmentation*, Academic Press: London.

Schoer, K. (1987), 'Part-time employment : Britain and West Germany', *Cambridge Journal of Economics*, Vol.11, pp. 83-94.

Shaw, L.B. (1983), *Unplanned Careers : The working lives of middle-aged women*, D.C. Heath and Company: Lexington.

Sheldrake, J. (1990), 'The changing pattern of collective bargaining in local government', in Trinder, C. (ed.), *Pay in the Public Sector*, Public Finance Foundation: London.

Simpson, W. (1986), 'Analysis of part-time pay in Canada', *Canadian Journal of Economics*, Vol.19, pp. 798-807.

Sloane, P. and Murphy, P. D. (1989), *The union/non-union wage differential revisited: an analysis of six local labour markets*, Working Paper No. 8. The Social Change and Economic Life Initiative.

Sloane, P. J. (1994), 'The gender wage differential and discrimination in the six SCELI local labour markets', in Scott, A. M. (ed.), *Gender Segregation and Social Change*, OUP: Oxford.

Sproull, A. (1989), *The Growth of Part-time Employment in the service sector : demand-side explanations*, unpublished Ph.D. thesis. University of Glasgow: Glasgow.

Stern, N.H. (1981), 'The participation of married women in paid work in the UK in the 1970's', Mimeo. Department of Economics, University of Warwick: Coventry.

Stewart, M. (1983), 'Relative earnings and individual union membership', *Economica*, Vol. 5, pp. 111-25.

Sundstrom, M. (1987), *A Study in the Growth of Part-time work in Sweden*, Arbetslivscentrum: Stockholm.

Sundstrom, M. (1993), 'The growth in full-time work among Swedish women in the 1980s', *Acta Sociologica*, Vol.36, pp.139-50.

Tilly, C. (1991), 'Reasons for the continuing growth of part-time employment', *Monthly Labour Review*, Vol.114, pp. 10-18.

Tilly, C. (1992), 'Dualism in part-time employment', *Industrial Relations*, Vol. 31, pp. 330-47.

Thomson, K. (1996), 'Working mothers : choice or circumstance?', *British Social Attitudes - 12th Report*, Aldershot: Dartmouth

Ultee, W., et al. (1988), 'Why does unemployment come in couples?'

European Sociological Review, Vol. 4, pp.111-22.

Vainiomaki, J. and Wadhwani, S. (1991), *The effects of changes in a firm's product market power on wages*, Centre for Economic Performance, Discussion paper no. 18, London.

Vecchio, R.P. (1980), 'The functional meaning of work and the job: Morse and Weiss 1955 revisited', *Academy of Management Journal*, Vol. 23, pp. 361-67.

Volger, C. (1994), 'Segregation, sexism, and labour supply', in Scott, A. M. (ed.), *Gender Segregation and Social Change*, OUP: Oxford.

Walker, J. and Moore, R. (1987), 'The impact of privatization on the United Kingdom local government labour market', in Tarling, R. (ed.), *Flexibility in the Labour Market*, Academic Press: London.

Walker, J. (1988), 'Women, the state and the family in Britain : Thatcher economics and the experience of women', in Rubery, J. (ed.), *Women and Recession*, RKP: London.

Walsh, T.J. (1990), 'Flexible labour utilization in the private service sector', *Work, Employment and Society*, Vol. 4, pp. 517-30.

Warr, P. (1982), 'A national study of non-financial employment commitment', *Journal of Occupational Psychology*, Vol. 55, pp. 297-312.

Watson, G. and Fothergil, B. (1993), 'Part-time employment and attitudes to part-time work', *Employment Gazette*, Vol.101, pp. 213-20.

Wilkinson, F. and White, M. (1994), 'Product market pressures and employers' responses', in Rubery, J. and Wilkinson, F. (eds.), *Employer Strategy and the Labour Market*, Oxford University Press: Oxford.

Wilson, R.A., et al. (1991), 'Occupational assessment', *Review of the Economy and Employment*, Institute for Employment Research, University of Warwick: Warwick.

Witherspoon, S. and Prior, G. (1991), 'Working mothers : free to choose?', in Jowell, R., et al. (eds.), *British Social Attitudes : the 8th Report* , Dartmouth: Aldershot.

Wood, D. and Smith, P. (1989), *Employers' Labour Use Strategies : First Report on the 1987 Survey*, Department of Employment, Research Paper No. 63, HMSO: London.

Wright, J. D. and Hamilton, R. F. (1978), 'Work satisfaction and age : some evidence for the "job change" hypothesis', *Social Forces*, Vol. 56, pp.1140-58.

Wright, R.E. and Hinde, R.A.A. (1991), 'The dynamics of full-time and part-time female labour force participation in Great Britain', *European Journal of Population*, Vol. 7, pp. 201-30.

Yankelovitch, D., et al. (1983), *Work and Human Values : an international report on jobs in the 1980s and 1990s*, Aspen Institute for Humanistic Studies: New York.

Yaron, G. (1991), *Sex Discrimination and Low Pay : an empirical analysis using UK data.*, Discussion Paper 108, Applied Economics, University of Oxford: Oxford.

Zabala, A. (1983), 'The CES utility function, non-linear budget constraints and labour supply results from female participation and hours', *The Economics Journal*, Vol. 93, pp. 312-30.

'03